ORDER OF BATTLE
GERMAN PANZERS
IN
WWII

ORDER OF BATTLE
GERMAN PANZERS
IN
WWII

CHRIS BISHOP

ZENITH PRESS

ISBN-13: 978-0-7603-3116-3
ISBN-10: 0-7603-3116-2

Produced by:
Amber Books Ltd
Bradley's Close
74–77 White Lion Street
London N1 9PF
United Kingdom
www.amberbooks.co.uk

Project Editor: Michael Spilling
Design: Hawes Design
Picture Research: Terry Forshaw

Printed in Dubai

CONTENTS

The *Panzerwaffe* of the German Army

Although they existed for less than a decade from the foundation of the first units in 1935, the panzer divisions of the German Army changed the face of modern warfare by intoducing a new style of fast-moving combat known as *Blitzkrieg.*

German Panzer I tanks parade through Wenceslas Square, Prague, following the occupation of Czechoslovakia, March 1939.

*B*LITZKRIEG ENABLED THE *WEHRMACHT* to overcome the bloody attrition strategies of Word War I, and to humble enemy after enemy at minimum cost to the German nation.

The roots of *Blitzkrieg* lay in the German infiltration tactics of 1918. Special assault divisions with heavily armed 'Storm Troopers' broke through weak points in the Allied lines. The troops carried heavy loads of grenades, machine-guns and trench mortars, giving them superior firepower at the point of contact. They were supported by precision artillery fire and ground attack aircraft. Isolated pockets of defenders were dealt with by follow-up units: the Storm Troopers raged on through the Allied rear areas.

Between the wars, British theories regarding a balanced armoured force were examined in great detail by the *Truppenamt*, the clandestine General Staff of the *Reichswehr*. One of the most important of the officers involved was Colonel Heinz Guderian. Guderian proposed that any future armoured force had to be a balance of all arms, with the main striking force being provided by a mobile spearhead of tanks, mechanized infantry and artillery.

Guderian had some opposition within the German Army, but much of the General Staff looked on his ideas with favour. When the Nazis came to power, he found an even greater supporter in Hitler, who encouraged the efforts of the panzer troops at every stage.

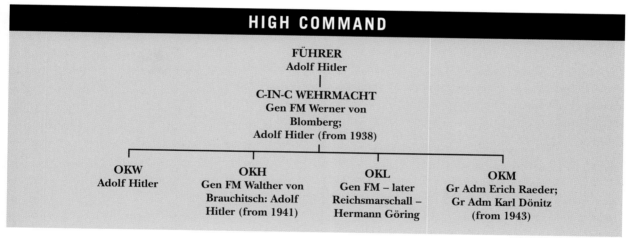

HIGH COMMAND

FÜHRER
Adolf Hitler

C-IN-C WEHRMACHT
Gen FM Werner von Blomberg;
Adolf Hitler (from 1938)

OKW	OKH	OKL	OKM
Adolf Hitler	Gen FM Walther von Brauchitsch: Adolf Hitler (from 1941)	Gen FM – later Reichsmarschall – Hermann Göring	Gr Adm Erich Raeder; Gr Adm Karl Dönitz (from 1943)

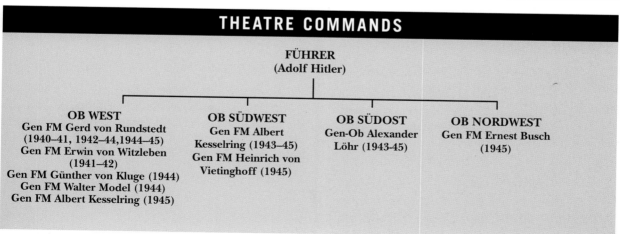

THEATRE COMMANDS

FÜHRER
(Adolf Hitler)

OB WEST	OB SÜDWEST	OB SÜDOST	OB NORDWEST
Gen FM Gerd von Rundstedt (1940–41, 1942–44,1944–45) Gen FM Erwin von Witzleben (1941–42) Gen FM Günther von Kluge (1944) Gen FM Walter Model (1944) Gen FM Albert Kesselring (1945)	Gen FM Albert Kesselring (1943–45) Gen FM Heinrich von Vietinghoff (1945)	Gen-Ob Alexander Löhr (1943-45)	Gen FM Ernest Busch (1945)

Pre-War Organization

In a manual written soon after its establishment, the function of the panzer arm was defined as 'the creation of rapid concentrations of considerable fighting power, obtaining quick decisions by breakthroughs, deep penetration on wide fronts and the destruction of the enemy'.

This policy was being advocated at a time when other armies were still slowing their armour to move at the pace of the marching soldier. The Germans preferred to increase the speed of their infantry, initially by carrying them on trucks and later by mounting them in specialized half-tracks.

But making the infantry more mobile was not enough. To be truly effective, all the formations involved in the attack needed to be motorized, including reconnaissance units, artillery, combat engineers and support units. A shortage of suitable artillery meant that in the early days of *Blitzkrieg* fire support for the panzers had to be provided by the *Luftwaffe*. Thanks to Hitler's support, Heinz Guderian was able to put some of his ideas into practice as the first experimental tank formations appeared in 1934, and the first true panzer divisions were formed a year later.

The first panzers

Although the tanks were to be the key to the success of *Blitzkrieg*, the first panzers were primarily training machines that were never intended to have a major combat role. They were small, lightly armed and armoured, and had definite tactical limitations; production of better designs was slow and expensive. But they were highly mobile, which was vital since speed was the essence of the newly emerging concept of *Blitzkrieg*.

Mobile infantry

The reformed German Army announced in 1935 was based on the *Reichswehr* formations permitted under the treaty of Versailles. Most infantry units were just that – infantry, expected to march into battle. However, the mobile warfare theories inspired by Guderian meant that infantrymen on foot would not be able to keep up with the new, fast-moving panzer divisions then being created. At the very least, some infantry divisions would have to be motorized, to make possible the all-arms means of waging war that would come to be known as *Blitzkrieg*.

Although the bulk of German Army was still largely horse drawn, the panzer divisions that raced through France in 1940 were entirely motorized with infantry and support units being carried on trucks.

Panzer division organization

The spearhead of the early panzer divisions was provided by a panzer brigade of two panzer regiments. The regiment in turn was divided into two light companies operating Panzer Is and IIs, and a medium company with Panzer IIs and IVs. Typically, a panzer division would have a strength of some 300 tanks.

In addition to two regiments of tanks, the new panzer divisions would include a *Schützen-Brigade* (rifle brigade) with one *leichte Schützen-Regiment* (light rifle regiment) and one *Kradeschützen-Bataillon* (motorcycle rifle battalion).

Motorcycles were used in large numbers, primarily because the German Army did not have enough wheeled transport to carry the infantry, though the motorcycle battalions also served an important reconnaissance function.

Infantry in panzer divisions were classed as *Panzertruppen*: they wore the same rose pink *waffenfarbe*, or uniform piping, as the tank crews.

In 1938, Hitler appointed Guderian, now a *General der Panzertruppen*, as Chief of *Schnelle Truppen* (mobile troops), with authority over the development and training of Germany's mechanized forces, including: *Panzer, Schützen, Kavallerieschützen, Motorisierte Infanterie, Panzerabwehr* (anti-tank) and *Kavallerie truppen*.

PANZER ARMIES 1942–45

CHEF DES GENERALSTABES DES HEERES
Gen-Ob Ludwig Beck (1935–38)
Gen-Ob Franz Halder (1938–42)
Gen-Ob Kurt Zeitzler (1942–44)
Gen-Ob Heinz Guderian (1944–45)
Gen Hans Krebs (1945)

FIRST PANZER ARMY
Gen-Ob Ewald von Kleist
(1940–42)

Gen-Ob Eberhard von
Mackensen (1942–43)

Gen-Ob Hans-Valentin Hube
(1943–44)

Gen der Inf Kurt
von der Chevallerie (1944)

Gen-Ob Gotthard Heinrici
(1944–45)

Gen der Pz Walther Nehring
(1945)

Gen der Inf Wilhelm Hasse
(1945)

SECOND PANZER ARMY
Gen-Ob Heinz Guderian
(1940–41)

Gen-Ob Rudolf Schmidt
(1941–43)

Gen der Inf Heinrich
Clößner (1943)

Gen FM Walter Model
(1943)

Gen-Ob Dr. Lothar Rendulic
(1943–44)

Gen der Inf Franz Böhme
(1944)

Gen der Art Maximilian
de Angelis (1944–45)

THIRD PANZER ARMY
Gen-Ob Hermann Hoth
(1940–41)

Gen-Ob Hans-Georg
Reinhardt (1941–44)

Gen-Ob Erhard Raus
(1944–45)

Gen der Pz
Hasso-Eccard
von Manteuffel (1945)

FOURTH PANZER ARMY
Gen-Ob Erich Höppner
(1941–42)

Gen-Ob Richard Ruoff
(1942)

Gen-Ob Hermann Hoth
(1942–43)

Gen-Ob Erhard Raus
(1943–44)

Gen der Pz Walther Nehring
(1944)

Gen der Pz Hermann Balck
(1944)

Gen der Pz Fritz-Hubert
Gräser (1944–45)

FIFTH PANZER ARMY
PANZERGRUPPE WEST:
Gen der Pz Leo Geyr von
Schweppenburg (1944)
Gen der Pztrp Heinrich
Eberbach (1944)

FRANCE:
Gen der Pz Heinrich
Eberbach (1944)

SS-ObstGF Josef Dietrich
(1944)

Gen der Pz
Hasso-Eccard
von Manteuffel (1944–45)

Gen-Ob Josef Harpe (1945)

SIXTH SS PANZER ARMY
SS-Oberst-GF
Josef Dietrich (1944–45)

ELEVENTH SS
PANZER ARMY
SS-ObGF Felix Steiner
(1945)

PANZER ARMY AFRICA
Gen der Pz Erwin Rommel
(1941–42)

Gen der Pz Ludwig Crüwell
(1942)

Gen-Ob Erwin Rommel
(1942)

Gen der Kav
Georg Stumme (1942)

Gen der Pz Wilhelm Ritter
von Thoma (1942)

Gen FM Erwin Rommel
(1942)

Gen der Pz
Gustav Fehn (1942)

Gen FM Erwin Rommel
(1942–43)

Gen-Lt Karl Bülowius (1943)

Maresciallo d'Italia Giovanni
Messe (1943)

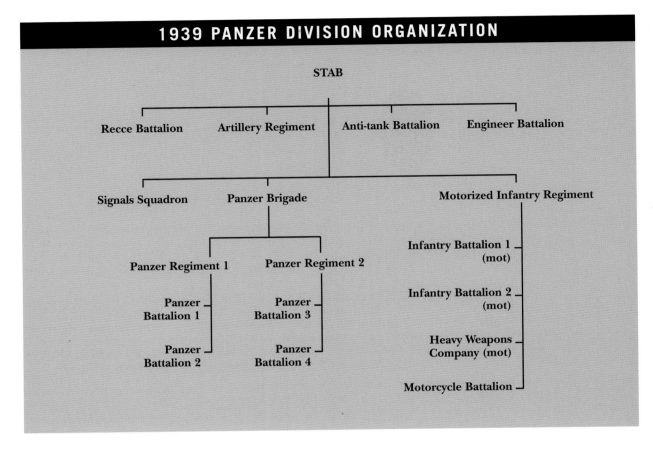

1939 PANZER DIVISION ORGANIZATION

STAB

Recce Battalion — Artillery Regiment — Anti-tank Battalion — Engineer Battalion

Signals Squadron — Panzer Brigade — Motorized Infantry Regiment

Panzer Regiment 1 — Panzer Regiment 2

Panzer Battalion 1 — Panzer Battalion 3

Panzer Battalion 2 — Panzer Battalion 4

Infantry Battalion 1 (mot)

Infantry Battalion 2 (mot)

Heavy Weapons Company (mot)

Motorcycle Battalion

Organization of 1st Panzer Division
1939

1. *Schützen-Brigade*
   Schützen-Regiment 1 (2 battalions)
   Kradschützen-Bataillon 1 (motorcyle battalion)
1. *Panzer-Brigade*
   Panzer-Regiment 1 (2 *abteilungen*)
   Panzer-Regiment 2 (2 *abteilungen*)
73. *Artillerie-Regiment* (2 *abteilungen*)
Aufklärungs-Abteilung 4
Panzerjäger-Abteilung 37
Pionier-Bataillon 37
Nachrichten-Abteilung 37
37th Divisional Support Units

Experience in Poland had shown that the panzer brigade formation was too large and unwieldy for tactical use, so after the invasion of France most divisions were reduced to a single panzer regiment, and the armoured and infantry brigade headquarters were dissolved. Total tank strength of a division in the invasion of the west was typically 150.

1st Panzer Division
1940

Schützen-Regiment 1 (2 battalions)
Schützen-Regiment 113 (2 battalions)
Panzer-Regiment 1 (2 *abteilungen*)
Artillerie-Regiment 73 (3 *abteilungen*)
Kradschützen-Abteilung 1
Aufklärungs-Abteilung 4
Panzerjäger-Abteilung 37
Pionier-Bataillon 37
Nachrichten-Abteilung 37
37th Divisional Support Units

HITLER'S ANNEXATIONS

Hitler's Annexations
1935–39

- Germany after 1919
- Troops into demilitarized Rhineland March 1936
- *Anschluss* (union with Austria), March 1938
- Occupation of Sudetenland October 1938
- Original Czechoslovakian border
- Formerly Czechoslovakia occupied March 1939
- Moravian territory to Poland October 1938
- Memel territory to Germany March 1939
- Protectorate of Slovakia territory to Hungary Nov 1938
- Czechoslovakian territory to Hungary March 1939

1936–39

Hitler's first territorial acquisitions were Germany's traditional industrial heartlands of the Saar and the Rhineland – demilitarized areas until recently occupied by the Allied powers of 1918. The Saar he regained in January 1935 by plebiscite. In March 1936, he re-occupied the Rhineland.

On 12 March 1938, Hitler sent his troops across the Austrian border and into Vienna to a rapturous welcome. The following day, he himself travelled to Vienna to declare the *Anschluss* – the indissoluble reunion of Austria and Germany into the Greater German Reich. The German General Staff used the operation as an exercise in moving large numbers of troops by road.

In Czechoslovakia, the Sudetenland, the western and northern border areas facing Germany and Austria had a German-speaking population of three million. The area had rich mineral resources, and it also housed major munitions factories at Pilsen. At Munich in September 1939, Britain, France, Italy and Germany agreed that the German-speaking Sudetenland should be transferred to the Reich – as the final stage of Hitler's territorial aggrandizement. Hitler had no intention of abiding by the agreement, however, and in March 1939 German troops moved forward from the Sudetenland, first to Prague and then on into the whole of Bohemia and Moravia.

Polish Campaign: 1939

The first opportunity to test the new *Panzerwaffe* in battle came in Poland in September 1939. Hitler gambled that Britain and France would do nothing militarily while his armed forces conquered Germany's eastern neighbour.

German soldiers crouch behind a Panzerkampfwagen I tank on the outskirts of Warsaw during the invasion of Poland, September 1939.

AT 4.45 ON THE MORNING of 1 September 1939, without a formal declaration of war, aircraft of the *Luftwaffe* crossed the Polish frontier. The mission of almost 1400 fighters, bombers and dive-bombers: the systematic destruction of Poland.

German Messerchmitts rapidly established air superiority, ruthlessly knocking Polish fighters from the skies while German bombers pounded Polish military and civil targets. Working under the protective fighter cover, German forces were unleashed against the Polish Army. The outcome was never in doubt from the start.

In little more than a month, all resistance had been crushed and the Polish state ceased to exist. Poland had succumbed to a new form of warfare that would conquer most of western Europe in the next eight months. The Nazis called it *Blitzkrieg*, or 'Lightning war'.

The attack on Poland was a natural development of Hitler's hunger for conquest. He had already absorbed Austria and Czechoslovakia; Poland was his next target. Rivalry between the two countries had already soured relations and armies on both sides of the German–Polish border were preparing for war.

Planning for the invasion of Poland had begun in April 1939, when Hitler ordered the German General Staff to launch the operation, known as *Fall Weiss* ('Case White'), five months later.

In many ways, Poland was an ideal theatre for the new kind of combined arms operations being developed by the *Wehrmacht*. It was fairly flat, and therefore suitable for mechanized operations, while its long borders meant that the Polish Army was overstretched.

One hour after the initial *Luftwaffe* strikes, it was the turn of German ground forces to swing into action. Over 40 German divisions were committed to the Polish campaign. Providing the spearhead of the German invasion force were six panzer divisions and eight motorized infantry divisions. These were supported by 27 foot-slogging infantry divisions.

The main role of the infantry was to engage the bulk of the Polish Army while the German mobile forces raced around the flanks, cutting through supply lines and striking at command centres to the rear.

The role of the *Luftwaffe* was to provide close air support for the German ground forces. However, German aircraft also played a more strategic role, striking at Polish airfields and aircraft, road and rail centres, concentrations of troop reserves and military headquarters. A number of Polish aircraft survived the initial atttacks and put up stiff – if limited – resistance over the following week. But it was too little, too late.

The world was stunned by the pace of the attack. While German panzers crossed the River Warta, Britain and France demanded the instant withdrawal of all German forces. Given the contemptuous silence with which this was greeted in Berlin, the Allies consulted on how best to implement their promises to Poland. A final ultimatum was sent to Berlin – and ignored.

At 11 a.m. on Sunday 3 September, British Prime Minister Neville Chamberlain broadcast the news that Britain was now at war with Germany. The world would realize, he felt sure, what a bitter personal disappointment this was. After all, Hitler had given his word not to attack.

Lightning war

The campaign was planned as a massive double pincer movement. The inner pincer was designed to close on the Vistula River, surrounding the bulk of the Polish field army, while the outer, faster-moving forces were targeted on the Bug, cutting off any possibility of escape.

The plan worked brilliantly. Never before had so much territory been gained in such a short space of time. After just three days of fighting, leading elements of the German Army had pushed 80km (50 miles) into Poland. Whole Polish armies were in danger of being isolated.

By the end of the first week, the Polish government had fled from Warsaw.

In spite of some successful counterattacks early in the campaign, the Polish air force had been all but wiped out. German Stuka dive-bombers were free to probe ahead of advancing panzer columns.

The momentum of the German advance continued virtually unchecked. By 8 September, the German 4th Panzer Division had advanced nearly 241km (150 miles), an average of more than 30km (18 miles) per day. By the same time, the Poles began to prepare Warsaw's defences.

The next day, initial German attempts to storm Warsaw were rebuffed. This was followed by a spirited

GERD VON RUNDSTEDT
(1875–1953)

The most senior German Army officer of World War II, Karl Rudolf Gerd von Rundstedt was born in Aschersleben in 1875. He served as a General Staff officer in the Great War. He commanded some of the largest armoured campaigns in history, from the Ardennes attack in 1940 to the overall command in the Battle of the Bulge in 1944.

• Rundstedt commanded Army Group South in Poland in 1939. In 1940, he commanded Army Group A in the invasion of France. He was promoted to Field Marshal after the fall of France on 19 July 1940.

• Rundstedt commanded Army Group South during Operation Barbarossa. Hitler sacked him on 12 December 1941 for a tactical withdrawal near Rostov.

• He was appointed commander-in-chief of Army Group West in France in March 1942. Hitler sacked him on 2 July 1944 for failing to stop the D-Day landings.

• Rundstedt was reluctantly brought out of retirement one final time to command the Ardennes Offensive of December 1944.

Polish counterattack in the Bzura region, marking the start of the biggest battle of the campaign.

But, by now, the entire Polish Army was becoming trapped inside an ever-decreasing circle of German forces. On 10 September, the *Luftwaffe* began to launch heavy raids on Warsaw, and the Polish government ordered a general military withdrawal to the south east.

On 15 September, the Germans issued an ultimatum to Warsaw – surrender or be destroyed. The garrison, supported by as many as 100,000 civilians, chose to fight on.

Army Groups North and South met at Wlodawa on 17 September, completing the outer ring of the German double pincer. From this double encirclement only a small fraction of the Polish Army could hope to escape, and on the same day even this hope was dashed. Surrounded and besieged, the Poles received yet another crushing blow with the news that Soviet forces had entered the war on the German side.

Russian invasion

Signed the previous month, the secret Soviet–German Pact called for the division of Poland. While the Germans crushed any remaining Polish resistance in the east, the Red Army advanced on two fronts north and south of the impassable Pripet marshes, meeting negligible opposition. The Polish government, which had already changed its location five times, fled into Romania.

On 19 September, the Polish Army in the Bzura pocket was finally defeated: more than 100,000 men were taken prisoner.

Two days later, the Germans launched a massive bombardment of Warsaw. The next day, the Soviets occupied Lvov and, with the Germans, mounted a joint victory parade in Brest-Litovsk.

A further ultimatum was issued on 25 September to the citizens and defenders of Warsaw, emphasized by attacks by more than 400 bombers. Polish resistance began to weaken, and on 26 September the *Wehrmacht* launched an infantry assault on the city.

Within a day, the Germans had taken control of the outer suburbs, and the Polish commander, recognizing a lost cause, offered to surrender. A ceasefire came into effect the next day, 28 September.

PANZER *ABTEILUNG*, POLISH CAMPAIGN

When the *Panzerwaffe* was established in 1935, each Panzer *Abteilung* (battalion) had four light companies. Each company had a command platoon and three further platoons. Each platoon, or *Zug*, was equipped with five tanks – initially one PzKpfw II and four PzKpfw I, and later three PzKpfw II and two PzKpfw I. By the time of the invasion of Poland in 1939, Panzer Is and IIs still formed the bulk of Germany's tank forces, but a sufficient quantity of Panzer IIIs and IVs had been completed to allow each *Abteilung* to replace two of its *Leichte* (light) companies with a single *Mittlere* (medium) company. This had far fewer tanks, but was far more effective in combat.

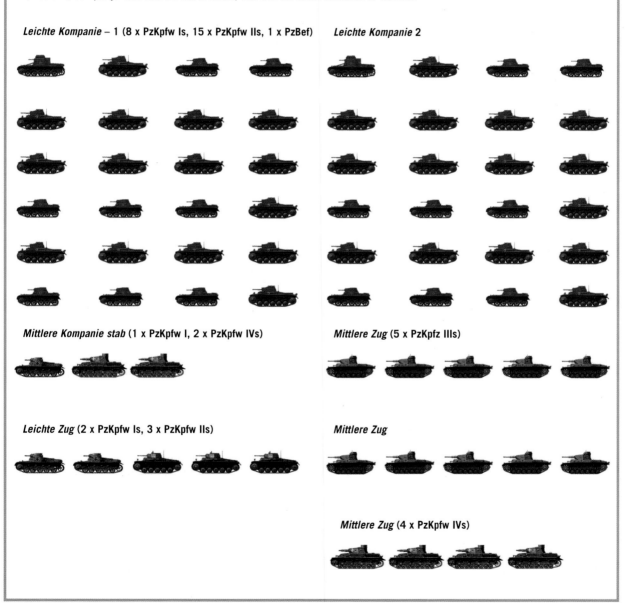

Leichte Kompanie – 1 (8 x PzKpfw Is, 15 x PzKpfw IIs, 1 x PzBef)

Leichte Kompanie 2

Mittlere Kompanie stab (1 x PzKpfw I, 2 x PzKpfw IVs)

Mittlere Zug (5 x PzKpfz IIIs)

Leichte Zug (2 x PzKpfw Is, 3 x PzKpfw IIs)

Mittlere Zug

Mittlere Zug (4 x PzKpfw IVs)

Army Group North

Although Army Group North was the weaker of the two massive forces concentrated by the Germans for the invasion of Poland, it included Guderian's crack XIX Corps, which was expected to prove its commander's theories of armoured warfare.

Army Group North was to control the Third and Fourth Armies, under command of *General der Artillerie* Georg von Küchler and *General der Artillerie* Gunther von Kluge. The headquarters for the Third Army would be formed from Küchler's I Corps in East Prussia; Fourth Army, from Kluge's Group Command. While Third

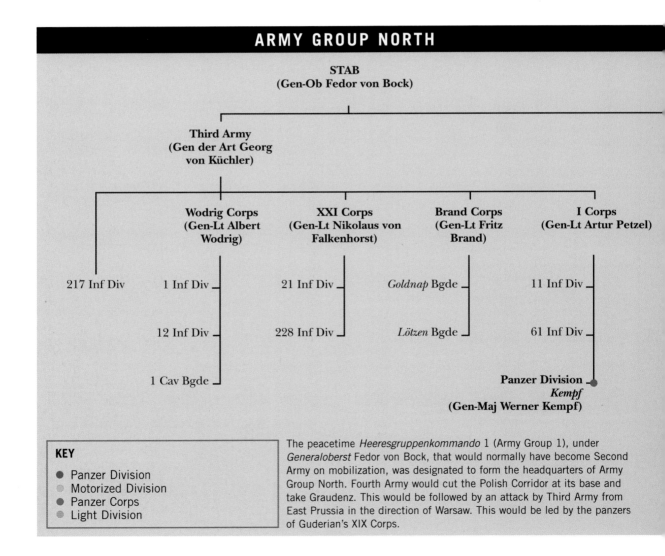

ARMY GROUP NORTH

STAB
(Gen-Ob Fedor von Bock)

Third Army
(Gen der Art Georg
von Küchler)

Wodrig Corps (Gen-Lt Albert Wodrig)	XXI Corps (Gen-Lt Nikolaus von Falkenhorst)	Brand Corps (Gen-Lt Fritz Brand)	I Corps (Gen-Lt Artur Petzel)

217 Inf Div

1 Inf Div — 21 Inf Div — *Goldnap* Bgde — 11 Inf Div —

12 Inf Div — 228 Inf Div — *Lötzen* Bgde — 61 Inf Div —

1 Cav Bgde —

Panzer Division
Kempf
(Gen-Maj Werner Kempf)

KEY
- Panzer Division
- Motorized Division
- Panzer Corps
- Light Division

The peacetime *Heeresgruppenkommando* 1 (Army Group 1), under *Generaloberst* Fedor von Bock, that would normally have become Second Army on mobilization, was designated to form the headquarters of Army Group North. Fourth Army would cut the Polish Corridor at its base and take Graudenz. This would be followed by an attack by Third Army from East Prussia in the direction of Warsaw. This would be led by the panzers of Guderian's XIX Corps.

Army commenced operations from East Prussia, Fourth Army would make its attack from Pomerania on Germany's Baltic Coast.

Third Army would comprise seven infantry divisions, a panzer brigade and a cavalry brigade (later combined and designated Panzer Division *Kempf*). Fourth Army would comprise six standard infantry divisions, two motorized infantry divisions and a panzer division. Two infantry divisions would be the army group reserve. Army Group North would thus include 13 standard infantry divisions, two motorized infantry divisions, a panzer

ARMY GROUP NORTH – PANZER STRENGTH (SEPT 1939)					
Tank type	Pz I	Pz II	Pz III	Pz IV	Pz Bef
3RD PANZER DIVISION					
5th Pz Rgt	63	77	3	9	8
6th Pz Rgt	59	79	3	9	8
Pz Lehr Abt	0	20	37	14	2
10TH PANZER DIVISION					
8th Pz Rgt	57	74	3	7	9

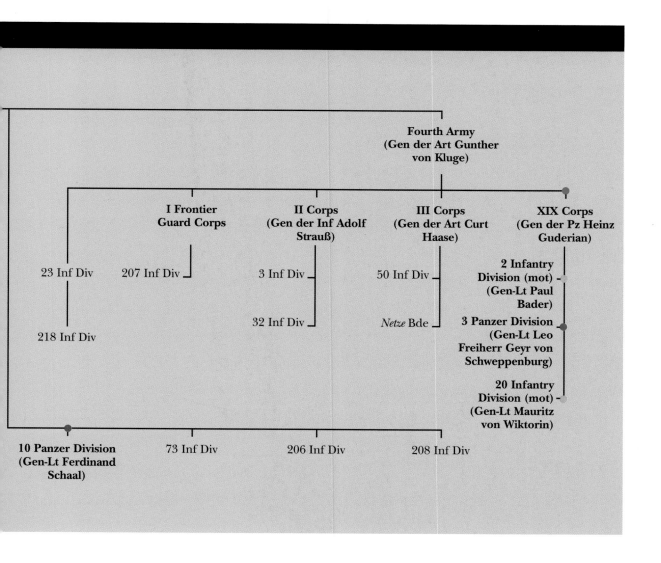

Fourth Army
(Gen der Art Gunther von Kluge)

I Frontier Guard Corps

II Corps (Gen der Inf Adolf Strauß)

III Corps (Gen der Art Curt Haase)

XIX Corps (Gen der Pz Heinz Guderian)

23 Inf Div   207 Inf Div   3 Inf Div   50 Inf Div   2 Infantry Division (mot) (Gen-Lt Paul Bader)

32 Inf Div   *Netze* Bde   3 Panzer Division (Gen-Lt Leo Freiherr Geyr von Schweppenburg)

218 Inf Div

20 Infantry Division (mot) (Gen-Lt Mauritz von Wiktorin)

10 Panzer Division (Gen-Lt Ferdinand Schaal)   73 Inf Div   206 Inf Div   208 Inf Div

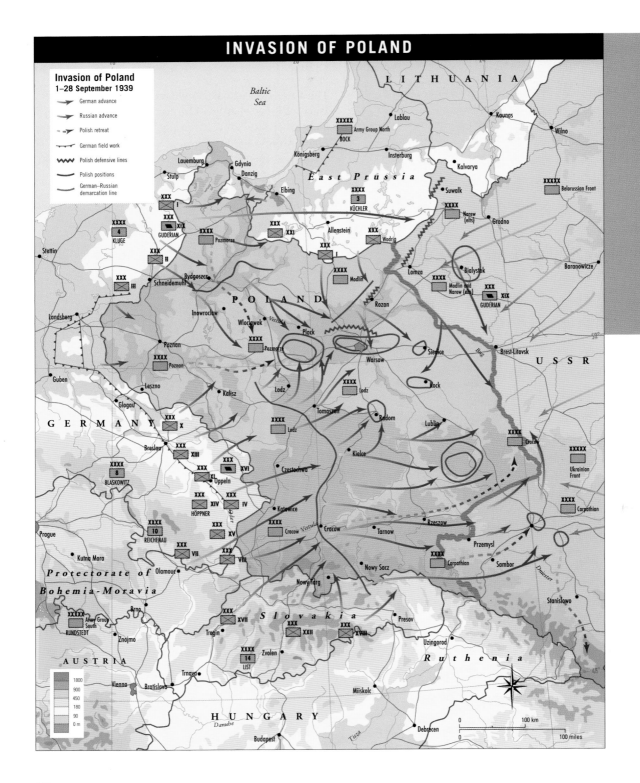

INVASION OF POLAND

Invasion of Poland
1–28 September 1939

- German advance
- Russian advance
- Polish retreat
- German field work
- Polish defensive lines
- Polish positions
- German–Russian demarcation line

1–28 September 1939

The invasion of Poland saw five German armies, amassing a total of more than 40 divisions, cross the border on 1 September 1939.

The panzer divisions of the newly created *Panzerwaffe*, supported by light armoured divisions and motorized infantry divisions, formed the spearhead of the German drive on Warsaw, reaching the outskirts of the city within a week.

The campaign was not a true *Blitzkrieg* operation as envisaged by Guderian and others: rather, it was a massive double pincer movement, the inner pincer designed to close on the Vistula River, while the outer pincer, comprising faster-moving forces, was targeted on the Bug River.

Poland's fate was sealed when the Soviets invaded from the east on 17 September 1939.

Third Army would attack simultaneously with the Fourth Army and send a strong force to assist Fourth Army in seizing crossings on the Vistula. The major force of Third Army, meanwhile, would attack in the direction of Warsaw without waiting for Fourth Army to establish land contact between the Reich proper and East Prussia. The Polish Army would be destroyed in the western part of Poland, and reserves would be prevented from mobilizing or concentrating to resist the German advance.

Fourth Army attack

The Fourth Army would attack to the east and south, cutting off the Polish forces in the northern part of the Corridor and securing the communication and transportation lines between Germany proper and East Prussia.

The force of the Third Army that attacked to the southwest and the Fourth Army would join in the attack towards Warsaw when their mission in the Corridor area was completed. The capture of Danzig would be accomplished by German reservists and SS forces already in the city.

division, a panzer brigade and a cavalry brigade, together with army group, army and corps troops.

Army Group South

Army Group South, the stronger of the two Groups, would include the Eighth, Tenth and Fourteenth Armies, under *General der Infanterie* Johannes Blaskowitz, *General der Artillerie* Walther von Reichenau and *Generaloberst* Wilhelm List.

Eighth Army would be formed from Blaskowitz's Group Command 3; Tenth Army, from Reichenau's Group Command 4; Fourteenth Army, from List's Group Command 5. The Eighth and Tenth Armies would attack from northern Silesia; Fourteenth Army, from southern Silesia and the satellite state of Slovakia.

Eighth Army would comprise four infantry divisions. Tenth Army would be composed of six infantry, two motorized infantry, two panzer, and three light divisions. Fourteenth Army would include five infantry, one light and two panzer divisions. Three mountain and six infantry divisions would be the army group reserve.

Army Group South would thus have 21 infantry, four panzer, two motorized infantry, four light and three mountain divisions.

Tenth Army, the strongest of the three, would make the main effort, striking towards Warsaw. Eighth Army would move on Lodz and secure the left (north) flank of Tenth Army against strong Polish forces in the Poznan-Kutno area capable of interfering with Tenth Army's mission. On the right (southeast) flank of Army Group South, Fourteenth Army would take Cracow and push to the east to protect the right flank of Tenth Army from attack by Polish forces moving into western Galicia from Lwow.

ARMY GROUP SOUTH

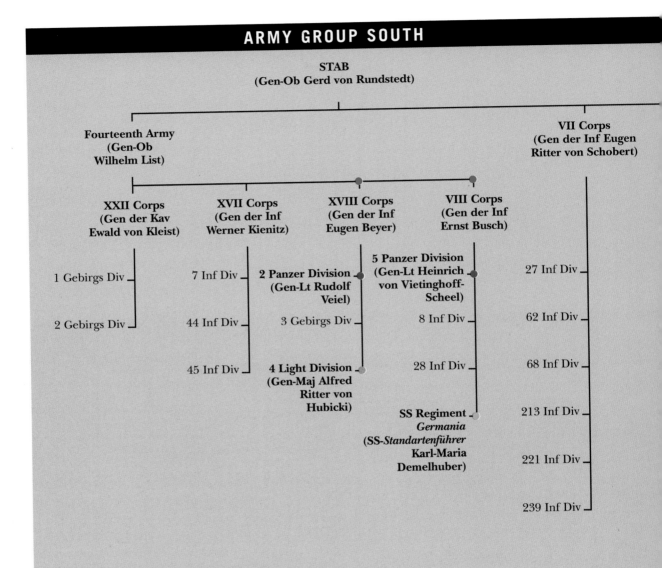

STAB
(Gen-Ob Gerd von Rundstedt)

Fourteenth Army
(Gen-Ob
Wilhelm List)

VII Corps
(Gen der Inf Eugen
Ritter von Schobert)

XXII Corps
(Gen der Kav
Ewald von Kleist)

XVII Corps
(Gen der Inf
Werner Kienitz)

XVIII Corps
(Gen der Inf
Eugen Beyer)

VIII Corps
(Gen der Inf
Ernst Busch)

1 Gebirgs Div

2 Gebirgs Div

7 Inf Div

44 Inf Div

45 Inf Div

2 Panzer Division
(Gen-Lt Rudolf
Veiel)

3 Gebirgs Div

4 Light Division
(Gen-Maj Alfred
Ritter von
Hubicki)

5 Panzer Division
(Gen-Lt Heinrich
von Vietinghoff-
Scheel)

8 Inf Div

28 Inf Div

SS Regiment
Germania
(SS-*Standartenführer*
Karl-Maria
Demelhuber)

27 Inf Div

62 Inf Div

68 Inf Div

213 Inf Div

221 Inf Div

239 Inf Div

KEY

- ● Panzer Division
- ○ Motorized Division/Unit
- ● Panzer Corps
- ○ Light Division

Army Group South, the stronger of the two major German ground forces, would include the Eighth, Tenth and Fourteenth Armies, under *General der Infanterie* Johannes Blaskowitz, *General der Artillerie* Walther von Reichenau, and *Generaloberst* Wilhelm List, in that order. It had the lion's share of the German Army's mobile forces, including four panzer divisions, four *leichte* divisions and two motorized infantry divisions, deploying a total of around 2000 panzers.

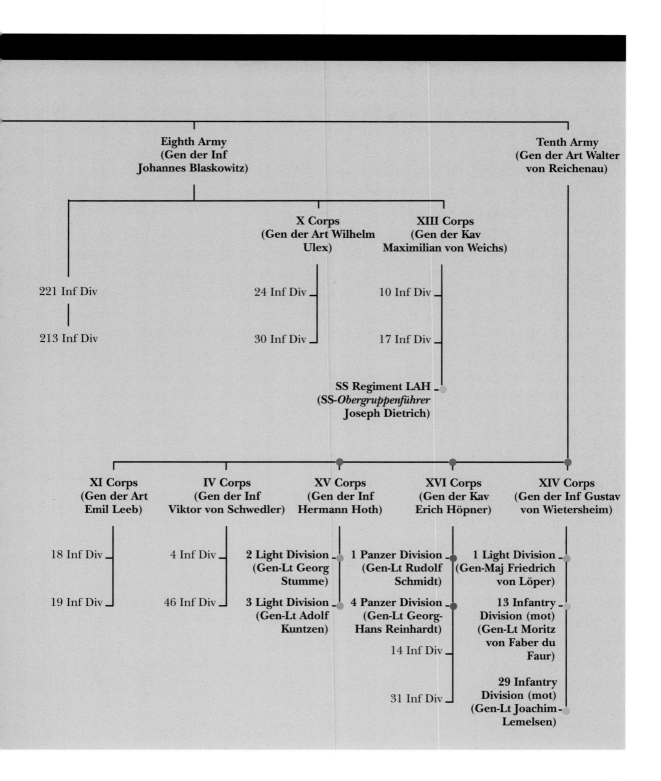

Eighth Army
(Gen der Inf
Johannes Blaskowitz)

Tenth Army
(Gen der Art Walter
von Reichenau)

X Corps
(Gen der Art Wilhelm
Ulex)

XIII Corps
(Gen der Kav
Maximilian von Weichs)

221 Inf Div

213 Inf Div

24 Inf Div

30 Inf Div

10 Inf Div

17 Inf Div

SS Regiment LAH
(SS-*Obergruppenführer*
Joseph Dietrich)

XI Corps
(Gen der Art
Emil Leeb)

IV Corps
(Gen der Inf
Viktor von Schwedler)

XV Corps
(Gen der Inf
Hermann Hoth)

XVI Corps
(Gen der Kav
Erich Höpner)

XIV Corps
(Gen der Inf Gustav
von Wietersheim)

18 Inf Div

19 Inf Div

4 Inf Div

46 Inf Div

2 Light Division
(Gen-Lt Georg
Stumme)

3 Light Division
(Gen-Lt Adolf
Kuntzen)

1 Panzer Division
(Gen-Lt Rudolf
Schmidt)

4 Panzer Division
(Gen-Lt Georg-
Hans Reinhardt)

14 Inf Div

31 Inf Div

1 Light Division
(Gen-Maj Friedrich
von Löper)

13 Infantry
Division (mot)
(Gen-Lt Moritz
von Faber du
Faur)

29 Infantry
Division (mot)
(Gen-Lt Joachim-
Lemelsen)

Combat lessons learned

The whirlwind German campaign introduced a new type of warfare, making use of classic principles of fire and manoeuvre allied to the utilization of the latest weapons in both the air and on the ground.

To the victors went the spoils of war. The Soviet–German partition of Poland came into force immediately with the signing of a 'treaty of frontier regulation and friendship' on 29 September. Poland as a nation ceased to exist.

To seal his triumph, Hitler flew into Warsaw on 5 October and took the salute at a victory parade. Organized Polish resistance ceased the next day with the surrender of 8000 troops southeast of Warsaw. For the Poles, defeat was now complete.

Despite the desperate gallantry of its soldiers, the Polish Army had been outclassed by a vastly more efficient military force. The fatal weakness in Poland's defences lay in its lack of armour and mobile forces. At the start of the war, 30 Polish infantry divisions had been supported by 13 cavalry brigades, just two of which were motorized: the remaining 11 still used horses.

The cost to the *Wehrmacht* of the campaign in Poland had been surprisingly light. According to the German sources, only 89 PzKpfw I, 83 PzKpfw II, 26 PzKpfw III, 19 PzKpfw IV, five command tanks, seven PzKpfw 35(t) and seven PzKpfw 38(t) were complete combat losses, though many more were damaged and needed extensive repair work.

Casualty bills

Overall, German casualties came to 10,572 killed, 30,000 wounded and up to 5029 troops missing in action. These were far lower than Polish losses, which have been estimated at 66,300 killed, 133,700 wounded and more than 420,000 taken prisoner.

The *Wehrmacht*'s triumph was recorded by scores of Propaganda Company cameramen, whose work was soon being shown in cinemas all over the world. This contributed greatly to the myth of *Blitzkrieg*, which would soon be terrifying Germany's enemies.

Curiously, many Western military professionals did not give the new tactics much attention, wrongly assuming the magnitude of the *Wehrmacht*'s victory to be due to the incompetence of the Poles.

Hitler's gamble

For Hitler, the Polish campaign had been a gamble that he had taken . . . and won. The *Wehrmacht* had committed most of its forces to operations in Poland. No more than a token covering force in the west was left to face an overwhelming French Army of 70 divisions and a small British Expeditionary Force.

Although dangerously overexposed, Hitler had calculated correctly that the Allies would do nothing if he invaded Poland. Once the subjugation of Poland was completed in early October, Hitler was free to turn his attention to further campaigns in the west. Without real combat experience in the new kind of mobile warfare

Tank type	Pz I	Pz II	Pz III	Pz IV	Pz Bef
ARMY GROUP SOUTH – PANZER STRENGTH (SEPT 1939)					
1ST PANZER DIVISION					
1st Pz Rgt	39	60	20	28	6
2nd Pz Rgt	54	62	6	28	6
2ND PANZER DIVISION					
3rd Pz Rgt	62	78	3	8	9
4th Pz Rgt	62	77	3	9	11
4TH PANZER DIVISION					
35th Pz Rgt	99	64	0	6	8
36 Pz Rgt	84	66	0	6	18
5TH PANZER DIVISION					
15th Pz Rgt	51	61	24	16	15
31st Pz Rgt	46	59	28	16	11

introduced with the tank and extensive motorization, the German Army made an intensive analysis of the progress and outcome of the campaign.

Mobile warfare

Speed was a major contribution to the *Wehrmacht*'s success, as was good intelligence. German troops unerringly found the weak spots in the Polish defences, which were exploited by fast-moving armour and mechanized infantry that all but ignored flank security. They relied on their speed of penetration to disrupt Polish counterattacks, leaving consolidation to the slower-moving infantry following on foot.

Tanks

Clearly, the Panzer Is and Panzer IIs that made up the bulk of the German armoured force were far from ideal in real fighting. Introduced as training machines, they were effective in Poland because the Polish Army lacked the the means to stop them. Nevertheless, they proved to be vulnerable to any kind of organized anti-tank defence, and their thin armour meant that they also sustained losses to improvised weapons in urban areas.

The Panzer IIIs and Panzer IVs were real combat machines, but German industry had been unable to build enough vehicles to bring the medium companies of the original panzer divisions to full strength.

Panzer production was pushed up to 125 tanks a month, but that would not be enough to meet demand in the campaign in the West. As a stop-gap, the *Wehrmacht* issed Czech-built tanks to the new panzer divisions being converted from the light divisions.

As early as the Anschluss with Austria early in 1938, it was clear that reliability was going to be a problem for the emerging Panzerwaffe. Many of the light tanks involved in that operation broke down, and by the time of the Polish campaign things had improved very little. According to the Army High Command, about a quarter of the German Army's panzer inventory was out of action at any one time, due to combat damage, breakdowns or scheduled maintenance.

Divisional reorganization

The panzer brigade of two regiments looked impressive on paper, but in practice it proved rather difficult to command effectively. After Poland, it was decided to reduce the panzer division's armoured strength to a single regiment, halving the number of tanks but making each tank unit more easy to command. The surplus tanks could then be used to form the nucleus of new panzer divisions being formed, in the first instance from the four existing Light divisions.

The light divisions had been created before the war to give the influential cavalry faction in the German Army a piece of the armoured cake. However, while they were as complex and expensive to run as a panzer division, they had less than half the tank strength. They had a large motorized infantry component, but were less cost-effective than a regular motorized infantry division.

After Poland, it was decided to convert the four Light divisions into regular panzer divisions.

Tactics and operations

Two of the decisive components of *Blitzkrieg* had proved themselves in Poland, and the panzers and the *Luftwaffe* had also shown that they could work effectively together to take advantage of weaknesses in the enemy lines.

Tank forces and motorized infantry had moved with unprecedented speed: von Reichenau's Tenth Army advanced more than 250km (155 miles) in the first week of the campaign. The Germans were lucky in being able to complete their campaign before the onset of the Autumn rains: they were even less prepared to deal with deep mud in 1939 than they would be in the Soviet Union two years later.

The only doubt in the minds of German panzer commanders was the lack of any tank-versus-tank combat in the campaign. The Poles had only one fully equipped tank unit at the outbreak of war, and it was over-run and destroyed while forming up at the outset of the campaign. German tankmen knew that in any war in the West, they would be outnumbered by the French Army, and French tanks were, on paper, more powerful and better protected than German machines, although they had yet to prove themselves in combat.

In the event, they had no need to worry. What the campaign in Poland had shown was that it was the way you used your tanks that brought victory on the *Blitzkrieg* battlefield, and nobody did that better than the German Army.

France and the
Low Countries: 1940

Having proved their abilities in a conventional campaign in Poland, Germany's panzers were now to use fully the deep penetration, fast-moving panzer tactics of *Blitzkrieg* to achieve a smashing victory against the Western Allies.

Light Panzer Is and IIs move through a burning French village in June 1940. The speed and mobility of the *Panzerwaffe* enabled German tanks and motorized infantry and artillery to run riot through French rear areas and lines of communication

THE ORIGINAL GERMAN PLAN for the invasion of western Europe was based on the opening attack of World War I. Hitler's High Command intended to occupy Belgium and France's northern industrial regions but no further. They had no intention of repeating the ill-fated march on Paris they tried in 1914.

But Hitler had other ideas. He had fought in Belgium, in the shattered villages around Ypres. He knew the terrain. Countless small rivers and streams offered endless obstruction to an invader. Surely it would be better to attack further south, perhaps through the forested hills of the Ardennes?

The Manstein Plan

By the time the postponed offensive was ready to roll in the spring, Hitler discovered that at least some officers shared his vision. General von Manstein, von Rundstedt's Chief of Staff, had studied the Ardennes and had come to the same conclusion as the Führer.

Along with General Heinz Guderian, he argued for a radical strategy: to rush German panzer divisions along the narrow forest tracks and out onto the gently rolling hills of northern France.

Guderian and his tank men were confident they could storm the French defences. The *Luftwaffe*'s bombers, especially its fearsome Stukas, would provide close support in place of artillery.

Hitler adopted von Manstein's plan and changed the orders to his commanders in the west. Manstein would receive due credit in time, but the orthodox generals resented having a relatively junior officer's plan thrust upon them, and posted von Manstein to command an infantry corps in the rear.

Panzers outnumbered

One thing Hitler could not change was the odds. Although Germany enjoyed superiority in the air, the *Wehrmacht* had only 141 divisions with which to attack 144 Allied divisions.

In terms of armour, the Allies had the clear advantage, with nearly 3500 tanks compared to the German total of just over 2300. Worse for the Germans, many of these were light tanks of limited fighting ability. But it was the way the *Wehrmacht* used its panzers that would prove decisive in the end.

HEINZ GUDERIAN (1888–1954)

Commissioned into the light infantry in 1907, Guderian served as a staff officer in World War I. Between the wars he developed *Blitzkrieg* – the tactics that enabled Germany's victories up to 1941.

• More than a theoretician, he proved to be an aggressive and capable panzer commander in Poland, France and in the first months of the invasion of the USSR. However, he was relieved of his command in 1941 where he withdrew his Panzer Group from Moscow as it came under intense Soviet attack.

• He was made Inspector of Panzer Troops in 1943, responsible for the training and equipment of the Panzer Arm.

• In July 1944, he was promoted to army chief-of-staff and held this post until 22 March, 1945.

He died at Schwangau-bei-Fussen in Bavaria on 15 May 1954

Army Group A

Renamed from Army Group South in October 1939 as German troops redeployed westwards after the Polish Campaign, Army Group A was to be the principal German strike force in the campaign that was launched in the West in May 1940.

With the Allied field army lured from France into Belgium, the real German punch came through the Ardennes. Runstedt's Army Group A had 44 divisions, including seven panzer divisions under von Kleist, with the spearhead provided by Heinz Guderian's XIX Corps.

Encountering little resistance from Belgian troops in the Ardennes, the panzers headed down the dirt roads in dense columns and, by the evening of 12 May, German spearheads had reached the River Meuse.

Guderian's tanks crashed through the 'impassable' Ardennes as though on a peacetime exercise, brushing aside the French light cavalry unit that had been sent out to 'delay' them.

Across the Meuse

On 13 May, Guderian's infantry paddled across the Meuse in rubber dinghies while the French defences were pulverized by attacks from 300 twin-engine bombers and 200 Stukas. The dive-bombers attacked with particular accuracy, knocking out key French gun positions.

By the morning of the next day, Guderian had two bridgeheads. Up at Dinant, the 7th Panzer Division – under the command of Major-General Erwin Rommel – had formed yet another bridgehead in the face of desperate but sporadic French defences.

Early on 15 May, the German flood burst into France. From each of the bridgeheads the panzers roared out, preceded by swarms of screaming Stukas. These were protected from British and French fighter attack by roving Messerschmitts.

The Channel coast

By the evening of 20 May, Guderian's panzer spearheads had reached Abbeville at the mouth of the Somme, and at this point their line was as thinned out as it ever would be.

The Germans were vulnerable to a determined counterattack, but the only one that threatened the speeding panzers was by British tanks at Arras on 21 May. The Allies inflicted a stinging reverse on the SS *Totenkopf* division, but they quickly found themselves blocked by Rommel's panzers. After a brisk battle, the British were driven back to their original positions and threatened with encirclement.

Dunkirk evacuation

Trapped in a shrinking pocket around Dunkirk, the British seemed certain to be destroyed. But then the Führer ordered his panzers to stop, allowing the British a breathing space. A fleet of 1000 civilian boats helped the Royal Navy evacuate over 338,000 soldiers, including 100,000 Frenchmen.

By 5 June, the 10 panzer divisions of both army groups had been redeployed into five armoured corps, three under von Bock, two under von Rundstedt. Over the next 10 days, they would race through France, utterly defeating the French Army.

XIX PANZER CORPS – PANZER STRENGTH (MAY 1940)					
Tank type	Pz I	Pz II	Pz III	Pz IV	Pz Bef
1ST PANZER DIVISION					
1st Pz Rgt	26	49	28	20	4
2nd Pz Rgt	26	49	30	20	4
2ND PANZER DIVISION					
3rd Pz Rgt	22	55	29	16	8
4th Pz Rgt	23	60	29	16	8
10TH PANZER DIVISION					
7th Pz Rgt	22	58	29	16	9
8th Pz Rgt	22	55	29	16	9

PANZER *ABTEILUNG*, 25TH PZ REGIMENT (MAY 1940)

The panzer regiment in 1940 was very little changed from the panzer regiment of 1939. Although production of medium tanks was being stepped up, there were still too few Panzer IIIs and IVs in service to replace the lightweight Panzer Is and IIs that still served in large numbers. However, large numbers of Czech-built Panzer 35(t) and Panzer 38(t) tanks were being deployed, especially in the new panzer divisions formed after the end of the Polish campaign.

Abteilung Stab Kompanie

1 *Leichte Kompanie*

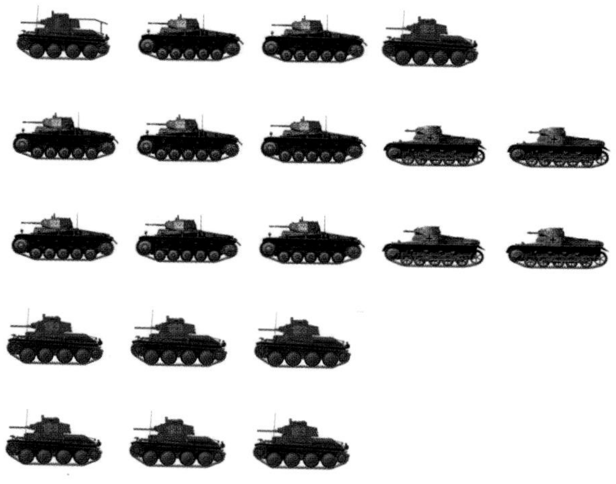

2 *Leichte Kompanie*

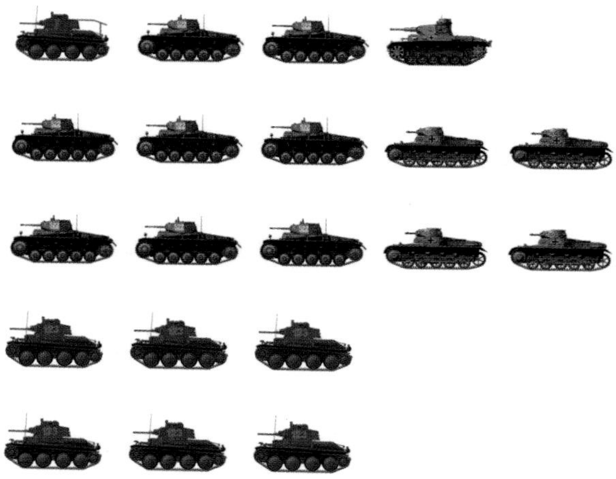

Mittlere Kompanie

ORGANIZATIONS

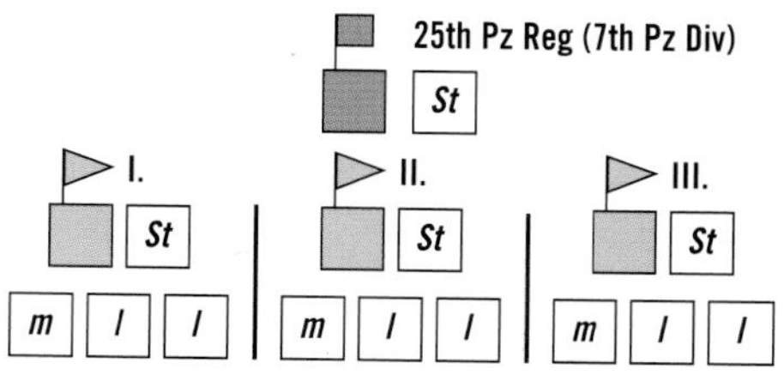

25th Pz Reg (7th Pz Div)
St

I.
St
m l l

II.
St
m l l

III.
St
m l l

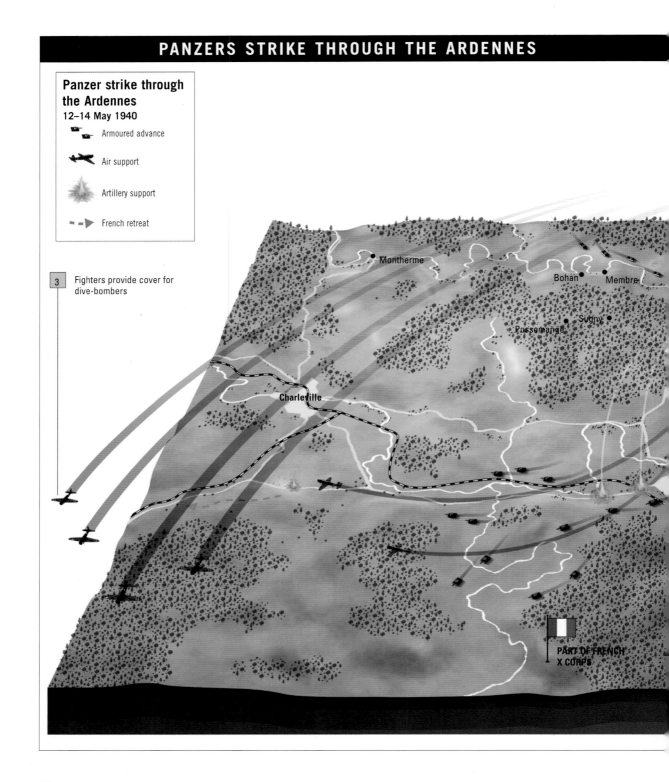

PANZERS STRIKE THROUGH THE ARDENNES

Panzer strike through the Ardennes
12–14 May 1940

- Armoured advance
- Air support
- Artillery support
- French retreat

3 Fighters provide cover for dive-bombers

Montherme

Bohan • Membre

Sugny
Pussemange

Charleville

PART OF FRENCH
X CORPS

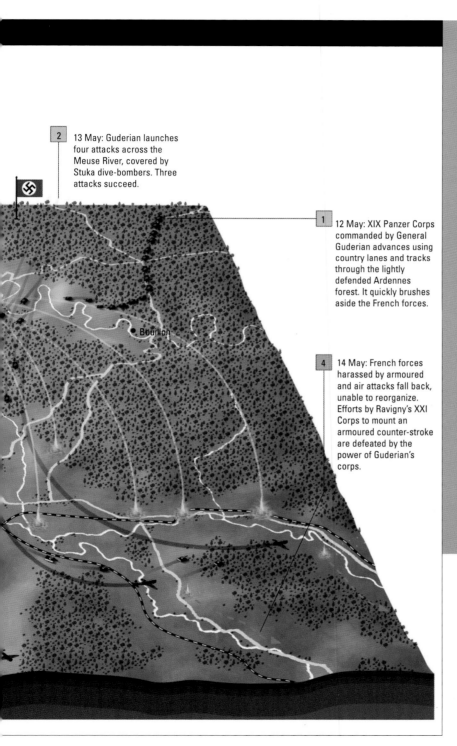

2   13 May: Guderian launches four attacks across the Meuse River, covered by Stuka dive-bombers. Three attacks succeed.

1   12 May: XIX Panzer Corps commanded by General Guderian advances using country lanes and tracks through the lightly defended Ardennes forest. It quickly brushes aside the French forces.

Bouillon

4   14 May: French forces harassed by armoured and air attacks fall back, unable to reorganize. Efforts by Ravigny's XXI Corps to mount an armoured counter-stroke are defeated by the power of Guderian's corps.

12–14 May 1940

The German attack in the Low Countries was a massive feint designed to draw the Anglo–French field armies northwards into Belgium. The real punch came through the Ardennes, where the 44 divisions of von Rundstedt's Army Group A planned to catch the Allies by surprise.

The bulk of the French troops were in the Maginot Line, guarding against an attack across the German border. But the huge works did not cover the Belgian border, French planners having considered that a major attack through the Ardennes was impossible.

Encountering little resistance from Belgian troops in the Ardennes, the panzer divisions headed down the dirt roads in alarmingly dense columns. Crashing through the 'impassable' forests and hills, brushing aside the French light cavalry unit that had been sent out to 'delay' them, the three divisions of General Guderian's panzer corps were across the French frontier and had reached the River Meuse on each side of Sedan by the afternoon of 12 May.

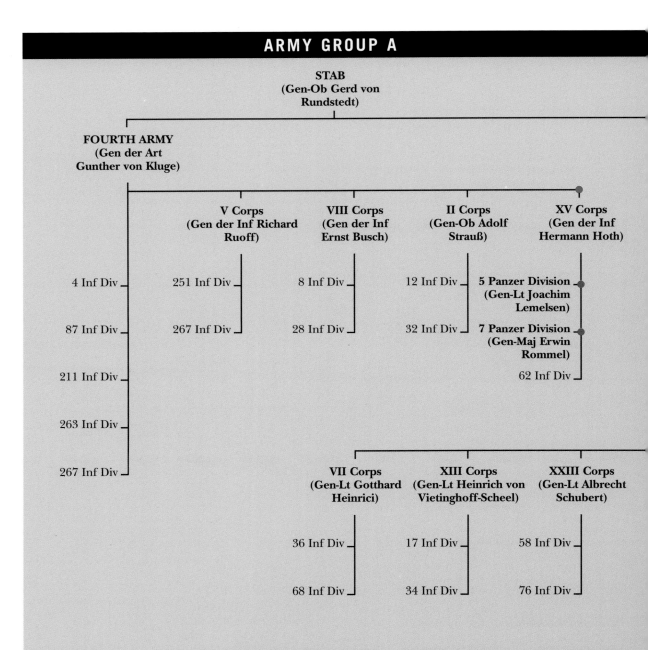

ARMY GROUP A

STAB
(Gen-Ob Gerd von Rundstedt)

FOURTH ARMY
(Gen der Art Gunther von Kluge)

V Corps **(Gen der Inf Richard Ruoff)**	**VIII Corps** **(Gen der Inf Ernst Busch)**	**II Corps** **(Gen-Ob Adolf Strauß)**	**XV Corps** **(Gen der Inf Hermann Hoth)**

4 Inf Div — 251 Inf Div — 8 Inf Div — 12 Inf Div — **5 Panzer Division (Gen-Lt Joachim Lemelsen)**

87 Inf Div — 267 Inf Div — 28 Inf Div — 32 Inf Div — **7 Panzer Division (Gen-Maj Erwin Rommel)**

211 Inf Div — 62 Inf Div

263 Inf Div

267 Inf Div

VII Corps **(Gen-Lt Gotthard Heinrici)**	**XIII Corps** **(Gen-Lt Heinrich von Vietinghoff-Scheel)**	**XXIII Corps** **(Gen-Lt Albrecht Schubert)**

36 Inf Div — 17 Inf Div — 58 Inf Div

68 Inf Div — 34 Inf Div — 76 Inf Div

KEY

● Panzer Division
● Motorized Division/unit
● Panzer Corps
● Light Division

Army Group A provided the *Wehrmacht's* main punch in the campaign in the West. It was spearheaded by three motorized corps, commanded by Generals Guderian, Reinhardt and Hoth (the former two subordinated to Panzer Group von Kleist). *Heeresgruppe* A (Army Group A) led the Ardennes breakout, the advance to the Somme and operations against Dunkirk. *Heeresgruppe* A was reorganized during the pause in the fighting after Dunkirk. In July, it advanced to the Swiss border in the French rear, isolating the Maginot Line.

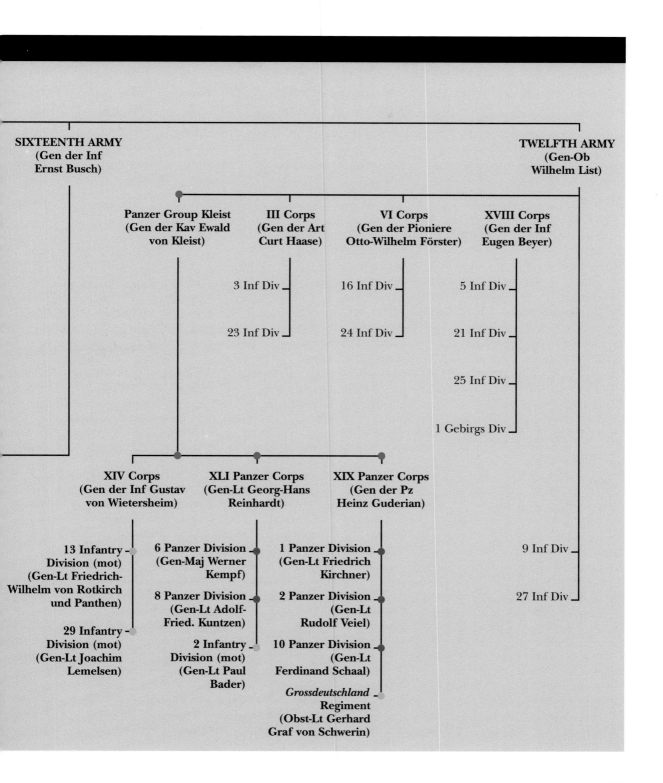

SIXTEENTH ARMY
(Gen der Inf
Ernst Busch)

TWELFTH ARMY
(Gen-Ob
Wilhelm List)

Panzer Group Kleist
(Gen der Kav Ewald
von Kleist)

III Corps
(Gen der Art
Curt Haase)

VI Corps
(Gen der Pioniere
Otto-Wilhelm Förster)

XVIII Corps
(Gen der Inf
Eugen Beyer)

3 Inf Div

16 Inf Div

5 Inf Div

23 Inf Div

24 Inf Div

21 Inf Div

25 Inf Div

1 Gebirgs Div

XIV Corps
(Gen der Inf Gustav
von Wietersheim)

XLI Panzer Corps
(Gen-Lt Georg-Hans
Reinhardt)

XIX Panzer Corps
(Gen der Pz
Heinz Guderian)

13 Infantry
Division (mot)
(Gen-Lt Friedrich-
Wilhelm von Rotkirch
und Panthen)

6 Panzer Division
(Gen-Maj Werner
Kempf)

1 Panzer Division
(Gen-Lt Friedrich
Kirchner)

9 Inf Div

8 Panzer Division
(Gen-Lt Adolf-
Fried. Kuntzen)

2 Panzer Division
(Gen-Lt
Rudolf Veiel)

27 Inf Div

29 Infantry
Division (mot)
(Gen-Lt Joachim
Lemelsen)

2 Infantry
Division (mot)
(Gen-Lt Paul
Bader)

10 Panzer Division
(Gen-Lt
Ferdinand Schaal)

Grossdeutschland
Regiment
(Obst-Lt Gerhard
Graf von Schwerin)

Army Group B

Army Group B was formed in the Autumn of 1939 after the campaign in Poland by the redesignation of Army Group North. Tasked with attacking the Low Countries, it had fewer armoured and motorized formations than Army Group A.

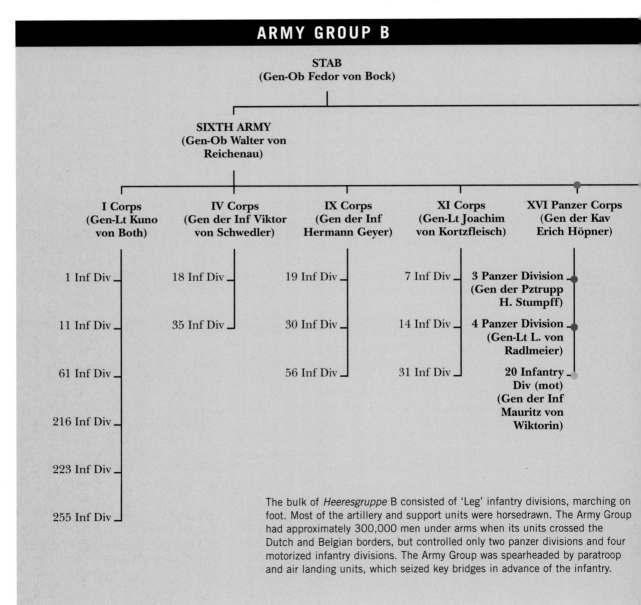

ARMY GROUP B

STAB
(Gen-Ob Fedor von Bock)

SIXTH ARMY
(Gen-Ob Walter von Reichenau)

I Corps (Gen-Lt Kuno von Both)	IV Corps (Gen der Inf Viktor von Schwedler)	IX Corps (Gen der Inf Hermann Geyer)	XI Corps (Gen-Lt Joachim von Kortzfleisch)	XVI Panzer Corps (Gen der Kav Erich Höpner)
1 Inf Div	18 Inf Div	19 Inf Div	7 Inf Div	3 Panzer Division (Gen der Pztrupp H. Stumpff)
11 Inf Div	35 Inf Div	30 Inf Div	14 Inf Div	4 Panzer Division (Gen-Lt L. von Radlmeier)
61 Inf Div		56 Inf Div	31 Inf Div	20 Infantry Div (mot) (Gen der Inf Mauritz von Wiktorin)
216 Inf Div				
223 Inf Div				
255 Inf Div				

The bulk of *Heeresgruppe* B consisted of 'Leg' infantry divisions, marching on foot. Most of the artillery and support units were horsedrawn. The Army Group had approximately 300,000 men under arms when its units crossed the Dutch and Belgian borders, but controlled only two panzer divisions and four motorized infantry divisions. The Army Group was spearheaded by paratroop and air landing units, which seized key bridges in advance of the infantry.

Shortly after 2.30 a.m., 10 May, 64 German troops crossed the Dutch frontier. Three hours later, glider-borne troops dropped over the Belgian border to capture and demolish the huge fortifications at Eben-Emael. The imposing concrete and steel fortress fell to a crack unit of *Fallschirmjäger* – paratroops – who landed by glider right on the roof of the fortress. At 5.35 a.m., the 30 divisions of General von Bock's Army Group B flooded forwards across the frontiers from Maastricht up to the coast at the Ems estuary.

The Allies were expecting the attack through the Low Countries and made their plans accordingly.

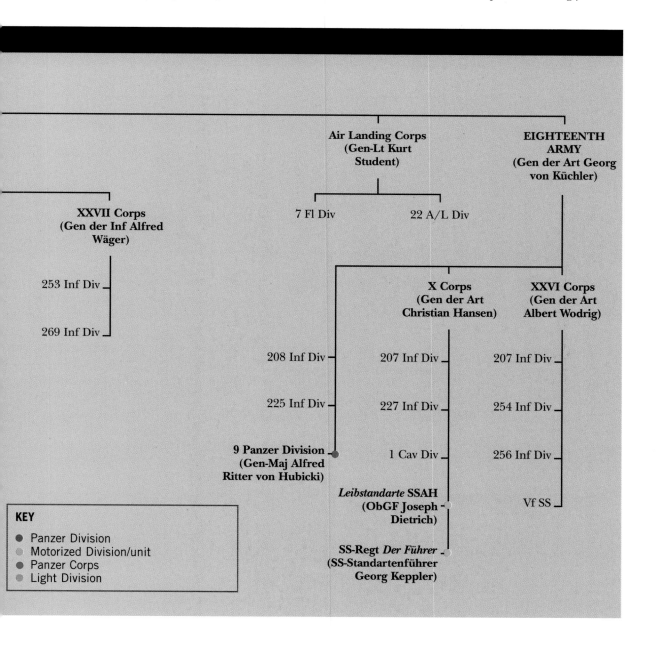

Air Landing Corps
(Gen-Lt Kurt Student)

7 Fl Div   22 A/L Div

EIGHTEENTH ARMY
(Gen der Art Georg von Küchler)

XXVII Corps
(Gen der Inf Alfred Wäger)

253 Inf Div

269 Inf Div

X Corps
(Gen der Art Christian Hansen)

XXVI Corps
(Gen der Art Albert Wodrig)

208 Inf Div   207 Inf Div   207 Inf Div

225 Inf Div   227 Inf Div   254 Inf Div

9 Panzer Division
(Gen-Maj Alfred Ritter von Hubicki)   1 Cav Div   256 Inf Div

Leibstandarte SSAH
(ObGF Joseph Dietrich)   Vf SS

SS-Regt *Der Führer*
(SS-Standartenführer Georg Keppler)

KEY
- Panzer Division
- Motorized Division/unit
- Panzer Corps
- Light Division

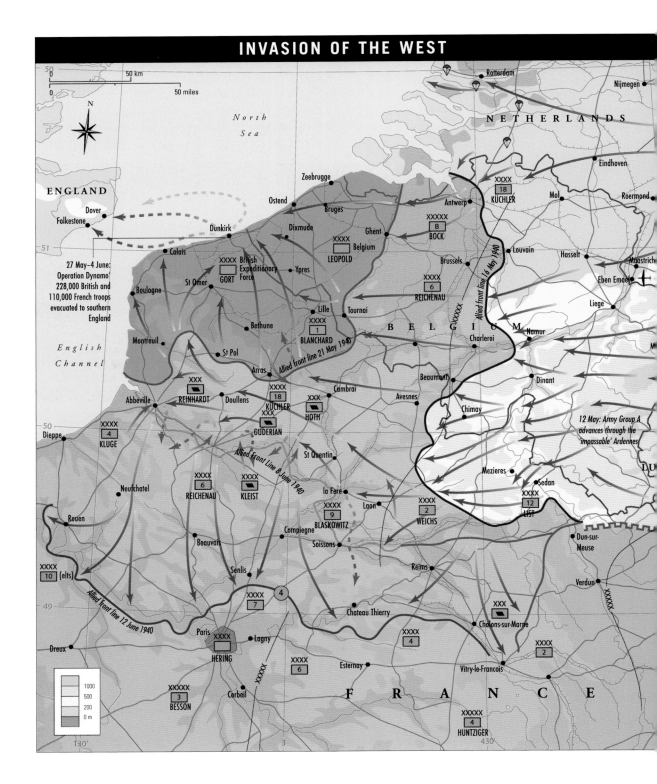

INVASION OF THE WEST

50 km

50 miles

N

North Sea

NETHERLANDS

Rotterdam

Nijmegen

Eindhoven

Roermond

ENGLAND

Dover

Folkestone

Zeebrugge

Ostend

Bruges

Dixmude

Ghent

Antwerp

XXXX
18
KÜCHLER

Mol

Maastricht

XXXXX
B
BOCK

Louvain

Hasselt

27 May–4 June:
Operation Dynamo:
228,000 British and
110,000 French troops
evacuated to southern
England

Calais

Dunkirk

XXXX
British
Expeditionary
Force
GORT

XXXX
Belgium
LEOPOLD

Ypres

Brussels

XXXX
6
REICHENAU

Eben Emael

Liege

Boulogne

St Omer

Lille

Tournai

B E L G I U M

Charleroi

Namur

English Channel

Montreuil

St Pol

Bethune

XXXX
1
BLANCHARD

Allied front line 21 May 1940

Beaumont

Dinant

Arras

XXX
REINHARDT

Doullens

Cambrai

Avesnes

Chimay

*12 May: Army Group A
advances through the
'impassable' Ardennes*

Abbeville

XXXX
18
KÜCHLER

XXX
HOTH

Dieppe

XXXX
4
KLUGE

GUDERIAN

St Quentin

Allied Front Line 8 June 1940

Mezieres

Sedan

XXXX
12
LIST

LU

Neufchatel

XXXX
6
REICHENAU

XXXX
KLEIST

la Fere

Laon

XXXX
2
WEICHS

Rouen

XXXX
9
BLASKOWITZ

Compiegne

Soissons

Reims

Dun-sur-
Meuse

Beauvais

XXXX
10 (elts)

Allied front line 12 June 1940

Senlis

XXXX
7

4

Chateau Thierry

Verdun

XXX

Chalons-sur-Marne

Paris

XXXX
HERING

Lagny

Dreux

XXXX
6

Esternay

XXXX
4

Vitry-le-Francois

XXXX
2

XXXXX
3
BESSON

Corbeil

XXXXX

F R A N C E

XXXXX
4
HUNTZIGER

1000
500
200
0 m

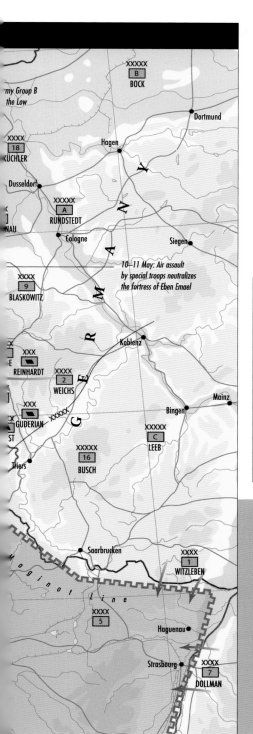

XVI PANZER CORPS – PANZER STRENGTH (MAY 1940)					
Tank type	Pz I	Pz II	Pz III	Pz IV	Pz Bef
3RD PANZER DIVISION					
5th Pz Rgt	22	55	29	16	8
6th Pz Rgt	23	60	29	16	8
4TH PANZER DIVISION					
35th Pz Rgt	69	50	20	12	5
66th Pz Rgt	66	55	20	12	5

But the 30 divisions of von Bock's Army Group B were actually a feint. They drew the Allied armies from the defensive positions they had so arduously prepared during the bitterly cold winter of 1939–40. By the evening of 14 May, the Allied line was formed as British and French troops moved forwards to join the Belgian Army. Movements were hampered by roads choked by refugees fleeing ahead of Bock's advancing infantry.

Allied commanders took too long to realize that Bock's slowly advancing Army Group was the lure to tempt them into a trap. It was too late: von Rundstedt's Army Group A had already launched the killing thrust through the Ardennes into France.

Invasion of the West
May–June 1940

➤ German attacks

➤ Allied counterattacks

- -➤ Allied retreats

⌒ Allied front lines

⊐⌐⊓ Allied defensive lines

⊻ German paratroop drops

✛ German glider assault

May–June 1940

After brushing aside the weak French resistance on the Meuse, Rundstedt's Army Group A, spearheaded by Guderian's panzer corps, broke out into the French countryside beyond. Instead of driving towards Paris, the panzers raced to the northwest, towards the Channel.

The French lacked the reserves to be able to react to the German challenge. A French tank counterattack on 17 May, led by Colonel Charles de Gaulle, was brushed aside without difficulty by the 1st Panzer Division. A British attack near Arras was much more threatening, and was held off only when General Erwin Rommel of the 7th Panzer Division used his 8.8cm Flak guns in the anti-tank role.

The attacks came too late: Guderian's panzers had already reached the Channel coast on the 20 May. The Allied armies were cut off.

Army Group C

The weakest of the *Wehrmacht's* formations in the West, Army Group C was tasked with threatening the French Maginot Line fortifications, tying down 400,000 French troops and preventing them from reinforcing Allied armies to the west.

Established on 26 August 1939 from the staff of *Heeresgruppenkommando* 2, Army Group C played no part in the invasion of Poland. Its mission was to command all German troops facing the Western allies while the conquest of Poland was completed.

After the successful conclusion of the Polish campaign, as German troops were hurried westwards in case of a major French attack across the border, Army Group C's area of responsibility was reduced to covering

the southern border comprising the Upper Rhine and the Palatinate.

Holding attacks

For the planned attack on France, Army Group C would be composed of 19 divisions under Wilhelm von Leeb. Its mission was primarily to support the larger Army Groups to the north. Its task was to prevent a French flanking movement from the east, and to do that it was

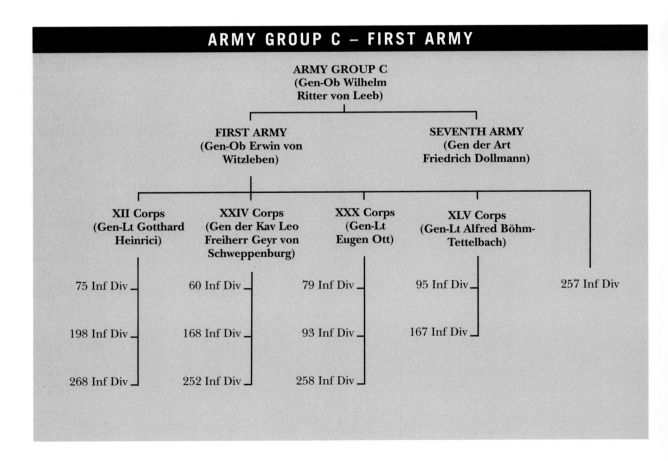

ARMY GROUP C – FIRST ARMY

ARMY GROUP C
(Gen-Ob Wilhelm
Ritter von Leeb)

FIRST ARMY
(Gen-Ob Erwin von
Witzleben)

SEVENTH ARMY
(Gen der Art
Friedrich Dollmann)

XII Corps
(Gen-Lt Gotthard
Heinrici)

XXIV Corps
(Gen der Kav Leo
Freiherr Geyr von
Schweppenburg)

XXX Corps
(Gen-Lt
Eugen Ott)

XLV Corps
(Gen-Lt Alfred Böhm-
Tettelbach)

75 Inf Div

198 Inf Div

268 Inf Div

60 Inf Div

168 Inf Div

252 Inf Div

79 Inf Div

93 Inf Div

258 Inf Div

95 Inf Div

167 Inf Div

257 Inf Div

DUNKIRK: OPERATION DYNAMO

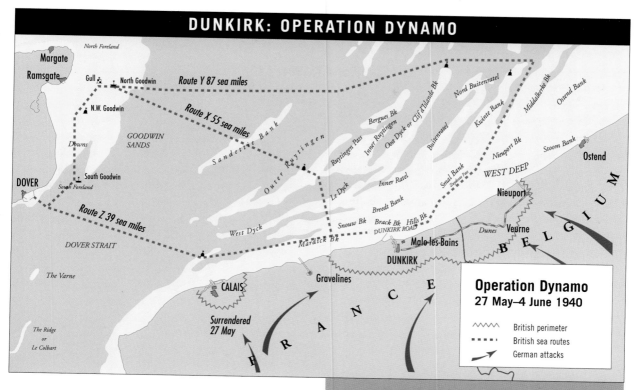

to launch a series of small holding attacks against the Maginot Line and the Upper Rhine.

The Army Group's main formations were the First Army on the right, facing the main strength of the Maginot fortifications, and the Seventh Army on the left, which was deployed along the Upper Rhine.

The Maginot Line

Facing them were the massive French fortifications built between the wars, which were intended to be impregnable to any German attack. The Maginot Line included interconnected bunker complexes for thousands of men, which supported 45 large fortresses about 15km (9 miles) apart with 97 smaller forts and 352 armoured gun turrets between.

However, the Line was not the monolith that pre-war French propaganda claimed: it was strongest around the industrial regions of Metz, Lauter and Alsace, but other stretches were weak.

On 14 June 1940, the day Paris fell, Army Group C, which had done very little as the other German armies

27 May – 4 June 1940

British and French forces in Belgium faced annihilation as the infantry of von Bock's army group pressed southwards from the Low Countries, while the panzers of von Rundstedt's army group raced northwards along the Channel coast. Only a rapid retreat to the coast at Dunkirk and evacuation to England would save even a quarter of the BEF.

But then, the Führer ordered his panzers to stop, allowing the British a breathing space. Operation Dynamo saw some 338,000 allied servicemen being lifted safely from the beaches, and small private craft being used to ferry the troops out to larger vessels waiting in deep water. Much was owed to the French troops who were fighting furiously to the south, holding back powerful German forces.

had swept through France, went over to the offensive in an attack code-named Operation Tiger.

Generaloberst Erwin von Witzleben's First Army attacked the Line between St. Avoid and Saarbrücken. After hard fighting, the Germans broke through the fortification

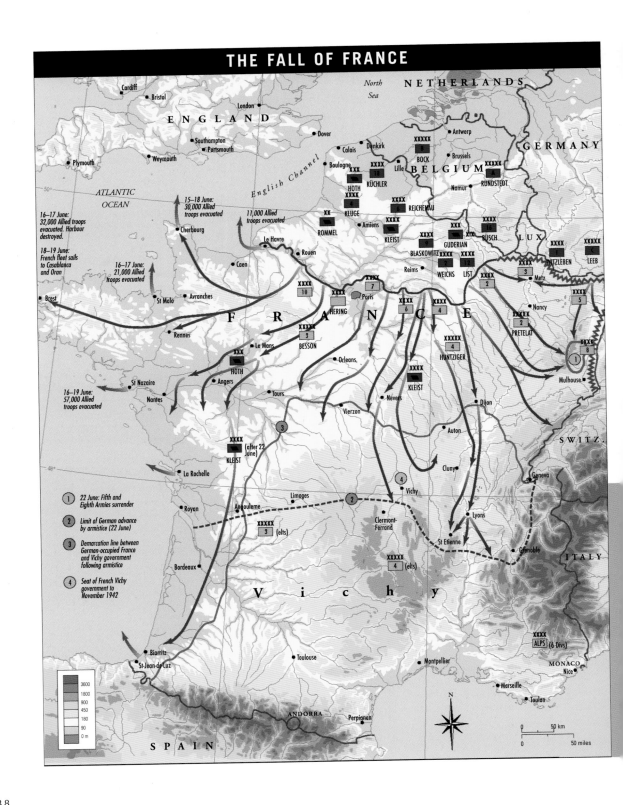

THE FALL OF FRANCE

15–18 June:
30,000 Allied
troops evacuated

16–17 June:
32,000 Allied troops
evacuated. Harbour
destroyed.

18–19 June:
French fleet sails
to Casablanca
and Oran

16–17 June:
21,000 Allied
troops evacuated

16–19 June:
57,000 Allied
troops evacuated

11,000 Allied
troops evacuated

① 22 June: Fifth and
Eighth Armies surrender

② Limit of German advance
by armistice (22 June)

③ Demarcation line between
German-occupied France
and Vichy government
following armistice

④ Seat of French Vichy
government to
November 1942

ARMY GROUP C – SEVENTH ARMY

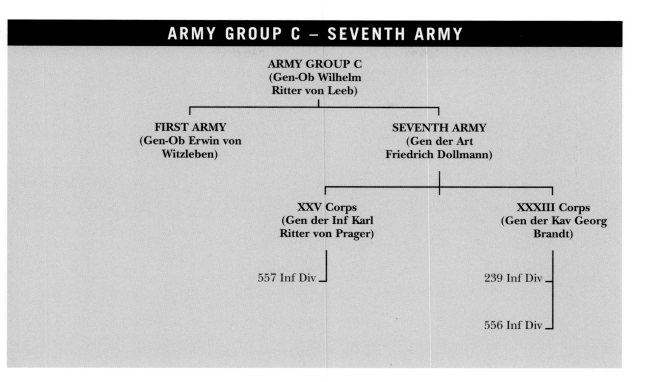

ARMY GROUP C
(Gen-Ob Wilhelm
Ritter von Leeb)

FIRST ARMY
(Gen-Ob Erwin von
Witzleben)

SEVENTH ARMY
(Gen der Art
Friedrich Dollmann)

XXV Corps
(Gen der Inf Karl
Ritter von Prager)

XXXIII Corps
(Gen der Kav Georg
Brandt)

557 Inf Div

239 Inf Div

556 Inf Div

line as defending French forces retreated southwards. In the following days, First Army attacked fortifications on each side of the penetration and mounted two attacks

June 1940

After a pause for reorganization, the Germans launched their assault on the rest of France on 5 June. As the panzers cut deeper and deeper into the heart of France, French morale plummeted and the French army moved ever closer to disintegration.

Resistance was light, though on occasion diehard French troops put up a stiff fight. The Germany infantrymen had to clear towns and villages street by street. More often than not, however, the ordinary French soldiers surrendered.

By 20 June, German troops were in Lyons and Grenoble in the south, along the Swiss border to the east and controlling much of the Biscay coast to the west. In just three weeks, they had forced the French government to sue for an armistice.

further to the east in northern Alsace. One successfully broke through a weak section of the Line in the Vosges Mountains, but the second faltered.

On 15 June, *General der Artillerie* Friedrich Dollmann's Seventh Army launched Operation Small Bear across the Rhine, capturing Colmar and Strasbourg.

The end of the Line

By the middle of June, von Leeb's forces had isolated the hundreds of thousands of French troops manning the Maginot Line. Army Group C mounted some attacks from the rear, but by now the French government was making overtures for an armistice.

Even so, the main fortifications of the Line were still mostly intact and fully manned, and many local commanders and troops wanted to hold out. But, on 19 June, General Maxime Weygand ordered the remaining French army formations at the Maginot Line, amounting to 400,000 troops, to 'ask for a cessation of fighting, with war honours'. The French Army was ordered out of its still powerful fortifications, to be taken to POW camps.

The Balkans and Crete: 1941–45

Following the fall of France, Hitler began planning his next great offensive, against the Soviet Union. However, his plans were disrupted early in 1941 when the *Wehrmacht* was obliged to come to the aid of Mussolini, whose forces were in trouble in the Balkans.

German armour in Nis, Serbia, April 1941. Panzer troops played a significant part in the conquest of Yugoslavia.

THE LAST THING THAT Adolf Hitler wanted in the spring of 1941 was a war in the Balkans – his mind was full of the forthcoming invasion of Russia. But his fellow dictator Mussolini was in serious trouble, and German troops and aircraft were needed to prevent catastrophe.

But the Führer got more than he bargained for: Yugoslavia's stand against the Nazis was rewarded with instant invasion, but the German foray into the Balkans became more extensive as the Greeks doggedly resisted conquest.

British attempts to help were unequal to the task, and further humiliation was to follow as German paratroopers seized Crete, inflicting yet another crushing defeat on the British Empire.

German plans

Hitler had already laid plans for a drive down through Bulgaria – 'to occupy the northeast coast of the Aegean'. This was intended to secure the southern flank of his planned onslaught on Soviet Russia. The operation, codenamed Marita, also provided for the conquest of the whole of mainland Greece if necessary.

But Hitler had hoped that the bonds between his own dictatorship and that of the Greek ruler, General Metaxas, would be sufficient to avoid actual battle. Hitler wanted a peaceful occupation, similar to those already in place in Romania and Hungary, and intended for Bulgaria.

He also hoped for a peaceful solution to the problem posed by Yugoslavia. Even before the war started, Germany had arranged to take Yugoslavia's entire production of copper, plus substantial quantities of lead and zinc, in return for supplies of aircraft and guns.

He summoned the Yugoslav Foreign Minister to Berchtesgaden on 27 November 1940 to suggest that his country place herself unreservedly upon the side of the Axis.

Anti-German coup

When it became necessary to take action against the Greeks, who were putting up a stiff fight against the Italians, Hitler bullied the Bulgarians and Yugoslavs into signing the Tripartite Pact. This allowed *Generalfeldmarschall* List's Twelfth Army to cross their borders on

EWALD VON KLEIST (1881–1954)

Commissioned into the Death's Head Hussars in 1900, he was a captain by 1914. Opposition to the SA led to his forced retirement as a general of cavalry in 1938.

• Recalled on the outbreak of war, he commanded a corps in Poland and led the *Wehrmacht*'s most powerful panzer strike through the Ardennes in 1940.

• Commanded in the Balkans and the Soviet Union in 1941–42.

• Led Army Group A in the 1942 drive for the Caucasus, displaying great military skill in conducting a fighting retreat after the fall of Stalingrad. He was promoted to Field Marshal the day Stalingrad fell. With von Manstein, he was dismissed by Hitler in March 1944.

PANZER GROUP I – PANZER STRENGTH (APRIL 1941)					
Tank type	Pz I	Pz II	Pz III	Pz IV	Pz Bef
5TH PANZER DIVISION					
31st Pz Rgt	9	40	51	16	5

Tank type	Pz II	Pz III (37)	Pz III (50)	Pz IV	Pz Bef
11TH PANZER DIVISION					
15th Pz Rgt	45	25	26	16	14
16TH PANZER DIVISION					
2nd Pz Rgt	45	23	48	20	10

its way to Greece. However, German plans were thrown awry when hardline Serb officers organized a military coup in the name of the young King Peter, overthrowing his uncle, the Regent Prince Paul. Within hours, the High Command of the *Wehrmacht* had received new and unequivocal orders for Operation *Strafgericht* (punishment).

Operation Punishment

'The Führer is determined … to make all preparations for the destruction of Yugoslavia, militarily and as a national unit …. Politically it is especially important that the blow against Yugoslavia is carried out with pitiless harshness …. The main task of the *Luftwaffe* is to start as early as possible … and to destroy the capital city, Belgrade, in waves of attack.'

Spearheaded by *Luftwaffe* bomber and dive-bomber attacks, *Generaloberst* Ewald von Kleist's *Panzergruppe* 1 attacked towards Belgrade. Kleists's group included three corps, with three panzer divisions, two motorized divisions incuding the SS Division Reich, two infantry divisions, the reinforced motorized infantry regiment *Grossdeutschland* and the *Hermann Göring* Brigade.

Generaloberst Maximilian von Weichs' Second Army, which included two panzer divisions and a motorized division, pushed south into Croatia. Two Croatian divisions mutinied and a breakaway Croat republic welcomed the Germans into Zagreb.

At the same time, the *Leibstandarte*-SS 'Adolf Hitler' and the 9th Panzer Division drove through Macedonia towards Skopje: the aim was to block any possible union of the Yugoslav and the Greek armies.

Bombing of Belgrade

The German onslaught began on Palm Sunday, 6 April, with spectacular strikes by the *Luftwaffe*. By 6.00 a.m., bombs were raining down on the railway station, the Royal Palace and the airfield at Zemun, where much of the Yugoslav air force was caught on the ground. By the following evening, 17,000 people had been killed and fires continued to rage.

German panzers raced through Yugoslavia. The 9th Panzer Division captured Skopje and 2nd Panzer blocked any possible Greek intervention. The 9th and 11th Panzer Divisions then drove northwards to Nis. The 8th and 14th Panzer Divisions of Second Army had taken Zagreb and Sarajevo by 15 April, and had competed with SS-Division *Reich* and the *Grossdeutschland* Regiment to be first to reach Belgrade.

Yugoslavia dismembered

The Yugoslav government requested an armistice on 14 April, and the country splintered along its pre-1914 boundaries. However, two separate groups of Serbs scattered into their barren mountains: Chetniks, loyal to the monarchy, and the Communist partisans dominated by Josip Broz, the guerrilla leader known as 'Tito'. The stage was set for an internecine war that has festered into the twenty-first century.

6–23 April 1941

The *Wehrmacht* had no plans to invade the Balkans, but Italy's ill-advised attack on Greece had come unstuck, and Hitler had to send troops to help his fellow dictator.

The *Wehrmacht* had been funnelling troops into Hungary and Romania since the autumn of 1940. By February 1941, more than 650,000 were in place, primarily to secure the southern flank of the invasion of the Soviet Union, which at that time was planned for May.

The Germans forced the Yugoslav government to allow their forces transit, but when the Yugoslav government was overthrown by an anti-German uprising, plans for the *Wehrmacht* to pass through Yugoslavia on its way to Greece became a full-scale invasion and conquest of the country.

INVASION OF THE BALKANS

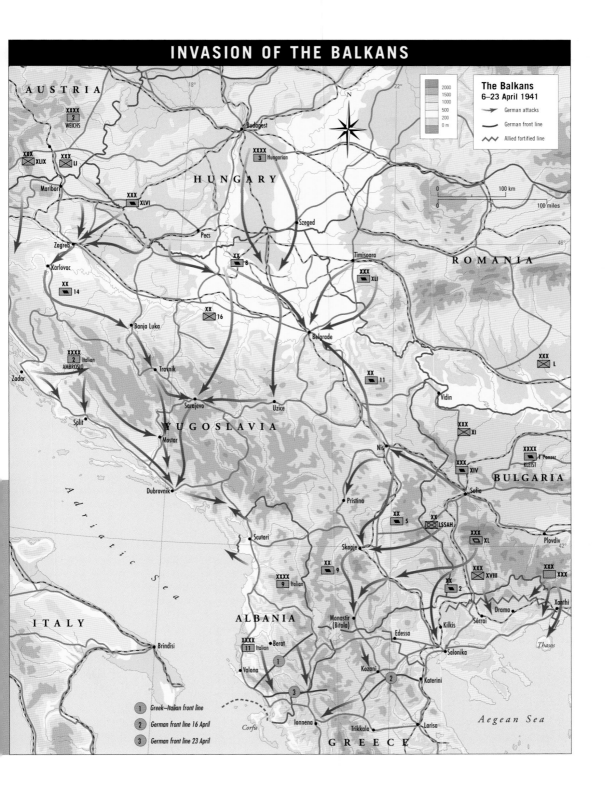

The Balkans
6–23 April 1941

2000	
1500	
1000	
500	
200	
0 m	

→ German attacks

— German front line

∿ Allied fortified line

1 Greek–Italian front line

2 German front line 16 April

3 German front line 23 April

AUSTRIA

XXXX 2 WEICHS

XXX XLIX

XXX LI

Maribor

HUNGARY

Budapest

XXXX 3 Hungarian

Szeged

Pecs

XXX XLVI

Zagreb

Karlovac

XX 14

XX 8

Banja Luka

XX 16

Timisoara

XXX XLI

ROMANIA

XXXX 2 Italian AMBROSIO

Zadar

Travnik

Sarajevo

Uzice

Belgrade

XX 11

Vidin

XXX L

YUGOSLAVIA

Split

Mostar

Dubrovnik

Scutari

Pristina

Niš

XXX XIV

XXX XI

XXXX KLEIST 1 Panzer

Sofia

BULGARIA

Skopje

XX 5

XX 9

XXX XL

Plovdiv

XXXX 9 Italian

Monastir (Bitola)

Edessa

XX 2

XXX XVIII

XXX XXX

Drama

Xanthi

Sérrai

Thasos

ITALY

Brindisi

ALBANIA

XXXX 11 Italian

Berat

Valona

Ionnena

GREECE

Trikkala

Kilkis

Salonika

Katerini

Kozani

Larisa

Aegean Sea

Corfu

Adriatic Sea

0 100 km

0 100 miles

BALKANS INVASION FORCE

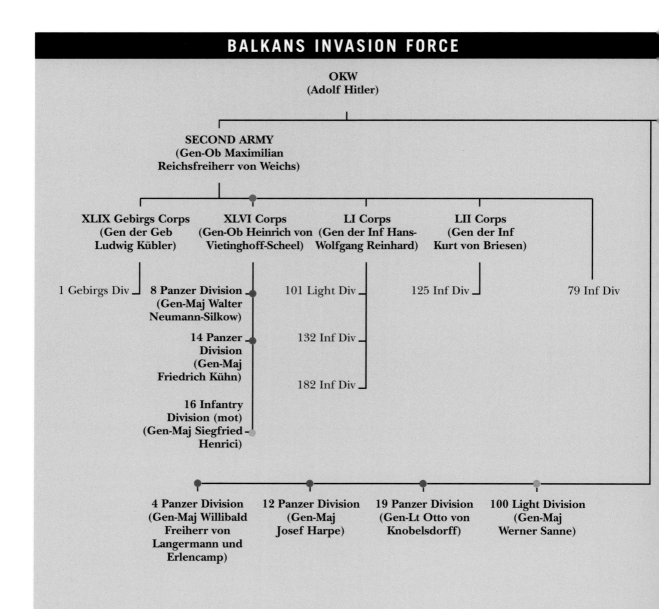

OKW
(Adolf Hitler)

SECOND ARMY
(Gen-Ob Maximilian
Reichsfreiherr von Weichs)

XLIX Gebirgs Corps
(Gen der Geb
Ludwig Kübler)

XLVI Corps
(Gen-Ob Heinrich von
Vietinghoff-Scheel)

LI Corps
(Gen der Inf Hans-
Wolfgang Reinhard)

LII Corps
(Gen der Inf
Kurt von Briesen)

1 Gebirgs Div

8 Panzer Division
(Gen-Maj Walter
Neumann-Silkow)

101 Light Div

125 Inf Div

79 Inf Div

14 Panzer
Division
(Gen-Maj
Friedrich Kühn)

132 Inf Div

182 Inf Div

16 Infantry
Division (mot)
(Gen-Maj Siegfried
Henrici)

4 Panzer Division
(Gen-Maj Willibald
Freiherr von
Langermann und
Erlencamp)

12 Panzer Division
(Gen-Maj
Josef Harpe)

19 Panzer Division
(Gen-Lt Otto von
Knobelsdorff)

100 Light Division
(Gen-Maj
Werner Sanne)

KEY

● Panzer Division
● Motorized Division/Unit
● Panzer Corps
● Light Division

Germany had begun amassing troops in Bulgaria and Romania early in 1941, aimed at countering any British actions in Greece that might threaten the southern flank of the planned attack on the Soviet Union. Field Marshal Wilhelm Lists's Twelfth Army was tasked with a possible invasion of Greece. However, further forces had to be deployed to Hungary and Austria with *Generaloberst* Maximilian von Weichs' Second Army when a coup in Yugoslavia necessitated the invasion of that country.

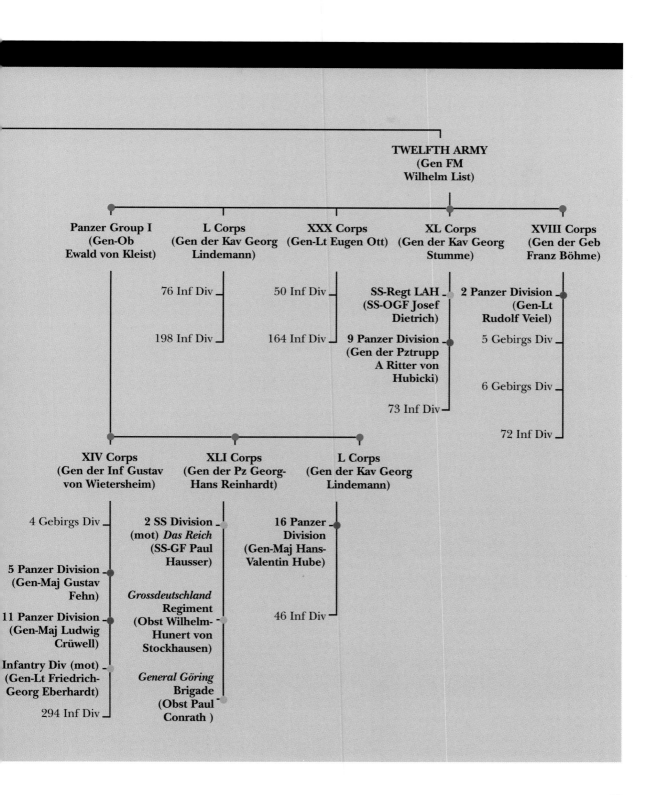

TWELFTH ARMY
(Gen FM
Wilhelm List)

Panzer Group I
(Gen-Ob
Ewald von Kleist)

L Corps
(Gen der Kav Georg
Lindemann)

XXX Corps
(Gen-Lt Eugen Ott)

XL Corps
(Gen der Kav Georg
Stumme)

XVIII Corps
(Gen der Geb
Franz Böhme)

76 Inf Div

50 Inf Div

SS-Regt LAH
(SS-OGF Josef
Dietrich)

2 Panzer Division
(Gen-Lt
Rudolf Veiel)

198 Inf Div

164 Inf Div

9 Panzer Division
(Gen der Pztrupp
A Ritter von
Hubicki)

5 Gebirgs Div

6 Gebirgs Div

73 Inf Div

72 Inf Div

XIV Corps
(Gen der Inf Gustav
von Wietersheim)

XLI Corps
(Gen der Pz Georg-
Hans Reinhardt)

L Corps
(Gen der Kav Georg
Lindemann)

4 Gebirgs Div

2 SS Division
(mot) *Das Reich*
(SS-GF Paul
Hausser)

16 Panzer
Division
(Gen-Maj Hans-
Valentin Hube)

5 Panzer Division
(Gen-Maj Gustav
Fehn)

11 Panzer Division
(Gen-Maj Ludwig
Crüwell)

Grossdeutschland
Regiment
(Obst Wilhelm-
Hunert von
Stockhausen)

46 Inf Div

Infantry Div (mot)
(Gen-Lt Friedrich-
Georg Eberhardt)

294 Inf Div

General Göring
Brigade
(Obst Paul
Conrath)

Greece and Crete

The German attack on Greece was conceived as two main thrusts: a combined SS and armoured drive would turn south along the Albanian border, while List's Twelfth Army would attack through Macedonia, piercing or bypassing the Greek defensive lines.

The attack began on 6 April when *Generalfeldmarschall* List's Twelfth Army punched through the Greek defences to the Aegean Sea. The German XL Corps, including the 5th Panzer Division and SS Brigade *Leibstandarte Adolf Hitler,* crossed the Yugoslav–Greek frontier at Monastir on 10 April. At the same time, the Italian Army launched a new offensive to coincide with Hitler's intervention.

Allied retreat

By 12 April, the British commander General Wilson knew that the Germans were about to outflank him on the east. He ordered an evacuation southwards. By 14 April, defences along the line of the Aliakmon River and the passes around Mount Olympus held the flood of German armour and infantry for four days while lorries full of exhausted men, trudging files of troops and farm carts full of bewildered Greek families and their belongings fled south.

The British fell back to the ancient battlefield of Thermopylae on 18 April. On 19 April, Commonwealth troops were streaming back past Thermopylae, the rearguards digging in for yet another 'last stand'.

Greece defeated

The Greek commander, General Papagos, advised his King on 21 April that the Greek Army could fight no more. The rearguards at Thermopylae held on until 24 April, then slipped away; General Wilson left Athens on the morning of 26 April and crossed the Corinth Bridge, glad to know that he had been preceded by over 40,000 men.

Shortly after dawn on 28 April, 5th Panzer Division and the SS *Leibstandarte* crossed the Corinth Canal and drove south. The panzers headed for Kalamata, where after a vicious fight the 7000 Imperial troops who had not been evacuated were taken prisoner.

German troops entered Athens on 27 April. Others embarked in commandeered local vessels to occupy the Ionian islands of Samothrace, Lesbos and Chios.

In keeping with the strict timetable for Operation *Barbarossa*, the invasion of the Soviet Union, the bulk of the German invasion force began withdrawing in May, leaving Greece to be held by a mixture of German reserve units and Italians.

XLVI CORPS – PANZER STRENGTH (APRIL 1941)					
Tank type	**Pz II**	**Pz 38(t)**	**Pz IV**	**Pz Bef(38)**	**Pz Bef**
8TH PANZER DIVISION					
10th Pz Rgt	49	118	30	7	8
Tank type	**Pz II**	**Pz III(37)**	**Pz III(50)**	**Pz IV**	**Pz Bef**
14TH PANZER DIVISION					
36th Pz Rgt	45	16	35	20	8

6–28 April 1941

When it became necessary to take action against the Greeks, who were putting up a stiff fight against the Italians, Hitler bullied the Bulgarians and Yugoslavs into signing the Tripartite Pact. After the lightning victory in Yugoslavia, the Germans moved on to Greece when *Generalfeldmarschall* List's Twelfth Army crossed the borders.

The Germans attacked the Metaxas line from Bulgaria, while mobile troops pressed southwards through Yugoslavia. The Greeks could do nothing to stop the Germans, and their British allies were forced to evacuate what forces they could to Crete.

A month later, the Germans mounted the world's first full-scale airborne assault and captured the island, suffering heavy casualties in the process.

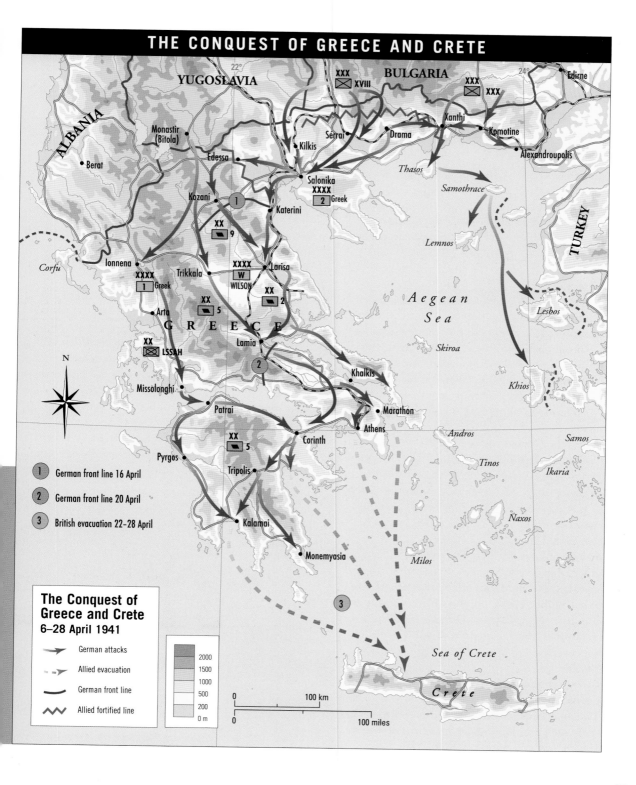

THE CONQUEST OF GREECE AND CRETE

YUGOSLAVIA

BULGARIA

ALBANIA

The Conquest of Greece and Crete
6–28 April 1941

1 German front line 16 April

2 German front line 20 April

3 British evacuation 22–28 April

German attacks

Allied evacuation

German front line

Allied fortified line

	2000
	1500
	1000
	500
	200
	0 m

0   100 km

0   100 miles

The Balkans: 1942–44

The conquest of the Balkans had been a relatively simple if hard-fought campaign. Occupying the Balkans was a much more bloody and protracted affair. Armoured troops played a peripheral but important part in the battles against the Partisans.

The Germans might have thought that they had conquered the Balkans, but nobody had told the locals. The withdrawal of the combat troops to the Soviet front was the signal for the start of one of the most brutal, most bitterly fought partisan campaigns the world has ever seen.

Balkan hatreds

Part of the problem was that it was several wars in one. The Croat puppet state was heavily involved, as were large numbers of German troops. At its most simplistic, the Italian, Germans and Fascist Croats were on one side, while Tito's communist guerrillas were on the other. The Serbian royalist forces, called Chetniks, fought either side, depending on circumstances. Croat fought Serb, Communist fought Royalist, and Muslim fought Christian.

Following the German victory, Yugoslavia was dismembered and divided among the victors – Germany, Italy, Hungary and Bulgaria. Croatia was granted independence as an axis puppet state under Ante Pavelic, the leader of the Fascist Ustase. As a reward for coming over to the Axis, Hitler ceded Bosnia-Herzegovina to Croatia.

Thousands of Jews, Serbs and Gypsies were exterminated in Croatian camps. At Jasenovac, the Croats showed that the German *Einsatzkommandos* had little to teach them about murder, with as many as 100,000 victims being shot or clubbed to death. In Bosnia, Muslims often assisted the Ustase killers.

Partisan war

As the war progressed, Partisan bands retaliated against the perpetrators of these crimes with massacres of their own. The horrors committed in Yugoslavia during the war, where over a million people perished, were not forgotten. In Croatia, Bosnia or Kosovo, there were few Serbs who had not lost friends or relatives during World War II.

Anti Partisan tactics

Nazi policy towards Partisans was severe, and is most clearly stated in Hitler's 'Partisan Order', issued on 16 December 1942:

'The enemy has thrown fanatic, Communist-trained fighters who will not stop at any act of violence… Troops are therefore authorized to take any measures without restriction even against women and children if these are needed for success. To show humanitarian consideration of any kind is a crime against the German Nation.'

The Partisans were by far the most effective opposition to the Germans, and by the end of the war they claimed almost 200,000 men and women under arms. Although Tito himself was a Croat, he did more

October–November 1944

In the aftermath of the Red Army's drive through Romania, the situation for German forces in the Balkans became precarious. To avoid being cut off in Crete, Greece and Albania, German units began withdrawing northwards in the early Autumn of 1944. SS and other troops held open the Vardar Corridor, which allowed 350,000 troops of Army Group *Lohr* to escape through Macedonia and Bulgaria.

Greek partisans had formed numerous anti-German groups during the years of occupation, but with the withdrawal of the Nazis, the mutual antipathy between the groups spilled over into violence. The Communists had hoped for support from Stalin, but the Soviet dictator had his eyes on other parts of the Balkans, and was quite happy for Greece to fall within the British sphere of influence. As a result, the Communists were left to fend for themselves.

than any other Yugoslav to bring the war home to the Germans and their Croatian allies.

Tito's Partisan army won the support of the Western allies in preference to the unreliable Serbian Chetniks, as they had tied down no less than 35 German divisions.

Yugoslavia was an important source of raw materials, it was strategically located on the Adriatic, and it was a source of manpower for the *Wehrmacht*. The growing partisan threat menaced German control of the area, so the war against the Partisans was given high priority.

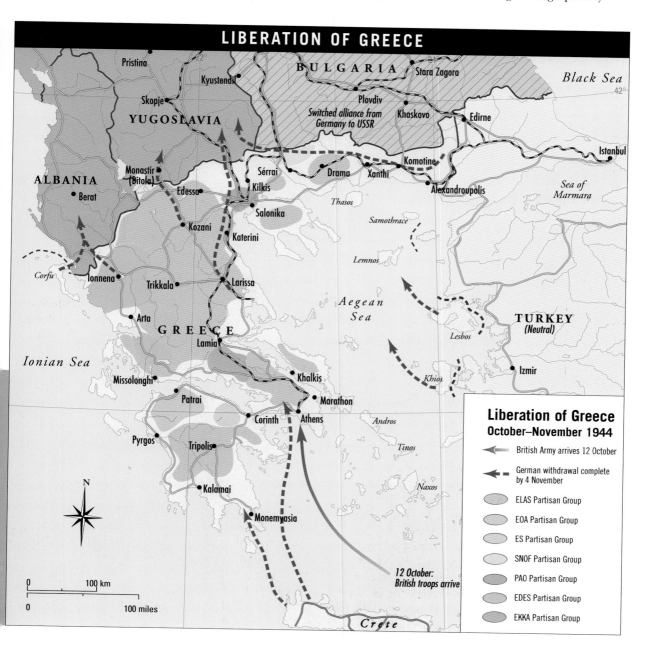

LIBERATION OF GREECE

Liberation of Greece
October–November 1944

- British Army arrives 12 October
- German withdrawal complete by 4 November
- ELAS Partisan Group
- EOA Partisan Group
- ES Partisan Group
- SNOF Partisan Group
- PAO Partisan Group
- EDES Partisan Group
- EKKA Partisan Group

Pristina · Kyustendil · BULGARIA · Stara Zagora · *Black Sea*

Skopje · Plovdiv · Khaskovo · Edirne

YUGOSLAVIA · Switched alliance from Germany to USSR

Komotine · Istanbul

Monastir (Bitola) · Sérrai · Drama · Xanthi · *Sea of Marmara*

ALBANIA · Edessa · Kilkis · Alexandroupolis

Berat · Salonika · *Thasos* · *Samothrace*

Kozani · Katerini · *Lemnos*

Corfu · Ionnena · *Aegean Sea* · TURKEY (Neutral)

Trikkala · Larissa · *Lesbos*

Arta · GREECE · *Khios* · Izmir

Ionian Sea · Lamia

Missolonghi · Khalkis

Patrai · Marathon · *Andros*

Pyrgos · Corinth · Athens · *Tinos*

Tripolis

Kalamai · *Naxos*

Monemvasia

12 October: British troops arrive

N

0 — 100 km
0 — 100 miles

Crete

Although there were few panzer divisions deployed in the Balkans, units such as the 7th SS Gebirgs-Division *Prinz Eugen* had a small panzer detachment equipped with Czech-built or captured French tanks. These were used to provide roadside and convoy security, though they were vulnerable to attack in the mountains.

Trying to capture Tito

In March 1943, a major campaign against the Partisans was launched around Slunj, Bihac, Petrovak and Zagreb. Operation White was supposed to seek out and destroy Tito's partisans, but although large numbers of bodies were counted, Tito escaped.

In September 1943, German troops in the former Yugoslavia had to disarm the Italian soldiers following Italy's armistice with the Allies.

The continuing failure to catch the communist leader had become costly. Over the previous three years, the Yugoslav Army of National Liberation (JANL) had grown from a few scattered bands of guerrillas into a major military force of more than 200,000 men and women under arms.

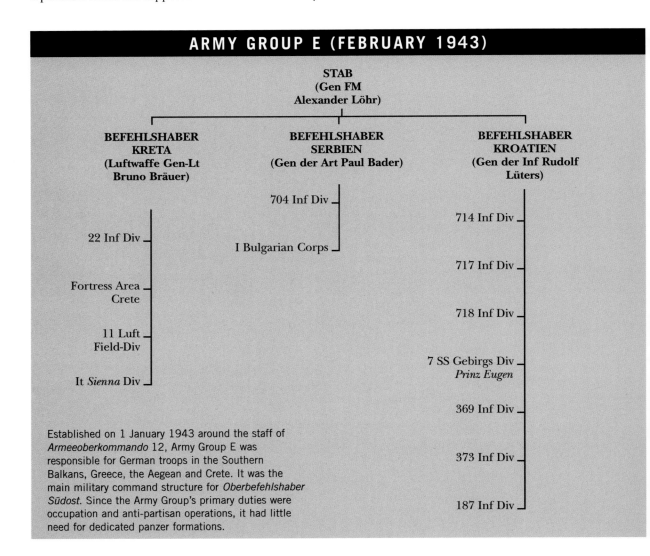

ARMY GROUP E (FEBRUARY 1943)

STAB
(Gen FM Alexander Löhr)

BEFEHLSHABER KRETA
(Luftwaffe Gen-Lt Bruno Bräuer)

- 22 Inf Div
- Fortress Area Crete
- 11 Luft Field-Div
- It *Sienna* Div

BEFEHLSHABER SERBIEN
(Gen der Art Paul Bader)

- 704 Inf Div
- I Bulgarian Corps

BEFEHLSHABER KROATIEN
(Gen der Inf Rudolf Lüters)

- 714 Inf Div
- 717 Inf Div
- 718 Inf Div
- 7 SS Gebirgs Div *Prinz Eugen*
- 369 Inf Div
- 373 Inf Div
- 187 Inf Div

Established on 1 January 1943 around the staff of *Armeeoberkommando 12*, Army Group E was responsible for German troops in the Southern Balkans, Greece, the Aegean and Crete. It was the main military command structure for *Oberbefehlshaber Südost*. Since the Army Group's primary duties were occupation and anti-partisan operations, it had little need for dedicated panzer formations.

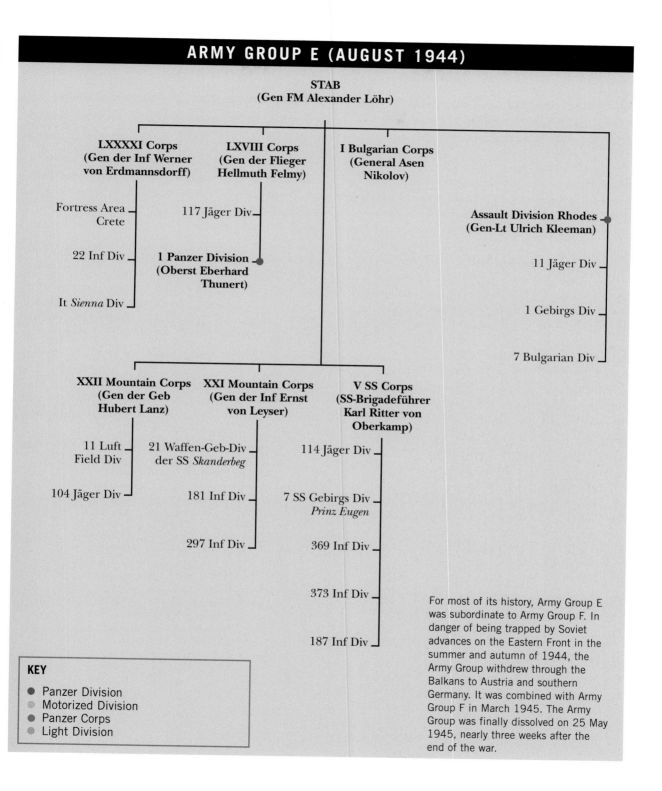

ARMY GROUP E (AUGUST 1944)

STAB
(Gen FM Alexander Löhr)

LXXXXI Corps
(Gen der Inf Werner von Erdmannsdorff)

LXVIII Corps
(Gen der Flieger Hellmuth Felmy)

I Bulgarian Corps
(General Asen Nikolov)

Fortress Area Crete

117 Jäger Div

Assault Division Rhodes
(Gen-Lt Ulrich Kleeman)

22 Inf Div

1 Panzer Division
(Oberst Eberhard Thunert)

11 Jäger Div

It *Sienna* Div

1 Gebirgs Div

7 Bulgarian Div

XXII Mountain Corps
(Gen der Geb Hubert Lanz)

XXI Mountain Corps
(Gen der Inf Ernst von Leyser)

V SS Corps
(SS-Brigadeführer Karl Ritter von Oberkamp)

11 Luft Field Div

21 Waffen-Geb-Div der SS *Skanderbeg*

114 Jäger Div

104 Jäger Div

181 Inf Div

7 SS Gebirgs Div *Prinz Eugen*

297 Inf Div

369 Inf Div

373 Inf Div

187 Inf Div

KEY

- ● Panzer Division
- ● Motorized Division
- ● Panzer Corps
- ● Light Division

For most of its history, Army Group E was subordinate to Army Group F. In danger of being trapped by Soviet advances on the Eastern Front in the summer and autumn of 1944, the Army Group withdrew through the Balkans to Austria and southern Germany. It was combined with Army Group F in March 1945. The Army Group was finally dissolved on 25 May 1945, nearly three weeks after the end of the war.

Retreat from the Balkans

Operation *Bagration*, the great Soviet summer offensive in June 1944, smashed the German defences on the Eastern Front. Soviet armies advanced towards Romania and Bulgaria, threatening to cut off the tens of thousands of German troops in the Balkans.

The Balkans were as great an attraction to Stalin as they had been for centuries to his imperial predecessors – the Romanovs. On 20 August, Malinovsky's 2nd Ukrainian Front broke through the defences of Army Group Ukraine in the Pruth valley opposite Jassy.

By 24 August, they were near Leovo, where they met two of Tolbukhin's mechanized corps, which had forced the lower Dniester into Bessarabia. They had isolated the German Sixth Army, reconstituted after Stalingrad, when political events intervened.

Axis disintegrating

A *coup d'état* took place in Bucharest. Marshal Antonescu was overthrown. King Michael took his place, the government promptly sued for peace, and two Romanian armies laid down their arms. Southern Bessarabia, the Danube delta and the Carpathian passes to the north lay open to the Soviet armies.

A group of pro-Allied officers now seized control in Sofia and welcomed the Red Army – so the invasion became 'a visit by friendly forces', who raced through the capital on 15 September. Collecting two Bulgarian armies, they pressed on to the Yugoslav border opposite Bor in the north and Skopje in the south.

By 8 September, Malinovsky's armies had joined Tolbukhin's. On 28 September, they moved forward together to link up with Marshal Tito's Partisans, while 2nd Ukrainian Front drove in over the Romanian border north of the Danube.

Escape from the Balkans

But the German Army Group F under Field Marshal von Weichs was holding open an escape route for both themselves and Army Group E under Field Marshal Löhr, rapidly retreating up through Greece.

The Germans put up such a stout resistance that it was 20 October before Belgrade was in Allied hands – and then only after the bulk of both German army groups had raced north through the gap. They joined a hastily forming defence line in Hungary, where yet another attempt to desert the Axis had been foiled.

German occupation of Hungary

Admiral Horthy had never been an enthusiastic follower of Nazi or even Fascist doctrine. He had only agreed to Hungarian co-operation in the war against the Soviet Union the previous March, when Hitler threatened a full-scale occupation of the country.

On 16 October, Horthy announced that he wanted an armistice with the Allies. Before he could implement it in any way, he was kidnapped by the German commando Otto Skorzeny. German armies from Austria poured in, later to be reinforced by the formations from Greece and Yugoslavia.

By the time Malinovksy's and Tolbukhin's armies had assembled for a drive up from the Lake Balaton area,

December 1944 – May 1945

From August 1944, as the Red Army drove through Romania and Bulgaria, Hitler's east European allies deserted him. As Army Groups E and F, under Field Marshal Maximilian von Weichs, were forced back through Yugoslavia, units like the ethnic volunteer 7th SS Freiwilligen-Gebirgs Division *Prinz Eugen* encountered the full force of the Soviet war machine. *Prinz Eugen* was shattered in actions to the south of Vukovar in January 1945, and the survivors withdrew into Austria. However, units of Army Group F, based in Croatia and Northern Serbia, held open a corridor for Army Group E, retreating from Greece through Kosovo, Macedonia, Montenegro and part of Serbia. In March 1945, Army Group F was formally disbanded, and Army Group E took command of what remained of German authority in Yugoslavia, including Slovenia.

BATTLE OF BUDAPEST AND VIENNA

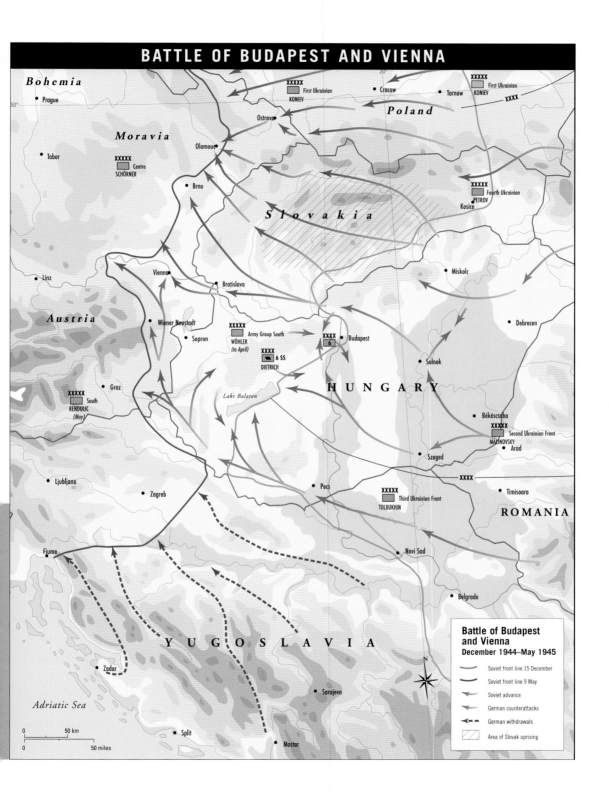

Bohemia

• Prague

Moravia

• Tabor

• Ostrava

• Olomouc

• Brno

XXXXX First Ukrainian KONIEV

• Cracow

• Tarnow

XXXXX First Ukrainian KONIEV

XXXX

Poland

Slovakia

XXXXX Centre SCHÖRNER

XXXXX Fourth Ukrainian PETROV

Košice

• Miskolc

Austria

• Linz

• Vienna

• Bratislava

• Wiener Neustadt

• Sopron

XXXXX Army Group South WÖHLER (to April)

XXXX 6 SS DIETRICH

XXXX 6 • Budapest

HUNGARY

• Solnok

• Debrecen

XXXXX South RENDULIC (May)

• Graz

Lake Balaton

XXXXX Second Ukrainian Front MALINOVSKY

• Békéscsaba

• Arad

• Ljubljana

• Zagreb

• Pecs

• Szeged

XXXX

XXXXX Third Ukrainian Front TOLBUKHIN

• Timisoara

ROMANIA

• Fiume

YUGOSLAVIA

• Novi Sad

• Belgrade

Adriatic Sea

• Zadar

• Sarajevo

0   50 km

0   50 miles

• Split

• Mostar

N

Battle of Budapest and Vienna
December 1944–May 1945

Soviet front line 15 December
Soviet front line 9 May
Soviet advance
German counterattacks
German withdrawals
Area of Slovak uprising

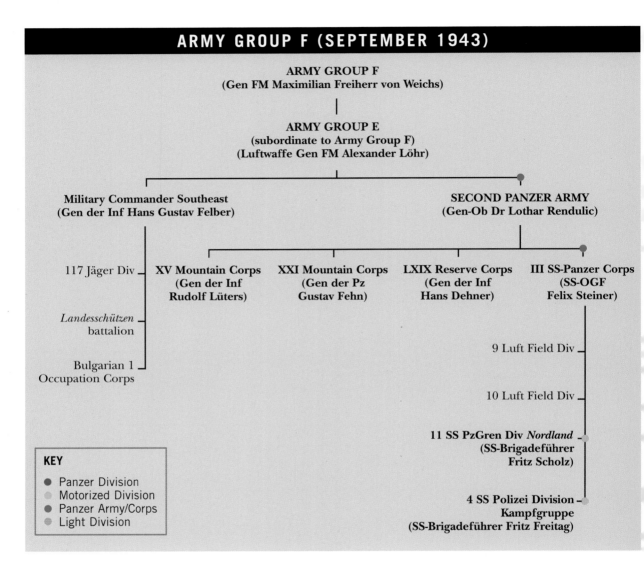

ARMY GROUP F (SEPTEMBER 1943)

ARMY GROUP F
(Gen FM Maximilian Freiherr von Weichs)

ARMY GROUP E
(subordinate to Army Group F)
(Luftwaffe Gen FM Alexander Löhr)

Military Commander Southeast
(Gen der Inf Hans Gustav Felber)

SECOND PANZER ARMY
(Gen-Ob Dr Lothar Rendulic)

117 Jäger Div

Landesschützen
battalion

Bulgarian 1
Occupation Corps

XV Mountain Corps
(Gen der Inf
Rudolf Lüters)

XXI Mountain Corps
(Gen der Pz
Gustav Fehn)

LXIX Reserve Corps
(Gen der Inf
Hans Dehner)

III SS-Panzer Corps
(SS-OGF
Felix Steiner)

9 Luft Field Div

10 Luft Field Div

11 SS PzGren Div *Nordland*
(SS-Brigadeführer
Fritz Scholz)

4 SS Polizei Division
Kampfgruppe
(SS-Brigadeführer Fritz Freitag)

KEY
- Panzer Division
- Motorized Division
- Panzer Army/Corps
- Light Division

not only were the Germans in some force throughout Hungary, but Budapest in particular was strongly held and fortified.

By November, the Soviet armies were fighting their way north on each side of the Hungarian capital, slowly, implacably, but at great cost and with little of the energy and momentum of the previous months.

On 25 December 1944, when divisions of the two Ukrainian fronts that had fought all the way from the Dniester met to the west of Budapest, it was decided that with 180,000 Germans and Hungarians encircled, there

was no chance of taking the city by storm. They therefore organized for a full-scale siege, calling up super-heavy artillery from hundreds of miles back in the Soviet Union, extra divisions from reserves, and supplies and food from wherever they could be found.

For the Germans, 1944 saw all hope of ultimate victory dashed. A few still believed in their Führer, but the Soviets had finally broken the once proud German war machine. Everywhere, the Nazis were in retreat, crushed between the Allies in west andin the east. Defeat was inevitable – but the final reckoning must wait until 1945.

ARMY GROUP F (SEPTEMBER 1944)

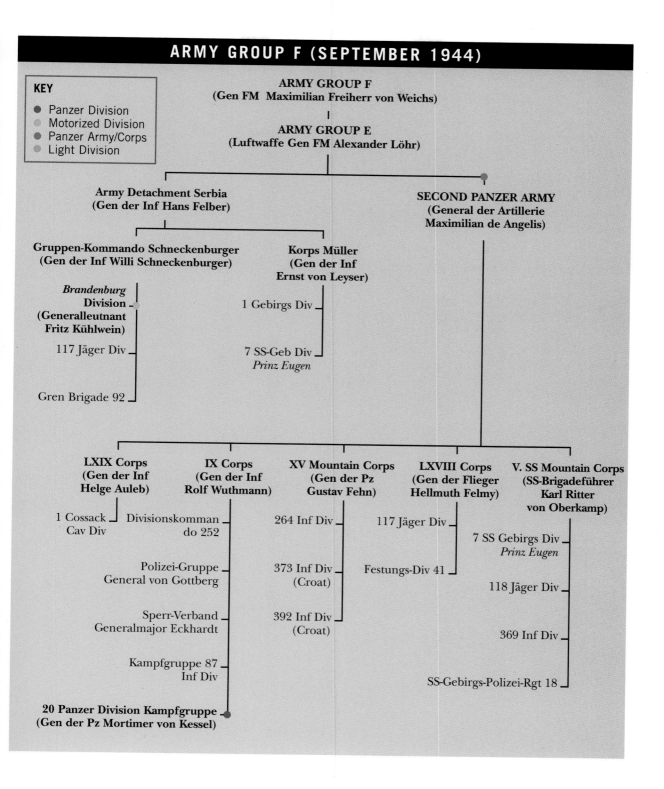

KEY

- ● Panzer Division
- ● Motorized Division
- ● Panzer Army/Corps
- ● Light Division

ARMY GROUP F
(Gen FM Maximilian Freiherr von Weichs)

ARMY GROUP E
(Luftwaffe Gen FM Alexander Löhr)

Army Detachment Serbia
(Gen der Inf Hans Felber)

SECOND PANZER ARMY
(General der Artillerie
Maximilian de Angelis)

Gruppen-Kommando Schneckenburger
(Gen der Inf Willi Schneckenburger)

Korps Müller
(Gen der Inf
Ernst von Leyser)

Brandenburg
Division
(Generalleutnant
Fritz Kühlwein)

117 Jäger Div

Gren Brigade 92

1 Gebirgs Div

7 SS-Geb Div
Prinz Eugen

LXIX Corps
(Gen der Inf
Helge Auleb)

1 Cossack
Cav Div

Divisionskomman
do 252

Polizei-Gruppe
General von Gottberg

Sperr-Verband
Generalmajor Eckhardt

Kampfgruppe 87
Inf Div

20 Panzer Division Kampfgruppe
(Gen der Pz Mortimer von Kessel)

IX Corps
(Gen der Inf
Rolf Wuthmann)

XV Mountain Corps
(Gen der Pz
Gustav Fehn)

264 Inf Div

373 Inf Div
(Croat)

392 Inf Div
(Croat)

LXVIII Corps
(Gen der Flieger
Hellmuth Felmy)

117 Jäger Div

Festungs-Div 41

V. SS Mountain Corps
(SS-Brigadeführer
Karl Ritter
von Oberkamp)

7 SS Gebirgs Div
Prinz Eugen

118 Jäger Div

369 Inf Div

SS-Gebirgs-Polizei-Rgt 18

Panzers in North Africa: 1941–43

In some ways, the North African desert is ideal country for tanks, with wide open terrain and few inhabitants. At the same time, the all-pervading sand and extremes of heat and cold put almost intolerable strains on both men and machines.

By February 1943, Allied forces had taken a decisive advantage in the Desert War. Even so, *Panzerarmee Afrika* could still inflict

THE WAR IN NORTH AFRICA began in earnest on 9 December 1940 as Benito Mussolini tried to expand the Italian empire in North Africa. Il Duce's armies crept tentatively from Libya into Egypt.

Mussolini confidently expected the large Italian force in Libya to over-run the relatively small British force in Egypt. At a stroke, he would seize the vital shipping route through the Suez canal and threaten further attacks on the vital oilfields of the Middle East. Unfortunately, his army was not up to the job.

Although the Italian Tenth Army outnumbered the British Desert Force by six to one, its advance into Egypt was tentative and came to a halt in a series of defensive lines south of Sidi Barrani.

The British launched a counterattack on 9 December 1940. Operation Compass was intended to be a 'five-day raid', but it caught the Italians completely by surprise. The British Matilda infantry tanks were impervious to Italian anti-tank guns, and soon the Italians were running. Over the next two months, the British under General Richard O'Connor advanced some 805km (500 miles), destroying the Italian Tenth Army and capturing 130,000 prisoners – including seven generals. They had captured Bardia, Tobruk, Derna, Barce and Benghazi and had come to rest at El Agheila.

Germany intervenes

The Italian disaster threatened Fortress Europe. For his own security, Hitler felt that he had no option but to intervene on behalf of his ally. By the middle of February 1941, the first contingent of German support had reached Tripoli. It was not very large – in fact, it consisted of one general and two staff officers – but the general was a man called Rommel.

As the commander of the 'Ghost' Division in France, Major-General Erwin Johannes Eugen Rommel had won a reputation as a brilliant commander. His orders were to stabilize the situation.

The Afrika Korps

Rarely more than a sideshow to the German High Command, the war in North Africa nevertheless showed that a small, experienced force under a charismatic leader like Erwin Rommel could have an inflence out of all proportion to its size.

Rommel's force initially included only the 5th Light Division. For the moment, he was expected only to stiffen Italian resistance. Perhaps in due course he would be given the resources to do more, but he was to await orders from above before contemplating offensive action.

But Rommel would not wait. Within days, he was planning a full-scale counterattack. And with that began two years of cut-and-thrust battles with British and Commonwealth forces. The battlefield was to be the Libyan desert, an area aptly described as a tactician's paradise and a quartermaster's nightmare.

Rommel's first attack: March 1941

Disobeying orders with a diligence that compels respect, Rommel moved the German 5th Light Division from Tripoli towards Agedabia on 24 March. There, on 3 April, Rommel set up his headquarters. He then cast aside all established principles of warfare by deliberately splitting the already tenuous forces at his disposal into three.

He sent a mixed German and Italian force under Graf von Schwerin eastwards in a wide arc. While this passed through Giof el Matar and Tengeder towards Mechili, he directed the bulk of the 5th Light Division to advance through Antelat and Msus. Rommel himself accompanied the armoured cars and light vehicles of the 3rd Reconnaissance Battalion to the north, towards Suluch.

Then, having heard rumours that the British were evacuating Benghazi, he ordered them to drive straight for the port. Here his troops were welcomed as

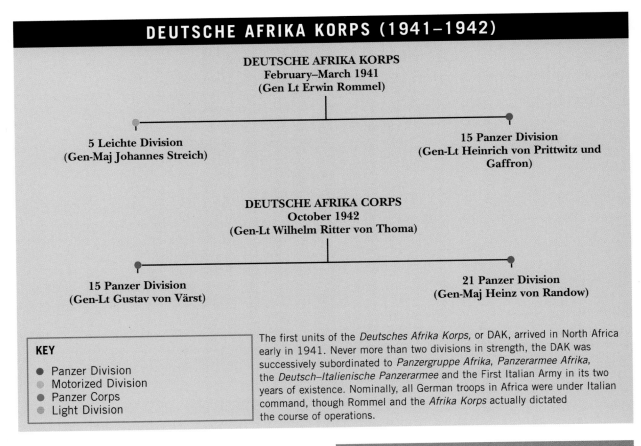

DEUTSCHE AFRIKA KORPS (1941–1942)

DEUTSCHE AFRIKA KORPS
February–March 1941
(Gen Lt Erwin Rommel)

5 Leichte Division
(Gen-Maj Johannes Streich)

15 Panzer Division
(Gen-Lt Heinrich von Prittwitz und Gaffron)

DEUTSCHE AFRIKA CORPS
October 1942
(Gen-Lt Wilhelm Ritter von Thoma)

15 Panzer Division
(Gen-Lt Gustav von Värst)

21 Panzer Division
(Gen-Maj Heinz von Randow)

KEY
- ● Panzer Division
- ● Motorized Division
- ● Panzer Corps
- ● Light Division

The first units of the *Deutsches Afrika Korps*, or DAK, arrived in North Africa early in 1941. Never more than two divisions in strength, the DAK was successively subordinated to *Panzergruppe Afrika*, *Panzerarmee Afrika*, the *Deutsch–Italienische Panzerarmee* and the First Italian Army in its two years of existence. Nominally, all German troops in Africa were under Italian command, though Rommel and the *Afrika Korps* actually dictated the course of operations.

conquering heroes. The *Afrika Korps* had come to liberate the Italian Empire in Cyrenaica, and the joy at seeing the advancing Germans appeared genuine. However, the wild enthusiasm exhibited by the inhabitants reminded one American observer of the jubilation with which the Australians had been received only a few months before. The desert taught lessons in pragmatism.

Master of mobile war

Now free to manoeuvre in open desert, Rommel pushed his reinforcements forwards. With numerical, and, more importantly, psychological advantage, the Germans surged east. The British were now in headlong retreat, being harried all the way by the Axis air forces, which enjoyed total control of the skies.

By 7 April, Rommel had captured Derna and isolated Mechili, and his reconnaissance units were probing

AFRIKA KORPS – PANZER STRENGTH (FEB 1941)					
Tank type	Pz I	Pz II	Pz III(50)	Pz IV	Pz Bef
15TH PANZER DIVISION					
8th Pz Rgt	0	45	71	20	10
5TH LEICHTE DIVISION					
5th Pz Rgt	25	45	67	22	7

eastwards south of Tobruk. Mechili fell to the Germans on the morning of 8 April and the victorious panzer troops encountered the all-too familiar evidence of a broken enemy. All around was the detritus of a fleeing army – abandoned tanks, troop carriers, trucks and, of course, the bodies of the fallen.

By 9 April, Rommel's reconnaissance units reached Bardia, with the Egyptian frontier, Halfaya Pass and

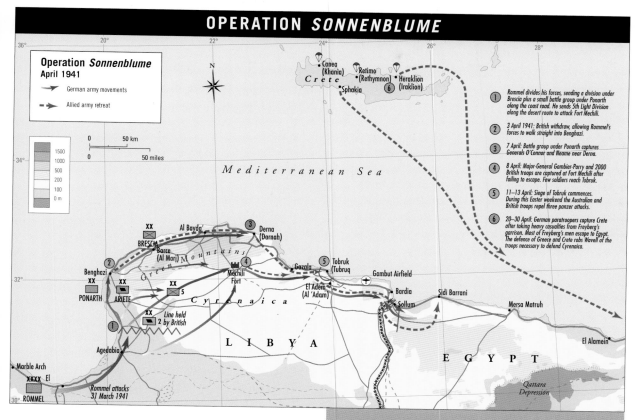

OPERATION *SONNENBLUME*

Operation *Sonnenblume*
April 1941

→ German army movements

⇢ Allied army retreat

1. Rommel divides his forces, sending a division under Brescia plus a small battle group under Ponarth along the coast road. He sends 5th Light Division along the desert route to attack Fort Mechili.

2. 3 April 1941: British withdraw, allowing Rommel's forces to walk straight into Benghazi.

3. 7 April: Battle group under Ponarth captures Generals O'Connor and Neame near Derna.

4. 8 April: Major-General Gambier-Parry and 2000 British troops are captured at Fort Mechili after failing to escape. Few soldiers reach Tobruk.

5. 11–13 April: Siege of Tobruk commences. During this Easter weekend the Australian and British troops repel three panzer attacks.

6. 20–30 April: German paratroopers capture Crete after taking heavy casualties from Freyberg's garrison. Most of Freyberg's men escape to Egypt. The defence of Greece and Crete robs Wavell of the troops necessary to defend Cyrenaica.

Sollum just a few miles further on. Some surviving British formations were scurrying past them towards the bases from which they had launched their own offensive only four months previously. But many had no opportunity to flee: large numbers were surrounded and others had already surrendered.

Back to the beginning
Rommel's headlong advance recovered all the territory lost by the Italians. He was soon talking to his staff about Egypt and the Suez canal. But he would have to take into account the reactions of the Italians.

It is worth noting that the Axis forces in North Africa remained under Italian command until early 1943. At this time, Rommel was only a corps commander. The theatre commander in Africa was Italian, as were the majority of Rommel's troops. However, such were Rommel's successes that he had an influence far greater than his official position as a corps commander.

April 1941
As in the Balkans, the Italian disasters in North Africa forced Hitler to send help to Mussolini's forces. Early in 1941, the *Wehrmacht* sent a force to Tunisia under the command of General Erwin Rommel. The Afrika Korps arrived when the British had been weakened after sending troops to reinforce Greece. Rommel saw this as an opportunity to launch an attack, codenamed Operation *Sonnenblume*.

Operation *Sonneblume*
Catching the Desert Force by surprise, Rommel showed how quickly he had mastered desert warfare by sending the 5th Light Division across the desert to try to cut off the British retreat. The Germans were unable to move fast enough to capture the key port of Tobruk, but they did send the Commonwealth forces into headlong retreat – in the process capturing General O'Connor. Rommel was now at the end of a long supply line, with tired troops and worn-out equipment, so he settled on the Egyptian border to prepare for a new attack.

Panzergruppe Afrika

In August 1941, the German High Command created a new headquarters to control all German panzer forces in the theatre called *Panzergruppe Afrika*. Rommel was in command, while command of the DAK was passed to Ludwig Crüwell.

Arguments about German offensive aims in Africa were rendered academic by a succession of British attacks. In May, General Wavell launched Operation Brevity, which was defeated. In June they tried again, this time reinforced with nearly 300 new tanks shipped from England. Operation Battleaxe showed Rommel and the *Afrika Korps* at their best.

Tanks and anti-tank guns

British armoured units tried to seek out and engage Rommel's armour in a tank-versus-tank battle. But the Germans made masterful use of their towed anti-tank guns, firing from well-concealed positions. They inflicted terrible losses before the panzers wheeled in from a flank to finish the business.

The *Luftwaffe*'s 88mm (3.5in) anti-aircraft guns were pressed into service in a ground role since the army's standard 37mm (1.5in) weapon could not penetrate the British Matilda and Valentine tanks. Ironically, the British had a similar weapon available, the equally high-velocity 3.7in (93mm) anti-aircraft gun; but lack of imagination and inter-service squabbling stopped them from using it the way the Germans employed their '88'.

Battle of Sollum

In three days' fighting, known by the Germans as the battle of Sollum, the *Afrika Korps* demonstrated its superior leadership and vastly better staffwork. Wavell was sacked and replaced by General Auchinleck, who was pressed by London to renew the attack and relieve Tobruk, still besieged by the Axis forces.

Both sides sent reinforcements, but Germany had little to spare, with the invasion of the Soviet Union in full swing. Rommel developed jaundice in August, but pressed on, his forces now designated *Panzergruppe Afrika*.

Tobruk was the key: by capturing the port, Rommel would get his supplies landed just behind the front,

instead of having them driven the hundreds of kilometres of coast road from Benghazi.

Operation Crusader

Thanks to the ULTRA code-breakers, the British knew all about Rommel's plans for Tobruk. They deliberately staged their own offensive within days of the planned German assault. On 17 November, Rommel's signals staff reported 'complete English radio silence'. He ignored them, and also ignored the first reports of a major British attack.

The British Eighth Army under Lieutenant-General Cunningham advanced to relieve Tobruk, its powerful tank force surging across the desert to find and destroy the German armour. On 19 November, the key airfield at Sidi Rezegh was overrun by British tanks.

Rommel was reluctant to abandon his own attack on Tobruk, but when he reacted, he did so with his usual vigour. Fighting raged around Sidi Rezegh until

January 1942: Rommel Returns

Although by January the war in North Africa seemed to have turned against the *Afrika Korps*, Rommel realized that the British position had weakened after Operation Crusader. Now it was they who were operating at the end of long supply lines. On 21 January 1942, Rommel launched a new attack from El Agheila, driving the British from Adjabiya. Near Msus, Rommel swung his forces northeast, striking out through rough but undefended terrain to try to reach Benghazi and cut off the retreating Commonwealth forces. Though the Germans reached the coast on 28 January, the British managed to smash through the lead elements of the *Afrika Korps* and continued their retreat eastwards. At this point, Rommel was forced to stop his advance while his troops were resupplied. The British used the pause to retreat to prepared positions around Gazala.

23 November, the combatants manoeuvring aggressively in the open terrain. There was no real front line. Both sides had headquarters units and supply columns taken by surprise by enemy tanks. Both sides suffered heavily, but had only a hazy idea of their opponents' losses.

Rommel in charge

In such a battle, psychological strength is a priceless asset. On 24 November, Rommel struck out behind the British, heading for the Egyptian frontier rather than staying to beat back the British assault along the coast road. It was a daring move, but it left the German commander out of touch with his own headquarters for several days.

Cunningham, who had narrowly avoided capture in the chaotic battle, was sacked by Auchinleck. The British commander-in-chief placed his own chief-of-staff, Lieutenant-General Ritchie, in command of the Eighth Army.

Rommel's 'dash to the wire' failed to relieve the small garrisons left in the wake of the British advance. His own staff regarded it as premature, and it was ended on his own initiative by *Oberstleutnant* Westphal at Rommel's HQ, who ordered 21st Panzer Division back to Tobruk. Rommel remained out of communication as he raced around the battlefield, micro-managing the operation.

Rommel retreats

Rommel admitted defeat and fell back towards Gazala. But there was no obvious defence line, and he soon announced that the retreat must go on back to the Gulf of Sirte. There, in bad weather and worse tempers, Operation Crusader, or 'The Winter Battle' as the Germans called it, fizzled out, in the desolate sands around El Agheila. It had been from there, nine long months before, that Rommel had launched the first spectacular advance of the *Afrika Korps*.

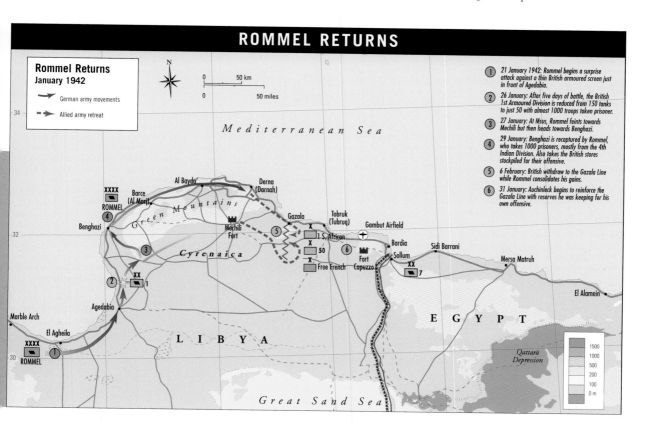

ROMMEL RETURNS

Rommel Returns
January 1942

→ German army movements
➤ Allied army retreat

1. 21 January 1942: Rommel begins a surprise attack against a thin British armoured screen just in front of Agedabia.
2. 26 January: After five days of battle, the British 1st Armoured Division is reduced from 150 tanks to just 50 with almost 1000 troops taken prisoner.
3. 27 January: At Msus, Rommel feints towards Mechili but then heads towards Benghazi.
4. 29 January: Benghazi is recaptured by Rommel, who takes 1000 prisoners, mostly from the 4th Indian Division. Also takes the British stores stockpiled for their offensive.
5. 6 February: British withdraw to the Gazala Line while Rommel consolidates his gains.
6. 31 January: Auchinleck begins to reinforce the Gazala Line with reserves he was keeping for his own offensive.

North Africa: 1942–43

Operating on a shoestring, at the end of extremely vulnerable supply lines across the Mediterranean, the German panzer forces at the end of 1942 were in no way prepared for the British offensive at Alamein or for the Allied landings of Operation Torch.

In the spring of 1942, Rommel decided that the time was ripe for *Panzerarmee Afrika* to finally take Tobruk. Seizure of the British bastion would remove a constant thorn in the side of the Axis forces, and promised to alleviate constant German and Italian supply problems, making a further attack on Egypt much more practical. However, the attack was risky since the British occupied strong defensive positions at Gazala.

Pre-emptive attack

Rommel pre-empted a possible British attack out of Gazala on 26 May 1942, by launching his own attack first. After a feint to the north, Axis mobile forces swung south around deep minefields and the tough French-

held position at Bir Hacheim. After a clash near Bir el Gubi, Rommel pressed on, shrugging off a series of disorganized British assaults. Pressing forwards on 13 June, the Axis forces inflicted heavy casualties on

AFRIKA KORPS – PANZER STRENGTH (NOV 1942)					
Tank type	**Pz II**	**Pz III (kz)**	**Pz III (lg)**	**Pz IV**	**Pz Bef**
15TH PANZER DIVISION					
8th Pz Rgt	14	43	44	18	2
21ST PANZER DIVISION					
5th Pz Rgt	16	53	43	22	2

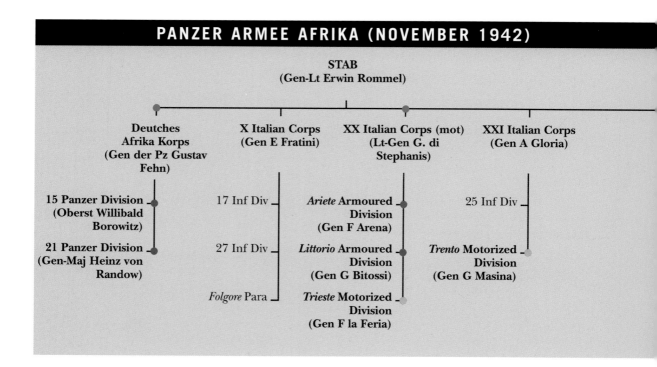

PANZER ARMEE AFRIKA (NOVEMBER 1942)

STAB
(Gen-Lt Erwin Rommel)

Deutches Afrika Korps (Gen der Pz Gustav Fehn)

X Italian Corps (Gen E Fratini)

XX Italian Corps (mot) (Lt-Gen G. di Stephanis)

XXI Italian Corps (Gen A Gloria)

15 Panzer Division (Oberst Willibald Borowitz)

21 Panzer Division (Gen-Maj Heinz von Randow)

17 Inf Div

27 Inf Div

Folgore Para

Ariete Armoured Division (Gen F Arena)

Littorio Armoured Division (Gen G Bitossi)

Trieste Motorized Division (Gen F la Feria)

25 Inf Div

Trento Motorized Division (Gen G Masina)

SCHWEREPANZERKOMPANIE, LATE 1942

The first heavy panzer companies were formed early in 1942, providing the cores of the first heavy panzer battalions later that year. The early organization of the companies saw the massive PzKpfw VI Tiger serving in mixed platoons with PzKpfw IIIs. The mobile Panzer IIIs provided flank protection for the ponderous Tigers.

The 501st and 503rd Battalions were sent to North Africa with the 10th Panzer Division at the end of 1942. In March 1943, the organization changed, with each battalion equipped only with Tigers.

Until their surrender, the Tigers of the 501st claimed to have destroyed 170 Allied tanks. The remnants of the 10th Panzer Division surrendered with the rest of the *Afrika Korps* in May 1943.

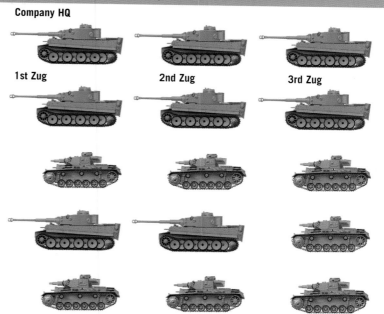

Company HQ

1st Zug   **2nd Zug**   **3rd Zug**

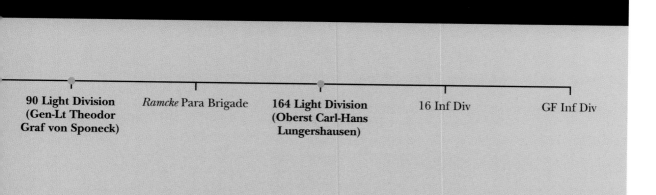

90 Light Division
(Gen-Lt Theodor
Graf von Sponeck)

Ramcke Para Brigade

164 Light Division
(Oberst Carl-Hans
Lungershausen)

16 Inf Div

GF Inf Div

KEY

● Panzer Division
● Motorized Division
● Panzer Corps
● Light Division

Panzergruppe Afrika controlled the *Afrika Korps* plus additional German panzer and motorized units that were sent to Africa, as well as two later three corps of Italian units. The term *Gruppe* was used by the Germans to describe a variety of different formations. In this case, the *Gruppe* was the size of an army in other armed forces. In fact, *Panzergruppe Afrika* was redesignated as *Panzerarmee Afrika* at the end of January, 1942.

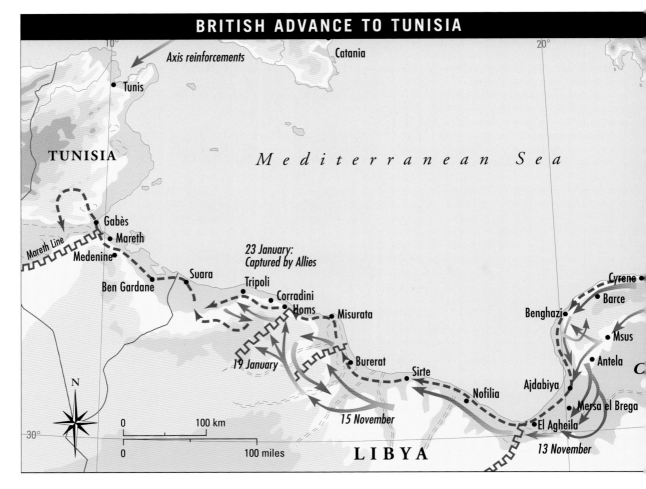

BRITISH ADVANCE TO TUNISIA

Commonwealth troops south of El Adam, before pushing the British further East past Sidi Rezegh. With only 70 tanks left, the British continued to retreat while Rommel turned back to smash through the defences of Tobruk and take the port.

Allied reinforcement

The early summer of 1942 had been a period of retreat for Commonwealth forces in North Africa, but from their powerful defensive line at El Alamein, the Eighth Army held off two powerful Axis attacks in June and August. Now, massively reinforced and with the Germans and Italians exhausted, it was time to strike back.

Safe behind strong defences, flanked to the north by the Mediterranean and to the south by the impassible sands of the Qattara Depression, the British could concentrate on building up forces for a major attack on the Axis forces. Under new commander General Bernard Law Montgomery, the Eighth Army soon had a massive materiel superiority over Rommel's command.

El Alamein

On the night of 23–24 October, Montgomery launched Operation Lightfoot, the first phase of a multi-stage offensive. XIII Corps launched a diversionary attack in the south. Then XXX Corps to the north cleared its way through minefields towards Kidney Ridge, covered by the largest artillery barrage ever seen in North Africa. It was followed by the tanks of X Armoured Corps.

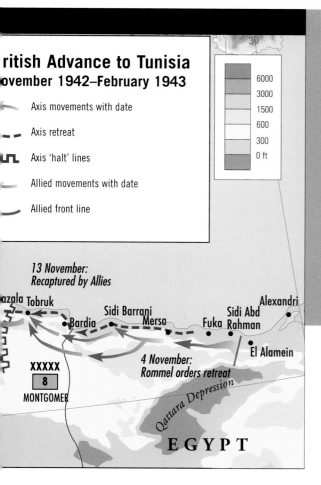

ritish Advance to Tunisia
ovember 1942–February 1943

Axis movements with date

Axis retreat

Axis 'halt' lines

Allied movements with date

Allied front line

	6000
	3000
	1500
	600
	300
	0 ft

13 November:
Recaptured by Allies

azala Tobruk   Alexandri
          Bardia   Sidi Barrani   Mersa   Sidi Abd   Rahman
                                  Fuka
          XXXXX   El Alamein
          8   *4 November:*
          MONTGOMER   *Rommel orders retreat*
                                  Qattara Depression

E G Y P T

November 1942 – Feb 1943

The Germans who did manage to make it to Rommel's first makeshift defensive line at Fuka after the Battle of Alamein were worth little more than a battalion, and even when joined by the 90th and 164th divisions constituted in battle-ready terms a brigade only. Ramcke's parachute formation made its own way back to the German lines virtually intact, but received only Rommel's scorn. The slower-moving Italian *Trieste* and *Littorio* divisions were, however, destroyed and many surrendered with scarcely a shot being fired. Montgomery failed to press home the advantage and finish off the remnants of the *Afrika Korps*. At that moment, Rommel's force consisted of just 4000 men, 11 tanks, 24 of the feared '88s', 25 other anti-tank guns and 40 assorted artillery pieces. However, he was able to hold off the advancing British thanks to the arrival of the Italian *Centauro* division at Antelat. Rommel was finally able to relax at Mersa Braga, due to the onset of winter. The new defence line was to be established at the Mareth Line, and Mersa Braga was to be given up whenever Montgomery felt like advancing again.

At 01.05 am, 2 November, another massive artillery barrage signalled the start of Operation Supercharge. By dawn on 4 November, British reconnaissance patrols had passed south of Tel el Akkakir only to find that the expected Axis defenses were not there. To save his army, Rommel had disobeyed his Führer, and was now withdrawing westwards. The battle was over. Now it was time for the pursuit.

And at the other end of the Mediterranean, for the first time in the European theatre, the Americans were about to make their massive presence felt. Operation Torch was the first major combined Anglo–American operation of the war. The landings in North West Africa would become a dress rehearsal for other, greater landings. Axis forces in Africa were caught between superior forces bent on its destruction. Barring miracles, there could only ever be one outcome.

ALLIED AND AXIS TANK STRENGTHS					
Date	**May 1941**	**November 1941**	**May 1942**	**October 1942**	**February 1943**
Battle	**Operation Battleaxe**	**Operation Crusader**	**Gazala**	**Alamein**	**Kasserine**
British	200	700	849	1100	0
American	0	0	0	0	160
Allied Total	200	700	849	1100	160
German	170	249	332	210	150
Italian	0	150	228	280	20
Axis Total	170	399	560 (390 operational)	490	170

Deutsch-Italienischen Panzer-Armee

At the end of January 1943, Italian General Giovanni Messe was appointed to command _Panzerarmee Afrika_, now known as the _Deutsch–Italienischen Panzerarmee_ in recognition of the fact that it consisted of one German and three Italian corps.

The Allies had believed that Tunisia would be taken before the end of 1942, but gradually, the Allied High Command came to a more realistic appreciation of the tactical situation. They recognized the enormous difficulty of covering the 2092km (1300 miles) from Casablanca to Tunis, given the appalling state of the

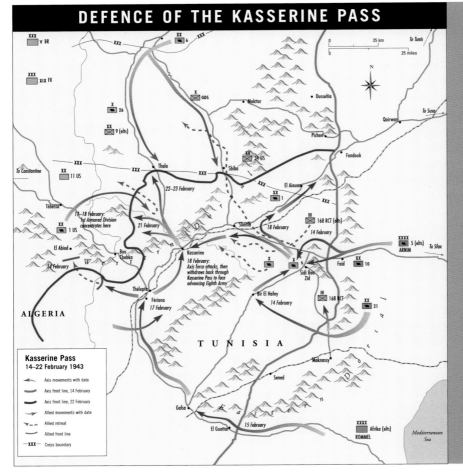

DEFENCE OF THE KASSERINE PASS

**Kasserine Pass
14–22 February 1943**

↞ Axis movements with date

⌇ Axis front line, 14 February

▬ Axis front line, 22 February

↠ Allied movements with date

┈┈► Allied retreat

⌇ Allied front line

–xxx– Corps boundary

14–22 February 1943

By early 1943, the Axis was being squeezed between the Eighth Army driving north and the Anglo–American armies driving east. Rommel did not favour being driven into the sea. Instead, he planned to sweep the Allies from Africa before their strength became too overwhelming. He chose for his target the Americans, whom he rightly assessed as still frighteningly green. The attack was launched on 14 February, and on 20 February the Germans burst through the Kasserine Pass. The attack smashed into the US II Corps, but it did not last. The Allies were just strong enough to hold the German attacks while reserves were rushed up. By the evening of 22 February, Rommel had to accept that his grandiose counterstroke was not working. He called off the assault. Within days, the lost ground was recovered by the British and Americans.

rudimentary African road system. It also began to dawn on the Allies that some very serious fighting lay ahead. Hitler, who had for so long starved Rommel of troops when victory had seemed in his grasp, now in extremis, poured in men and materials to bolster the Tunisian bridgehead. Although Montgomery was advancing steadily but slowly from the east, the Germans had placed Field Marshal Albert Kesselring in charge of the theatre. He quickly appreciated that his brief in Africa, especially after Operation Torch, was to fight a series of delaying actions, and he was to prove a master of this kind of defensive warfare.

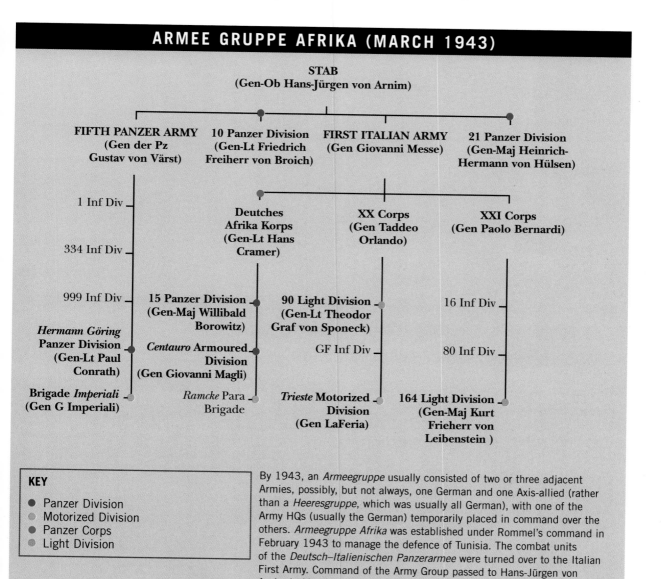

ARMEE GRUPPE AFRIKA (MARCH 1943)

STAB
(Gen-Ob Hans-Jürgen von Arnim)

FIFTH PANZER ARMY
(Gen der Pz Gustav von Värst)

10 Panzer Division
(Gen-Lt Friedrich Freiherr von Broich)

FIRST ITALIAN ARMY
(Gen Giovanni Messe)

21 Panzer Division
(Gen-Maj Heinrich-Hermann von Hülsen)

1 Inf Div

Deutches Afrika Korps
(Gen-Lt Hans Cramer)

XX Corps
(Gen Taddeo Orlando)

XXI Corps
(Gen Paolo Bernardi)

334 Inf Div

999 Inf Div

15 Panzer Division
(Gen-Maj Willibald Borowitz)

90 Light Division
(Gen-Lt Theodor Graf von Sponeck)

16 Inf Div

Hermann Göring **Panzer Division**
(Gen-Lt Paul Conrath)

Centauro **Armoured Division**
(Gen Giovanni Magli)

GF Inf Div

80 Inf Div

Brigade *Imperiali*
(Gen G Imperiali)

Ramcke Para Brigade

Trieste **Motorized Division**
(Gen LaFeria)

164 Light Division
(Gen-Maj Kurt Frieherr von Leibenstein)

KEY

- Panzer Division
- Motorized Division
- Panzer Corps
- Light Division

By 1943, an *Armeegruppe* usually consisted of two or three adjacent Armies, possibly, but not always, one German and one Axis-allied (rather than a *Heeresgruppe*, which was usually all German), with one of the Army HQs (usually the German) temporarily placed in command over the others. *Armeegruppe Afrika* was established under Rommel's command in February 1943 to manage the defence of Tunisia. The combat units of the *Deutsch–Italienischen Panzerarmee* were turned over to the Italian First Army. Command of the Army Group passed to Hans-Jürgen von Arnim in March.

Defeat in North Africa

Even though Hitler belatedly sent reinforcements to Tunisia in the spring of 1943, there was no way that the Axis armies could match the strength of the Allies advancing from east and west. Despite Rommel's best efforts, defeat was inevitable.

The Germans rushed their men into Tunis faster than the Allies could advance from their beachheads in Algeria. Within three days of the Allied landings, there were a thousand extra Axis soldiers in Africa; a week later, 4500. Some 20,000 German troops arrived over the following ten days, brought over from Sicily by some 673 transport aircraft.

False hopes
The German position had looked fairly promising at the end of 1942, in comparison to the dire predictions made two months previously at the beginning of Torch. But the delicate balance in the battlefield at the beginning of 1943 was tipped in the Allies' favour by their success in overcoming supply difficulties.

After the failure at Kasserine, a dispirited Rommel turned south against his old adversaries, the British. It was not Rommel's plan to attack the Eighth Army at Medenine, but was rather formulated by the Italian commanders Messe and Ziegler. The Germans were two-thirds under strength. The three panzer divisions had just 141 tanks between them.

Montgomery knew Rommel well and did not need particular intelligence to confirm his adversary's intentions. He concentrated two infantry brigades and two armoured brigades on a 39km (24-mile) front at right angles to Rommel's expected line of attack.

He had 810 medium artillery pieces and anti-tank guns, including some of the excellent new 17-pounders.

Killing ground
Although the artillery played havoc with the hapless German infantry, it was the anti-tank screen that did the real damage. Without armour, the German infantry was going nowhere. The killing ground in front of the British positions was a graveyard of German tanks – tanks that would be sorely missed by the Germans in the coming weeks of the campaign.

Two days later, Rommel left Africa for good and Arnim now took over as commander-in-chief. The *Afrika Korps* had launched its final offensive. It was now the turn of Montgomery to finish the job.

On 15 April, Army Group Africa was in place along a reduced 217km (135-mile) front. Arnim still theoretically had 16 divisions, but the nine German divisions numbered only 60,000 men with 100 tanks.

Final battles
The final battle began on 6 May. The Germans were pinned into a narrow bridgehead around Bizerta, Tunis and the Cape Bon peninsula. On the left, the US 2nd Corps, now commanded by Omar Bradley, pushed along the coast. First Army drove through Medjerda towards Tunis while the Eighth Army kept the attentions of Arnim around Enfidaville, so distracting him from the massive armoured punch at Tunis.

Organized resistance collapsed that morning, Arnim's weak divisions having so little fuel that counterattacks were no longer possible. By the afternoon of the following day, British troops were on the outskirts of Tunis and the defence had fragmented into isolated pockets. The last German pocket surrendered at Cape Bon on 13 May – only 800 troops out of 200,000 had made good their escape.

Tank type	Pz II	Pz III	Pz IV	Marder	Pz Bef
FIFTH PANZER ARMY – PANZER STRENGTH (FEB 1943)					
10TH PANZER DIVISION					
7th Pz Rgt	21	105	20	0	9
***HERMANN GÖRING* PANZER DIVISION**					
HG Pz Rgt	0	2	5	9	0

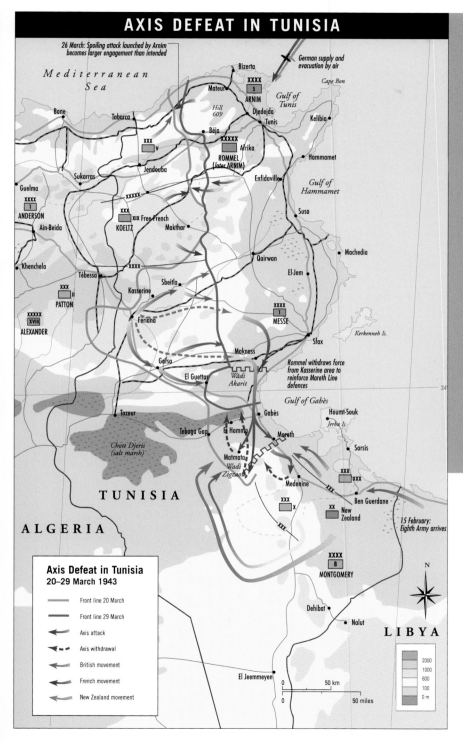

AXIS DEFEAT IN TUNISIA

26 March: Spoiling attack launched by Arnim becomes larger engagement than intended

German supply and evacuation by air

Mediterranean Sea

Bizerta

Cape Bon

XXXX 5 ARNIM

Mateur

Gulf of Tunis

Hill 609

Djedejda

Tunis

Kelibia

Bone

Tabarca

Béja

Hammamet

XXX V

XXXXX Afrika ROMMEL (later ARNIM)

Sukarras

Jendouba

Enfidaville

Gulf of Hammamet

Guelma

XXXX 1 ANDERSON

XXXXX

Susa

Ain-Beida

XXX XIX Free French KOELTZ

Makthar

Machedia

Khenchela

Qairwan

Tébessa

XXXX

El-Jem

Sbeitla

XXX II PATTON

Kasserine

XXXXX XVIII ALEXANDER

Feriana

XXXX 1 MESSE

Kerkenneh Is.

Gafsa

Maknass

Sfax

El Guettar

Wádi Akarit

Rommel withdraws force from Kasserine area to reinforce Mareth Line defences

341

Tozeur

Gulf of Gabès

Gabès

Houmt-Souk

Tebaga Gap

El Hamma

Jerba Is.

Mareth

Chott Djeris (salt marsh)

Matmata

Sarsis

Wadi Zigzaou

XXX XXX

Medenine

XXX X

TUNISIA

XX New Zealand

XXX

Ben Guerdane

ALGERIA

15 February: Eighth Army arrives

N

XXXX 8 MONTGOMERY

Axis Defeat in Tunisia
20–29 March 1943

——	Front line 20 March
——	Front line 29 March
◄—	Axis attack
◄--	Axis withdrawal
◄—	British movement
◄—	French movement
◄—	New Zealand movement

Dehibat

Nalut

LIBYA

El Jeemmeyen

0   50 km

0   50 miles

	2000
	1000
	600
	100
	0 m

May 1943

Rommel launched an attack, a direct assault on Montgomery's positions at Medenine, but the British were waiting. The attack was smashed by massed tanks and anti-tank guns. Another assault against the British and Americans by von Arnim's forces in the north was equally unsuccessful. Even though Hitler had poured reinforcements into Tunisia, the Axis could not match Allied strength. Constant Allied pressure meant that by May 1943 the remnants of the Axis forces had been compressed into a small enclave. Once the Allied Operation Vulcan was launched on 6 May, the remnants of the once-mighty *Afrika Korps* disintegrated. Across the north of Tunis, Allied forces mopped up the last German resistance. When the dust had settled, more than 150,000 Axis troops had become prisoners, in a defeat of Stalingrad proportions.

The Eastern Front: 1941–45

The invasion of the Soviet Union launched on 22 June 1941 was the largest military operation up to that time. Over 3.5 million men led by 3600 tanks and 2700 aircraft were thrown into an attack designed to smash the Soviet Union by the autumn.

The vast expanses of the steppes were in some respects ideal tank country, but the sheer size and scale of the landscape meant that the *Wehrmacht* experienced logistics and maintenance problems never before encountered.

THE SCALE OF OPERATIONS was vast. The German armies massed along the Soviet frontier that summer of 1941 stretched from the Arctic Circle to the Black Sea. They represented the greatest concentration of military force the world had ever seen.

Hitler had long had plans for the Soviet Union. In August 1939, on the eve of the invasion of Poland, he said: 'I have sent my Death's Head formations eastwards. Poland will be depopulated and settled with Germans… the fate of Russia will be exactly the same.'

It was to be nearly two years before Hitler was ready to act. In 18 months his forces had overrun western Europe, smashing every army that stood in their way. Only Britain held out, for reasons Hitler was still unable to comprehend. But there was nothing to stop Germany now.

On 22 June 1941, Hitler launched the greatest invasion in military history. Three million German and Axis troops in three Army Groups attacked the Russian border from the Baltic coast to the Romanian frontier. More than 150 divisions were mobilized, including 19 panzer divisions, 1945 German aircraft and another 1000 Axis planes.

They faced some three million men of the Red Army, which had another million soldiers deployed across southern republics of the Soviet Union and in the Far East, where they had recently beaten the Japanese in a series of border clashes.

Operation *Barbarossa*

The Soviets were taken by surprise. Stalin had been determined to do nothing that could provoke a German invasion until he had a chance to reorganize his own forces. Apparently unable to believe that Hitler would break their cynical alliance so soon, he saw to it that the Soviet Union continued to deliver strategic materials to the Germans right up to the very night of the attack.

PANZER *ABTEILUNG STABSKOMPANIE*, JUNE 1941

Following the campaign in France in 1940, it was decided to change the organization of panzer units to incorporate combat lessons from Poland and the campaign in the West. In 1939, a panzer battalion staff had a signals platoon with three command tanks and a light panzer platoon with five Panzer IIs. Introduced in February 1941, the new organization consisted of a signals platoon with two command tanks and one Panzer III, a light platoon as before, and a command squadron of mixed Panzer IIs, Panzer IIIs and a Panzer IV.

Nachrichten Zug

Leichte Zug

Stab Schwadrone

HERMANN HOTH (1885–1971)

Hermann Hoth (pictured right, with Guderian, left) joined the Imperial German Army in 1904. Between the wars he served in the *Truppenamt* of the *Reichswehr*, where Oswald Lutz and Heinz Guderian were developing the panzer arm.

- Hoth commanded an infantry corps in Poland, and a panzer corps during the invasion of France.

- Hoth was an unflappable commander, and a good tactician and strategist. During Operation *Barbarossa* he commanded *Panzergruppe* 3. In October 1941, he commanded Seventeenth Army in the battle to take Kharkov, transferring to command Fourth Panzer Army in 1942.

- Hoth led von Manstein's vain attempt to break the siege of Stalingrad in December 1942. In 1943, he fought at Kursk, and at the end of the year he was dismissed by Hitler for failing to stop the Soviet advances in southern Ukraine.

- In April 1945, he was recalled to duty and assigned to command the defence of the Harz Mountains.

A German corporal who had deserted on 21 June with news of the attack was interrogated by the NKVD. His story was reported to Stalin, who paused, then whispered his familiar instruction into the telephone. The unfortunate soldier was taken outside and shot.

Air strikes

The *Luftwaffe* had been overflying Russian airbases for months before the invasion – at least one Russian officer was shot for firing on German photo-reconnaissance planes that blamed 'navigational errors' for their intrusion. Now it scored the greatest victory in its history, wiping out the Red Air Force in a matter of days.

Soviet bases were in the process of expansion, so many air regiments were doubled up on the airstrips. Aircraft were packed together so a single bomb could destroy a whole squadron.

If they got into the air, the Soviets had neither the skill nor the aircraft to challenge the Messerschmitt Bf 109, and many German fighter pilots began to run up incredible numbers of victories.

Panzers to the fore

Spearheading the attack were four *Panzergruppen* – in effect, the world's first armoured armies. Commanded by generals who had made the first *Blitzkrieg* campaigns so successful in Poland and France, each *Panzergruppe* included at least two fully motorized Corps, formed around 19 panzer divisions.

By the time the attack was launched in mid-June, enough fuel, ammunition and stores had been stockpiled to supply this vast force in a 600km (37-mile) advance. Half a million lorries waited in massed parks from East Prussia to Romania to rush those supplies forward on demand. These had been gathered from all over occupied Europe, and the multiplicity of vehicle types must have been a quartermaster's nightmare, but as long as the war did not last too long, the High Command did not envisage too many problems.

However, the vast bulk of the *Wehrmacht*'s divisions were only marginally motorized at best. To the modern mind, the only questionable, indeed alarming, figure to emerge from the tables of statistics is that for 'stabling': 300,000 horses were to play an apparently essential part in this monumental military exercise.

OPERATION *BARBAROSSA*

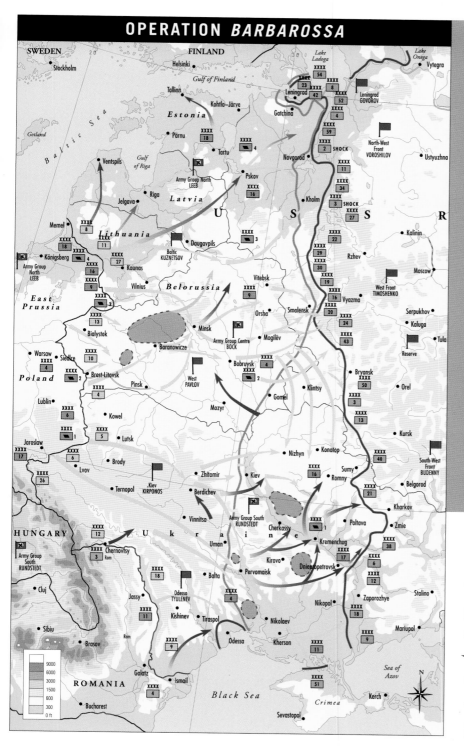

22 June–early October 1941

The German plan involved three Army Groups (North, South and Centre), with the bulk of the forces concentrated in Army Groups North and Centre. Army Group Centre, which contained around half the German armour, was to shatter Soviet forces in Belorussia before turning to assist Army Group North in the drive on Leningrad. Army Group South, meanwhile, was to deal with Soviet forces in the Ukraine. At 3.05 a.m., 22 June, Army Group North began the drive to Leningrad. By the evening of the first day the leading panzers were 60km (37 miles) into Lithuania. By the end of the second day, only the wrecks of 140 Soviet tanks lay between the panzer divisions and Pskov. But the *Panzergruppe*'s infantry could not keep up. The terrain encountered on the Soviet side of the border was so marshy and impenetrable that even the motorized infantry was reduced to the pace of the marching columns.

Operation *Barbarossa*
22 June–early October 1941

→ German attack

XXXX [6] Soviet positions 22 June

Soviet units encircled

◄ Soviet counterattacks

German front line, end of August

German front line, early October

XXXX [6] Soviet positions early October

73

The Push for Leningrad

Field Marshal von Leeb's Army Group North was aimed at the Baltic states and Leningrad. Two infantry armies contained 15 infantry divisions between them, while the armoured punch was provided by IV *Panzergruppe*, which comprised three panzer divisions, three motorized infantry divisions and two infantry divisions.

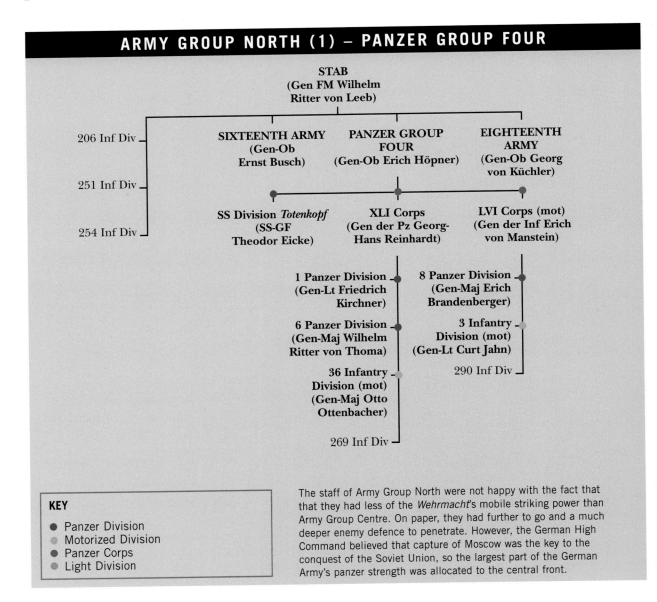

ARMY GROUP NORTH (1) – PANZER GROUP FOUR

STAB
(Gen FM Wilhelm Ritter von Leeb)

206 Inf Div
251 Inf Div
254 Inf Div

SIXTEENTH ARMY
(Gen-Ob Ernst Busch)

PANZER GROUP FOUR
(Gen-Ob Erich Höpner)

EIGHTEENTH ARMY
(Gen-Ob Georg von Küchler)

SS Division *Totenkopf*
(SS-GF Theodor Eicke)

XLI Corps
(Gen der Pz Georg-Hans Reinhardt)

LVI Corps (mot)
(Gen der Inf Erich von Manstein)

1 Panzer Division
(Gen-Lt Friedrich Kirchner)

6 Panzer Division
(Gen-Maj Wilhelm Ritter von Thoma)

36 Infantry Division (mot)
(Gen-Maj Otto Ottenbacher)

269 Inf Div

8 Panzer Division
(Gen-Maj Erich Brandenberger)

3 Infantry Division (mot)
(Gen-Lt Curt Jahn)

290 Inf Div

KEY

- Panzer Division
- Motorized Division
- Panzer Corps
- Light Division

The staff of Army Group North were not happy with the fact that that they had less of the *Wehrmacht*'s mobile striking power than Army Group Centre. On paper, they had further to go and a much deeper enemy defence to penetrate. However, the German High Command believed that capture of Moscow was the key to the conquest of the Soviet Union, so the largest part of the German Army's panzer strength was allocated to the central front.

ARMY GROUP NORTH (2)

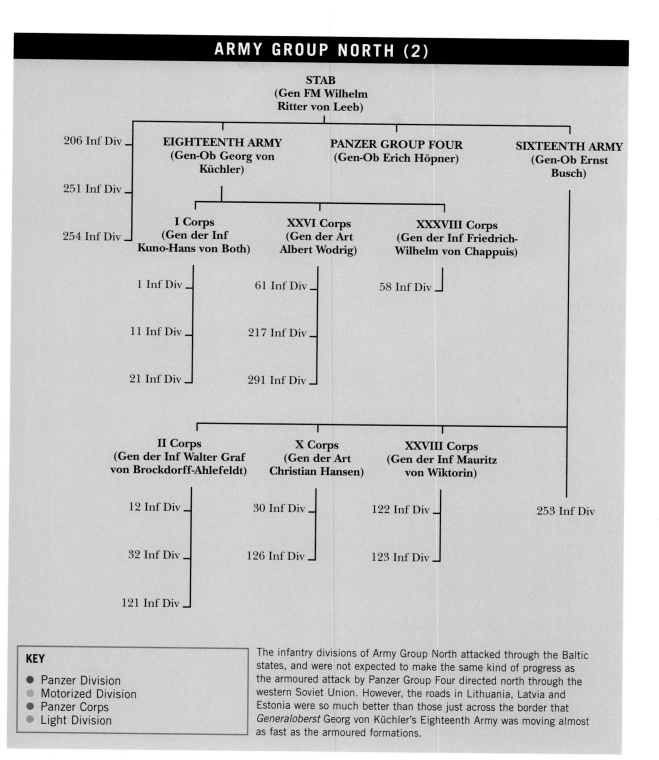

STAB
(Gen FM Wilhelm Ritter von Leeb)

206 Inf Div

EIGHTEENTH ARMY
(Gen-Ob Georg von Küchler)

PANZER GROUP FOUR
(Gen-Ob Erich Höpner)

SIXTEENTH ARMY
(Gen-Ob Ernst Busch)

251 Inf Div

254 Inf Div

I Corps
(Gen der Inf Kuno-Hans von Both)

XXVI Corps
(Gen der Art Albert Wodrig)

XXXVIII Corps
(Gen der Inf Friedrich-Wilhelm von Chappuis)

1 Inf Div

61 Inf Div

58 Inf Div

11 Inf Div

217 Inf Div

21 Inf Div

291 Inf Div

II Corps
(Gen der Inf Walter Graf von Brockdorff-Ahlefeldt)

X Corps
(Gen der Art Christian Hansen)

XXVIII Corps
(Gen der Inf Mauritz von Wiktorin)

12 Inf Div

30 Inf Div

122 Inf Div

253 Inf Div

32 Inf Div

126 Inf Div

123 Inf Div

121 Inf Div

KEY

- ● Panzer Division
- ○ Motorized Division
- ■ Panzer Corps
- ○ Light Division

The infantry divisions of Army Group North attacked through the Baltic states, and were not expected to make the same kind of progress as the armoured attack by Panzer Group Four directed north through the western Soviet Union. However, the roads in Lithuania, Latvia and Estonia were so much better than those just across the border that *Generaloberst* Georg von Küchler's Eighteenth Army was moving almost as fast as the armoured formations.

Objective Moscow

Under the command of Field Marshal Fedor von Bock, Army Group Centre comprised two infantry armies and two panzer groups – in effect, tank armies – under Generals Hoth and Guderian. Their task was to reach Moscow within two months.

These were the armies whose commanders intended to reduce Napoleon's feat of arms of 129 years earlier to historical obscurity. They planned to reach Moscow in less than eight weeks, and to annihilate the Soviet Army in the process.

In this hope, they were encouraged by Hitler, who had assured them: 'Before three months have passed, we shall witness a collapse in Russia, the like of which has never been seen in history. We have only to kick in the front door and the whole rotten Russian edifice will come tumbling down.'

Dual Panzer thrust

To Heinz Guderian, whose *Panzergruppe* II included four panzer divisions, this was the pinnacle of his military career. It was clear that he and Hoth jointly commanded the most significant forces in the entire operation, and could execute the most exciting and spectacular military feat of the century, perhaps of all history. The first few days seemed to confirm the prospect.

Guderian's first task was to throw his *Panzergruppe* across the River Bug on each side of the fortress of Brest-Litovsk, capture the fortress and then race with his armoured spearheads towards the city of Minsk. He would curve up to it from the south to meet Hoth's spearheads coming down from the north.

In this way, the Soviet frontline forces would be isolated in a huge cauldron. Once their supplies had run out, they would have little alternative but to surrender.

This was achieved in five days of breathtaking attack, which seemed to confirm Hitler's pronouncements and the optimism of the *Wehrmacht* leaders.

By 24 June, only 60 hours after the launch of the attack, 17th Panzer Division was driving into Slonim, more than 140km (87 miles) from the frontier and halfway to the Germans' first objective. Three days later, on the afternoon of 27 June, the leading tanks of the

PANZER GROUP THREE – PANZER STRENGTH (JUNE 1941)					
Tank type	Pz II	Pz 38(t)	Pz IV	PzBef38(t)	Pz Bef
7TH PANZER DIVISION					
25th Pz Rgt	53	167	30	7	8

Tank type	Pz I	Pz II	Pz 38(t)	Pz IV	PzBef38(t)
12TH PANZER DIVISION					
29th Pz Rgt	40	33	109	30	8
19TH PANZER DIVISION					
27th Pz Rgt	42	35	110	30	11
20TH PANZER DIVISION					
21st Pz Rgt	44	31	121	31	2

September–December 1941

In September, the German High Command decided to launch Operation Typhoon, the final, decisive offensive for the year to capture Moscow. The attack was launched in early October. The Soviets were taken by surprise, with over 600,000 men taken prisoner in pockets at Vyazma and Bryansk. The panzers raced towards Moscow, but desperate Soviet resistance held the Gernmans back until the weather broke. The autumn rains started in mid-October, and they quickly turned the dirt roads to mud. By the end of October, the Germans were approaching Tula on the southern route to the Soviet capital. At their closest, the Germans were now only 64km (40 miles) from Moscow. By 5 December, the Germans were halted along the entire front. Exhausted, the German forces had failed to take their objective. The next day, amidst the snows and intense cold of the onset of winter, the reinforced Soviets launched their winter counteroffensive.

OPERATION TYPHOON

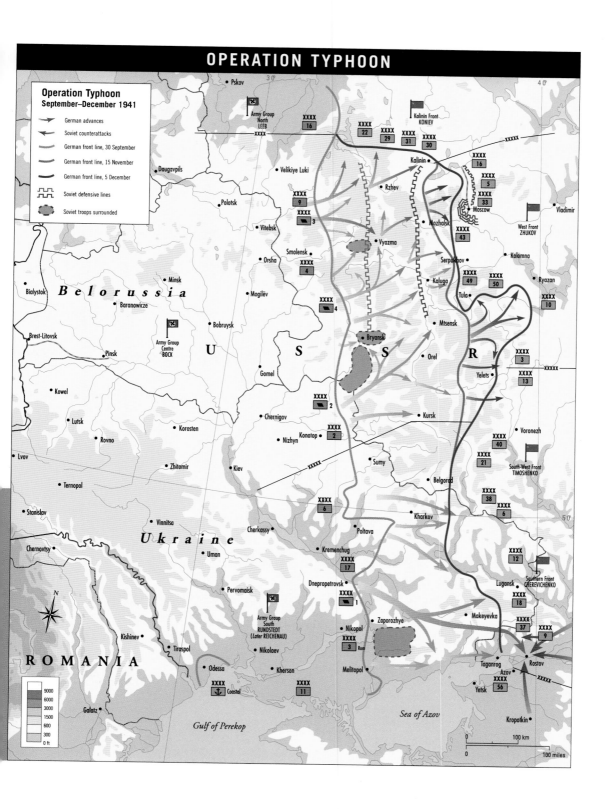

Operation Typhoon
September–December 1941

- German advances
- Soviet counterattacks
- German front line, 30 September
- German front line, 15 November
- German front line, 5 December
- Soviet defensive lines
- Soviet troops surrounded

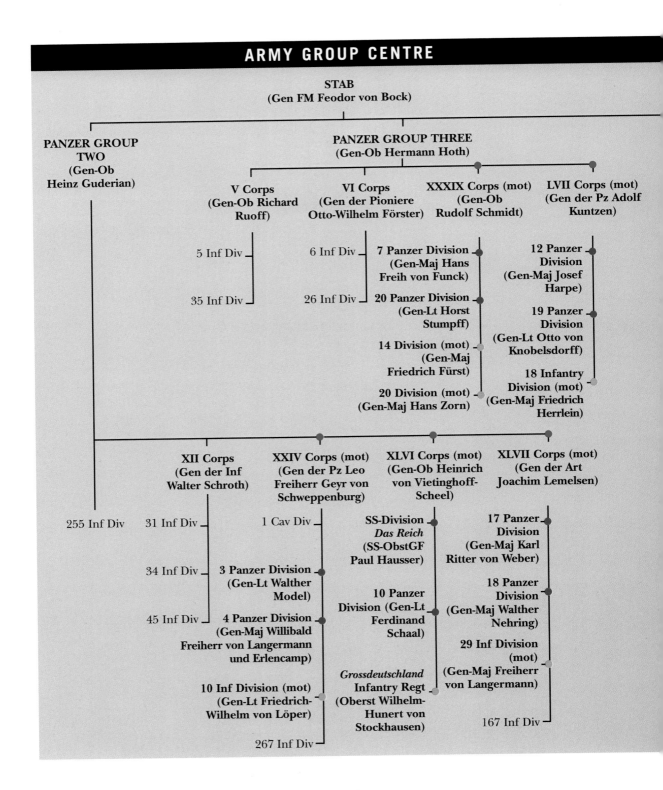

ARMY GROUP CENTRE

STAB
(Gen FM Feodor von Bock)

PANZER GROUP TWO
(Gen-Ob Heinz Guderian)

PANZER GROUP THREE
(Gen-Ob Hermann Hoth)

V Corps
(Gen-Ob Richard Ruoff)

VI Corps
(Gen der Pioniere Otto-Wilhelm Förster)

XXXIX Corps (mot)
(Gen-Ob Rudolf Schmidt)

LVII Corps (mot)
(Gen der Pz Adolf Kuntzen)

5 Inf Div

35 Inf Div

6 Inf Div

26 Inf Div

7 Panzer Division (Gen-Maj Hans Freih von Funck)

20 Panzer Division (Gen-Lt Horst Stumpff)

14 Division (mot) (Gen-Maj Friedrich Fürst)

20 Division (mot) (Gen-Maj Hans Zorn)

12 Panzer Division (Gen-Maj Josef Harpe)

19 Panzer Division (Gen-Lt Otto von Knobelsdorff)

18 Infantry Division (mot) (Gen-Maj Friedrich Herrlein)

XII Corps
(Gen der Inf Walter Schroth)

XXIV Corps (mot)
(Gen der Pz Leo Freiherr Geyr von Schweppenburg)

XLVI Corps (mot)
(Gen-Ob Heinrich von Vietinghoff-Scheel)

XLVII Corps (mot)
(Gen der Art Joachim Lemelsen)

255 Inf Div

31 Inf Div

34 Inf Div

45 Inf Div

1 Cav Div

3 Panzer Division (Gen-Lt Walther Model)

4 Panzer Division (Gen-Maj Willibald Freiherr von Langermann und Erlencamp)

10 Inf Division (mot) (Gen-Lt Friedrich-Wilhelm von Löper)

267 Inf Div

SS-Division Das Reich (SS-ObstGF Paul Hausser)

10 Panzer Division (Gen-Lt Ferdinand Schaal)

Grossdeutschland **Infantry Regt (Oberst Wilhelm-Hunert von Stockhausen)**

17 Panzer Division (Gen-Maj Karl Ritter von Weber)

18 Panzer Division (Gen-Maj Walther Nehring)

29 Inf Division (mot) (Gen-Maj Freiherr von Langermann)

167 Inf Div

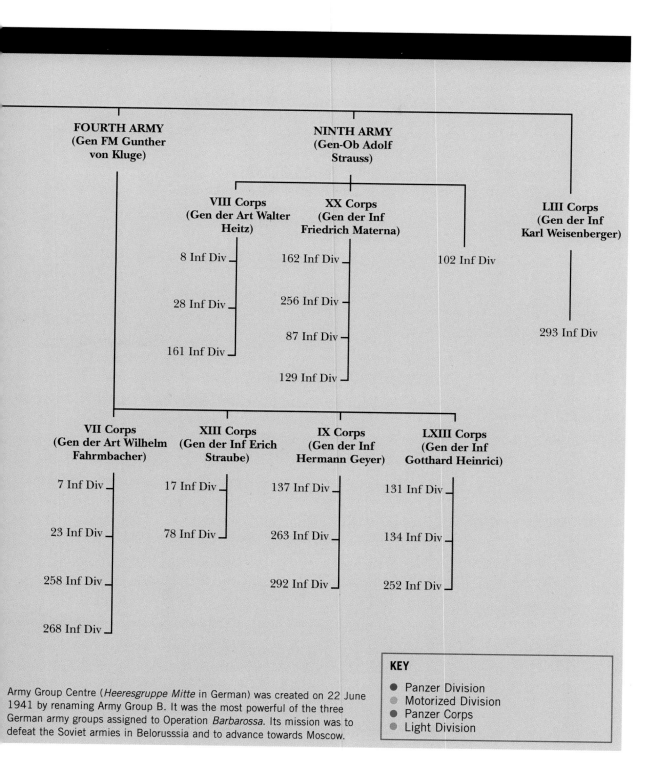

FOURTH ARMY
(Gen FM Gunther
von Kluge)

NINTH ARMY
(Gen-Ob Adolf
Strauss)

VIII Corps
(Gen der Art Walter
Heitz)

XX Corps
(Gen der Inf
Friedrich Materna)

LIII Corps
(Gen der Inf
Karl Weisenberger)

8 Inf Div

162 Inf Div

102 Inf Div

28 Inf Div

256 Inf Div

161 Inf Div

87 Inf Div

293 Inf Div

129 Inf Div

VII Corps
(Gen der Art Wilhelm
Fahrmbacher)

XIII Corps
(Gen der Inf Erich
Straube)

IX Corps
(Gen der Inf
Hermann Geyer)

LXIII Corps
(Gen der Inf
Gotthard Heinrici)

7 Inf Div

17 Inf Div

137 Inf Div

131 Inf Div

23 Inf Div

78 Inf Div

263 Inf Div

134 Inf Div

258 Inf Div

292 Inf Div

252 Inf Div

268 Inf Div

KEY

● Panzer Division
○ Motorized Division
● Panzer Corps
○ Light Division

Army Group Centre (*Heeresgruppe Mitte* in German) was created on 22 June 1941 by renaming Army Group B. It was the most powerful of the three German army groups assigned to Operation *Barbarossa*. Its mission was to defeat the Soviet armies in Belorusssia and to advance towards Moscow.

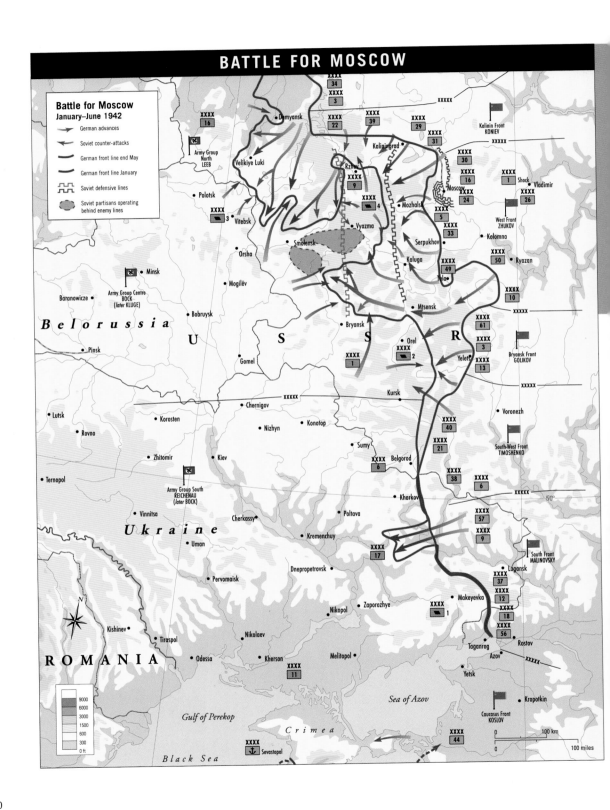

BATTLE FOR MOSCOW

Battle for Moscow
January–June 1942

→ German advances
← Soviet counter-attacks
— German front line end May
— German front line January
Soviet defensive lines
Soviet partisans operating behind enemy lines

January–March 1942

In January 1942, 12 German armies were locked in combat with 22 Soviet armies. On a front stretching from the Crimea to the Gulf of Finland, 141 divisions, including 11 from Axis allies, faced more than 300 Soviet formations. The very size of the war zone was in the *Wehrmacht*'s favour. Stalin was trying not only to relieve Moscow and Leningrad, but also to destroy Army Group Centre. His generals knew what happened to commanders who failed, and Red Army offensives were launched all along the line. It was too much. Despite tattered uniforms stuffed with straw and newspaper, weapons that jammed in the arctic temperatures and a grave lack of tanks or aircraft, the German Army defended itself with extraordinary professionalism and courage. The stubborn German defence revealed the Red Army's lack of experience. By March, even Stalin had to admit that his great offensive was over.

17th Panzer Division drove into Minsk to meet the Hoth's Third *Panzergruppe*, which had covered 350km (217 miles) in five days. Guderian and Hoth were convinced that they must immediately race further ahead, first to Smolensk and then to Moscow, confident that speed would prove the decisive factor in this campaign. On 1 July, in a burst of insubordination, the two panzer commanders released units towards the next obstacle, the River Beresina. They were threatened with court martial for doing so by their immediate superior, General Günther von Kluge.

On the same day, Guderian's panzers met for the first time the Soviet T-34. A single tank blocked their advance for three hours, knocking out five Panzer IIIs. It was only removed when attacked from the rear by an 88mm (3.5in) flak gun. Fortunately for the Germans, no more T-34s were encountered in the area.

Southern Front

Field Marshal Gerd von Rundstedt had originally been given command of the weakest Army Group in *Barbarossa*. His most powerful forces were Sixth Army under Reichenau, 1st *Panzergruppe* under Kleist and Seventeenth Army under Stulpnagel.

The principal objective of Army Group South was to capture Ukraine and its capital Kiev. Army Group South was then to advance as far as the Volga River, destroying a large part of the Red Army and clearing the way for Army Group North and Army Group Centre to take Leningrad and Moscow.

By August 1941, Hitler had decided that the southern prong of the *Wehrmacht*'s attack was the most important economically, so he diverted Guderian's panzers south from Army Group Centre to assist in the encirclement of Kiev.

By the end of October, Kleist's *Panzergruppe* was edging its way slowly into Rostov. Although they did not know it, they were edging into a Soviet trap.

On 19 November, the Red Army began to move forwards into Rostov. For the first time in World War II, the Germans had to face a major enemy attack. By 28 November, 1st *Panzergruppe* had been squeezed out of

ARMY GROUP SOUTH – PANZER STRENGTH (JUNE 1941)					
Tank type	Pz I	Pz II	Pz III	Pz IV	Pz Bef
9TH PANZER DIVISION					
33rd Pz Rgt	8	32	71	20	12
11TH PANZER DIVISION					
15th Pz Rgt	0	45	51	16	14
13TH PANZER DIVISION					
4th Pz Rgt	0	45	71	20	13
14TH PANZER DIVISION					
36th Pz Rgt	0	45	71	20	11
16TH PANZER DIVISION					
2nd Pz Rgt	0	45	70	20	9

Rostov, back through Taganrog to the line of the Mius River. The southern offensive had come to halt.

ARMY GROUP SOUTH

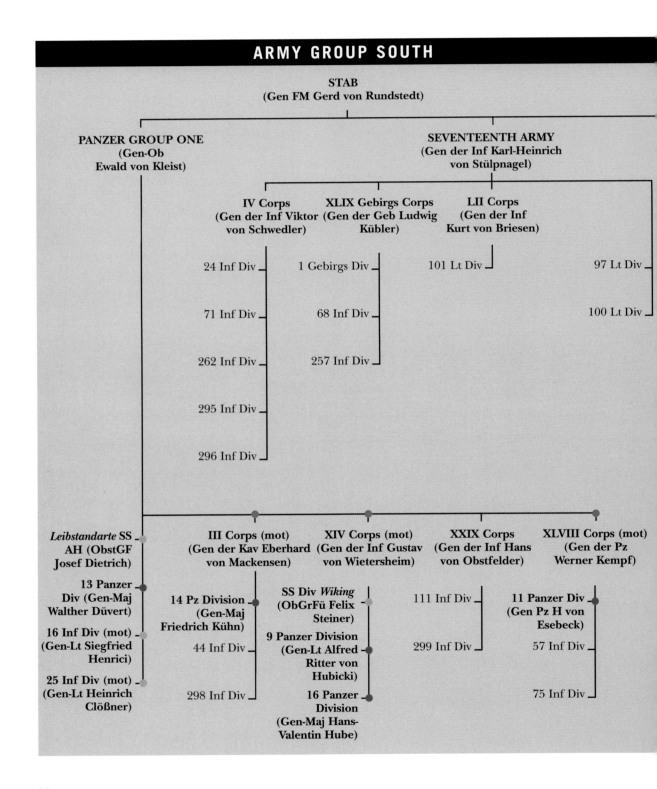

STAB
(Gen FM Gerd von Rundstedt)

PANZER GROUP ONE
(Gen-Ob
Ewald von Kleist)

SEVENTEENTH ARMY
(Gen der Inf Karl-Heinrich
von Stülpnagel)

IV Corps
(Gen der Inf Viktor
von Schwedler)

XLIX Gebirgs Corps
(Gen der Geb Ludwig
Kübler)

LII Corps
(Gen der Inf
Kurt von Briesen)

24 Inf Div

1 Gebirgs Div

101 Lt Div

97 Lt Div

71 Inf Div

68 Inf Div

100 Lt Div

262 Inf Div

257 Inf Div

295 Inf Div

296 Inf Div

Leibstandarte SS
AH (ObstGF
Josef Dietrich)

III Corps (mot)
(Gen der Kav Eberhard
von Mackensen)

XIV Corps (mot)
(Gen der Inf Gustav
von Wietersheim)

XXIX Corps
(Gen der Inf Hans
von Obstfelder)

XLVIII Corps (mot)
(Gen der Pz
Werner Kempf)

13 Panzer
Div (Gen-Maj
Walther Düvert)

14 Pz Division
(Gen-Maj
Friedrich Kühn)

SS Div *Wiking*
(ObGrFü Felix
Steiner)

111 Inf Div

11 Panzer Div
(Gen Pz H von
Esebeck)

16 Inf Div (mot)
(Gen-Lt Siegfried
Henrici)

44 Inf Div

9 Panzer Division
(Gen-Lt Alfred
Ritter von
Hubicki)

299 Inf Div

57 Inf Div

25 Inf Div (mot)
(Gen-Lt Heinrich
Clößner)

298 Inf Div

16 Panzer
Division
(Gen-Maj Hans-
Valentin Hube)

75 Inf Div

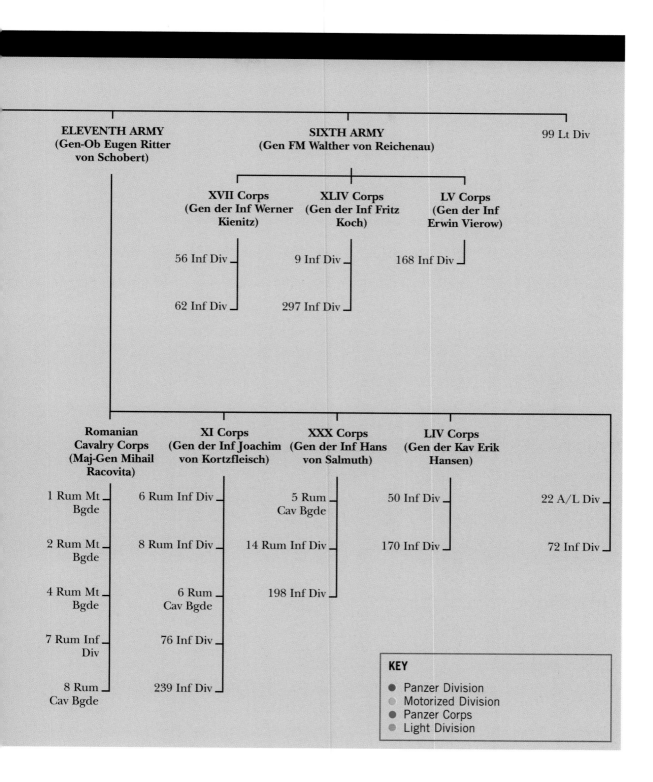

ELEVENTH ARMY
(Gen-Ob Eugen Ritter
von Schobert)

SIXTH ARMY
(Gen FM Walther von Reichenau)

99 Lt Div

XVII Corps
(Gen der Inf Werner
Kienitz)

XLIV Corps
(Gen der Inf Fritz
Koch)

LV Corps
(Gen der Inf
Erwin Vierow)

56 Inf Div

9 Inf Div

168 Inf Div

62 Inf Div

297 Inf Div

Romanian
Cavalry Corps
(Maj-Gen Mihail
Racovita)

XI Corps
(Gen der Inf Joachim
von Kortzfleisch)

XXX Corps
(Gen der Inf Hans
von Salmuth)

LIV Corps
(Gen der Kav Erik
Hansen)

1 Rum Mt
Bgde

6 Rum Inf Div

5 Rum
Cav Bgde

50 Inf Div

22 A/L Div

2 Rum Mt
Bgde

8 Rum Inf Div

14 Rum Inf Div

170 Inf Div

72 Inf Div

4 Rum Mt
Bgde

6 Rum
Cav Bgde

198 Inf Div

7 Rum Inf
Div

76 Inf Div

8 Rum
Cav Bgde

239 Inf Div

KEY
- Panzer Division
- Motorized Division
- Panzer Corps
- Light Division

Soviet Union: 1942

For the *Wehrmacht*'s campaigning season in 1942, Hitler refused to consider mere consolidation of 1941's huge territorial gains. Instead, he promised the German people that this was the year they would complete the conquest of the Soviet Union.

Moscow was no longer the key: the massed panzer and infantry formations were to drive southwestwards. They would sieze the city of Stalingrad – a strategic city to be sure, but made even more important in Hitler's eyes because it was named after his hated rival, Joseph Stalin. From there, they would be within striking distance of the real prize: the vital oilfields in the Caucasus.

Fall Blau

In Directive No. 41, dated 5 April, Hitler stated: 'The enemy has suffered enormous losses of men and materiel. In attempting to exploit their apparent initial successes, they have exhausted during this winter the mass of their reserves which were intended for later operations.'

In this mistaken belief, Hitler set out his objectives for the coming summer offensive, code-named Operation *Blau*. He set his revitalized armies, now numbering some 215 divisions, the task of destroying the last remaining enemy formations, and as far as possible, capturing the main sources of raw materials on which their war economy depended.

All available forces were to be concentrated on the southern sector. Their mission was firstly to annihilate the enemy on the Don. Then they were to swing north and take Stalingrad, followed by a combined assault to conquer the Caucasus oil areas. Without that oil, German panzers would go nowhere. Lastly, they were to capture the passes through the Caucasus mountains, giving access to the Middle East.

But first, they would have to deal with a renewed series of Soviet attacks.

Battle at Kharkov

The return of warmer weather was the signal for another Soviet offensive, but the Red Army's attempt to recapture Kharkov failed dismally. Ten days and nights of hectic thrust and counter-thrust in open country was turned by the German panzer and motorized formations into a master class in Blitzkrieg. The advancing Soviets were outmanoeuvred by the superbly co-ordinated German air and ground forces.

The *Luftwaffe* air fleets under Ritter von Greim dominated the skies. Swarms of Ju 88s, Stukas and Heinkel 111s pounded the Soviet positions, protected by the world's most experienced fighter pilots, who had been reinforced by Germany's Axis allies.

Three Soviet armies were surrounded and annihilated. Marshal Timoshenko was summoned to Moscow to explain the loss of another 200,000 men.

Crimea

As the German Sixth and Seventeenth armies shattered the Soviet offensive at Kharkov, the Eleventhth Army, under the command of General Erich von Manstein, broke through the heavily fortified Soviet positions on the Kerch peninsula. By April 1942, the Soviets had ferried 250,000 men into the Crimea, together with considerable tank and artillery support. But as in the previous year, the forces were committed piecemeal against overwhelming German opposition.

At dawn on 8 May, Manstein crossed the Kamenskoye isthmus to assault the positions covering Kerch. The nine German divisions were outnumbered two to one, but the Soviets were poorly placed and, as usual, the Germans placed their stongest forces at the weakest point in the enemy's front line. The sheer weight of German metal forced the Soviets back from Feodosia.

The panzers, supported by screaming Stukas, then drove through the waist of the peninsula towards Kerch itself. Between 15 and 20 May, the Caucasus front imploded and the Soviets were driven into the Black Sea. They left behind 170,000 prisoners, 1,380 guns and 258 tanks.

PANZER REGIMENT: 1942

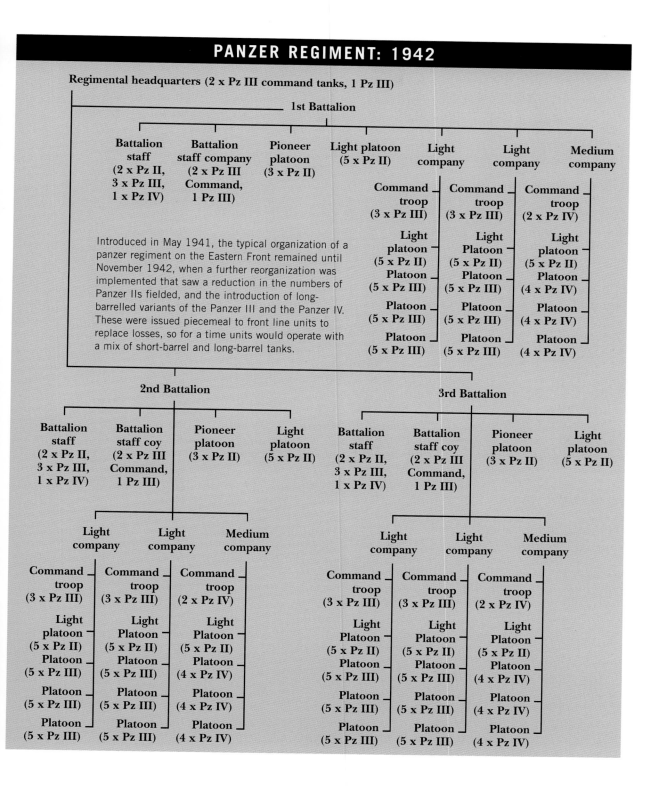

Regimental headquarters (2 x Pz III command tanks, 1 Pz III)

1st Battalion

| Battalion staff (2 x Pz II, 3 x Pz III, 1 x Pz IV) | Battalion staff company (2 x Pz III Command, 1 Pz III) | Pioneer platoon (3 x Pz II) | Light platoon (5 x Pz II) | Light company | Light company | Medium company |

Light company
Command troop (3 x Pz III)
Light platoon (5 x Pz II)
Platoon (5 x Pz III)
Platoon (5 x Pz III)
Platoon (5 x Pz III)

Light company
Command troop (3 x Pz III)
Light Platoon (5 x Pz II)
Platoon (5 x Pz III)
Platoon (5 x Pz III)
Platoon (5 x Pz III)

Medium company
Command troop (2 x Pz IV)
Light platoon (5 x Pz II)
Platoon (4 x Pz IV)
Platoon (4 x Pz IV)
Platoon (4 x Pz IV)

Introduced in May 1941, the typical organization of a panzer regiment on the Eastern Front remained until November 1942, when a further reorganization was implemented that saw a reduction in the numbers of Panzer IIs fielded, and the introduction of long-barrelled variants of the Panzer III and the Panzer IV. These were issued piecemeal to front line units to replace losses, so for a time units would operate with a mix of short-barrel and long-barrel tanks.

2nd Battalion

| Battalion staff (2 x Pz II, 3 x Pz III, 1 x Pz IV) | Battalion staff coy (2 x Pz III Command, 1 Pz III) | Pioneer platoon (3 x Pz II) | Light platoon (5 x Pz II) |

Light company
Command troop (3 x Pz III)
Light platoon (5 x Pz II)
Platoon (5 x Pz III)
Platoon (5 x Pz III)
Platoon (5 x Pz III)

Light company
Command troop (3 x Pz III)
Light Platoon (5 x Pz II)
Platoon (5 x Pz III)
Platoon (5 x Pz III)
Platoon (5 x Pz III)

Medium company
Command troop (2 x Pz IV)
Light Platoon (5 x Pz II)
Platoon (4 x Pz IV)
Platoon (4 x Pz IV)
Platoon (4 x Pz IV)

3rd Battalion

| Battalion staff (2 x Pz II, 3 x Pz III, 1 x Pz IV) | Battalion staff coy (2 x Pz III Command, 1 Pz III) | Pioneer platoon (3 x Pz II) | Light platoon (5 x Pz II) |

Light company
Command troop (3 x Pz III)
Light Platoon (5 x Pz II)
Platoon (5 x Pz III)
Platoon (5 x Pz III)
Platoon (5 x Pz III)

Light company
Command troop (3 x Pz III)
Light Platoon (5 x Pz II)
Platoon (5 x Pz III)
Platoon (5 x Pz III)
Platoon (5 x Pz III)

Medium company
Command troop (2 x Pz IV)
Light Platoon (5 x Pz II)
Platoon (4 x Pz IV)
Platoon (4 x Pz IV)
Platoon (4 x Pz IV)

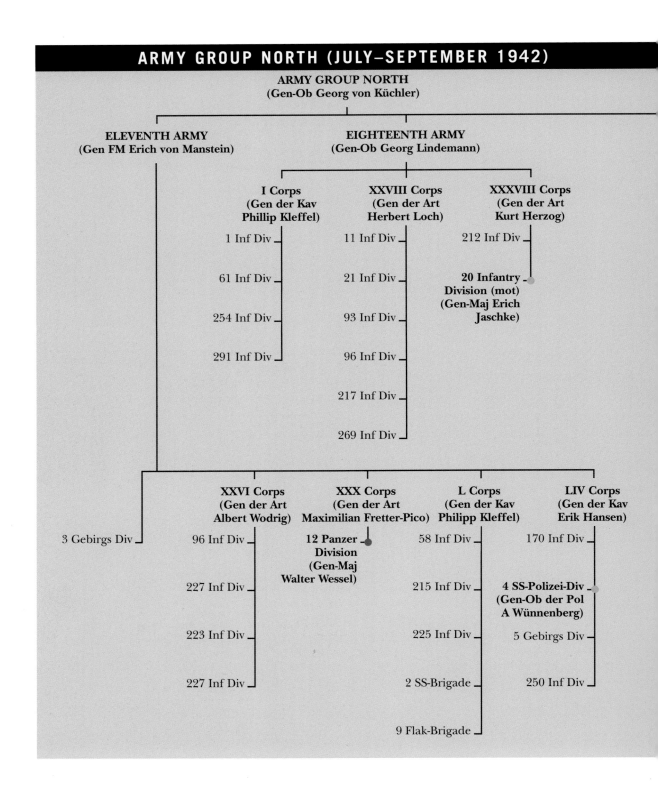

ARMY GROUP NORTH (JULY–SEPTEMBER 1942)

ARMY GROUP NORTH
(Gen-Ob Georg von Küchler)

ELEVENTH ARMY
(Gen FM Erich von Manstein)

EIGHTEENTH ARMY
(Gen-Ob Georg Lindemann)

I Corps
(Gen der Kav
Phillip Kleffel)

XXVIII Corps
(Gen der Art
Herbert Loch)

XXXVIII Corps
(Gen der Art
Kurt Herzog)

1 Inf Div

61 Inf Div

254 Inf Div

291 Inf Div

11 Inf Div

21 Inf Div

93 Inf Div

96 Inf Div

217 Inf Div

269 Inf Div

212 Inf Div

20 Infantry
Division (mot)
(Gen-Maj Erich
Jaschke)

3 Gebirgs Div

XXVI Corps
(Gen der Art
Albert Wodrig)

96 Inf Div

227 Inf Div

223 Inf Div

227 Inf Div

XXX Corps
(Gen der Art
Maximilian Fretter-Pico)

12 Panzer
Division
(Gen-Maj
Walter Wessel)

L Corps
(Gen der Kav
Philipp Kleffel)

58 Inf Div

215 Inf Div

225 Inf Div

2 SS-Brigade

9 Flak-Brigade

LIV Corps
(Gen der Kav
Erik Hansen)

170 Inf Div

4 SS-Polizei-Div
(Gen-Ob der Pol
A Wünnenberg)

5 Gebirgs Div

250 Inf Div

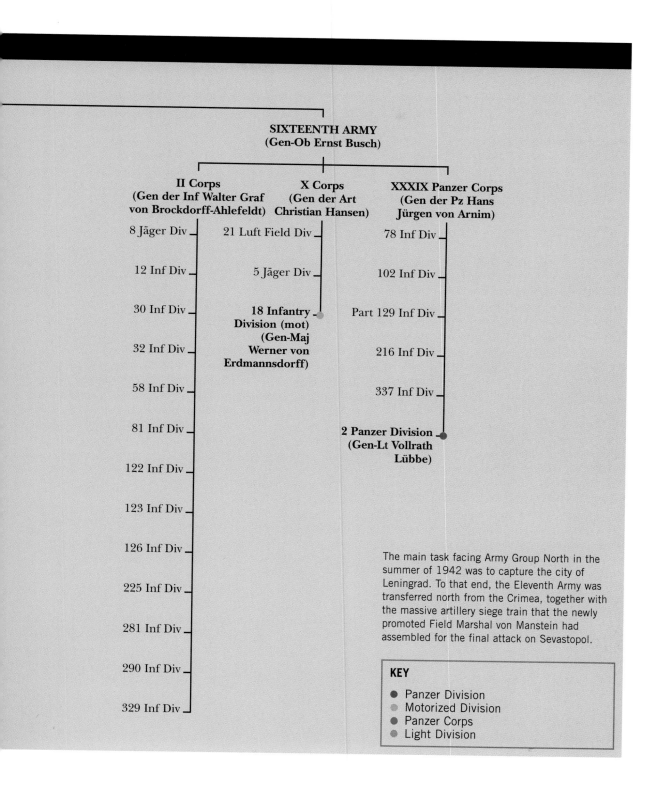

SIXTEENTH ARMY
(Gen-Ob Ernst Busch)

II Corps (Gen der Inf Walter Graf von Brockdorff-Ahlefeldt)	**X Corps** (Gen der Art Christian Hansen)	**XXXIX Panzer Corps** (Gen der Pz Hans Jürgen von Arnim)
8 Jäger Div	21 Luft Field Div	78 Inf Div
12 Inf Div	5 Jäger Div	102 Inf Div
30 Inf Div	**18 Infantry Division (mot) (Gen-Maj Werner von Erdmannsdorff)**	Part 129 Inf Div
32 Inf Div		216 Inf Div
58 Inf Div		337 Inf Div
81 Inf Div		**2 Panzer Division (Gen-Lt Vollrath Lübbe)**
122 Inf Div		
123 Inf Div		
126 Inf Div		
225 Inf Div		
281 Inf Div		
290 Inf Div		
329 Inf Div		

The main task facing Army Group North in the summer of 1942 was to capture the city of Leningrad. To that end, the Eleventh Army was transferred north from the Crimea, together with the massive artillery siege train that the newly promoted Field Marshal von Manstein had assembled for the final attack on Sevastopol.

KEY

● Panzer Division
● Motorized Division
● Panzer Corps
● Light Division

Northern Sector: 1942

Stalin's failure to relieve besieged Leningrad appeared to have doomed the city. Since Hitler had ordered that the cradle of the Bolshevik revolution be levelled, it seemed only a matter of time before it fell.

Its population swollen to over three million by refugees flooding into the city, Leningrad was cut off by Germans to the south and to the north by the Finns, eager to avenge the Winter War.

Communist Party chiefs anxiously calculated their food reserves: on 1 November, they realized there was only enough food for one more week. And with winter approaching, there was so little fuel that buildings could not be heated – electricity was rationed to an hour a day.

Siege of Leningrad

What followed was the most apalling siege in history, a long drawn-out agony in which nearly a million men, women and children died of cold and slow starvation – three times the total war dead suffered by Britain or the USA in the whole of World War II.

The German Army made no attempt to storm the city. Hitler believed – and had so instructed his generals – that once Leningrad had been surrounded and bombarded from the air and by artillery on the ground, the resolve of the city to continue the fight would disappear.

With unintercepted reconnaissance flights, the Germans trained their artillery with increasing accuracy on the Soviet defences. The bombardment was ceaseless; hunger and the bitter winter weather did the rest.

Only the barest of supplies reached the embattled population, being brought across the frozen ice of Lake Lagoda during the winter, or through the German lines. For the Germans themselves conditions were severe: the ground was iron hard, and could be shifted only with the liberal use of dynamite. However, throughout the winter and into the spring, they kept a relentless grip on the city, stopping all Soviet attempts to break through.

Battle for communications

Late in 1941, the Soviets formed the Volkhov Front to cover the sector north of Lake Ilmen to Lake Ladoga.

The major task of the Soviet North West Front now became to recapture the communications centre of Staraya Russa, to allow supplies to be moved towards Leningrad.

The fighting in the area lasted for more than two years, with the Soviets launching two major offensives against Army Group North as well as large numbers of smaller, more localized attacks. The Soviet attacks were generally unsuccessful, and consequently the Red Army suffered huge losses.

Cut off, but still fighting

However, the Germans did not have it all their own way at Leningrad. The fluid fighting of early 1942, driven by Soviet attempts to break the siege, isolated numerous pockets of the invaders. The Soviet Northwest Front broke through in the Valdai hills, encircling several divisions in turn. In each case, the trapped German troops were clustered around an airfield.

With the *Luftwaffe* flying in supplies, the Germans either continued to defend their perimeters until relief was at hand, or – in the case of General von Seydlitz's six divisions trapped for several months in the Demiansk pocket – broke out. Seydlitz's men took a month to battle their way to safety across the snow. Their epic escape was sustained by parachute drops and an iron determination never to surrender.

In the euphoria that greeted their escape, the German High Command overlooked the physical state of the exhausted survivors: months of combat on the frozen steppe, with inadequate rations, medical and sanitary facilities had left many men unfit for further service. The Germans also drew the comforting conclusion that they could keep encircled units supplied by air. It was an assumption that would be tested to destruction at Stalingrad before the end of the year.

Central Front: 1942

Stalin expected the main German summer offensive of 1942 to be against Moscow, so the bulk of the Soviet Army was deployed to defend the city. However, Army Group Centre's mission was to hold the line while the real offensive was launched to the south.

Early in December 1941, as the German offensive against Moscow stalled in the ice, a massive Red Army counteroffensive forced the invaders back from the Soviet capital. After several months of fighting, the Soviet advance was brought to a halt, leaving a huge German-held salient around the town of Rzhev. For the next year and a half, the divisions of Army Group Centre fought around Rzhev. It was the scene of heavy combat during the Red Army's Moscow counteroffensive in the winter of 1941–42.

In the spring of 1942, Army Group Centre was tasked with holding off any Soviet attacks as the German High Command planned its main summer offensive, *Fall Blau*, which was to smash the Soviet armies in Ukraine and capture the oilfields of the Caucasus.

However, Army Group Centre did not miss much in the way of fighting: the Red Army launched a series of offensives against Rzhev from July through to early September 1942. The most serious attempt by the Red Army to pinch out the salient was known as Operation Mars, with the heaviest fighting taking place in November and December 1942. Fighting continued into 1943. The *Wehrmacht's* panzer and motorized infantry divisions had been designed to fight an offensive war, but the action in Army Group Centre throughout 1942 was mainly defensive.

Mobile battlefield

Operation Mars, also known as the Second Rzhev-Sychevka Offensive, was launched by the combined forces of the Soviet Western and Kalinin Fronts, or army groups. Planned by Marshal Georgi Zhukhov, the operation was classified in official Soviet histories as a diversion, designed to pull German troops away from the Stalingrad sector.

However, recent research indicates that the offensive was a serious attempt by the Red Army to smash through

Army Group Centre. Certainly, the Soviets committed immense resources to the attack, and their losses led to the battle being known as the 'Rzhev mincing machine' to those soldiers taking part. Zhukov lost 335,000 killed and wounded in Operation Mars, which lasted less than a month, compared to the 485,000 casualties Vasilevsky suffered in the two-and-a-half months it took to destroy the Sixth Army at Stalingrad.

Although a defensive victory for the Germans, the battle was also costly. The remaining German divisions were weak, panzer forces had been worn down and artillery ammunition was approaching exhaustion.

The German motorized forces used their mobility in a series of 'Fire Brigade' actions, moving rapidly from sector to sector of the front to be deployed wherever the fighting was heaviest.

The units were assisted in their actions by the fact that Army Group Centre had heavily fortified the Rzhev salient and constructed a good road network, allowing the quick movement of reinforcements to the threatened zones.

ARMY GROUP CENTRE – PANZER STRENGTH (JUNE 1942)					
Tank type	**Pz II**	**Pz III**	**Pz 38 (t)**	**Pz IV**	**Pz Bef**
1ST PANZER DIVISION					
1st Pz Rgt	2	26	10	10	4
5TH PANZER DIVISION					
31st Pz Rgt	26	55	0	13	9
17TH PANZER DIVISION					
39th Pz Rgt	17	36	0	16	2
18TH PANZER DIVISION					
18th Pz Rgt	11	26	0	8	2
19TH PANZER DIVISION					
27th Pz Rgt	6	12	35	4	0

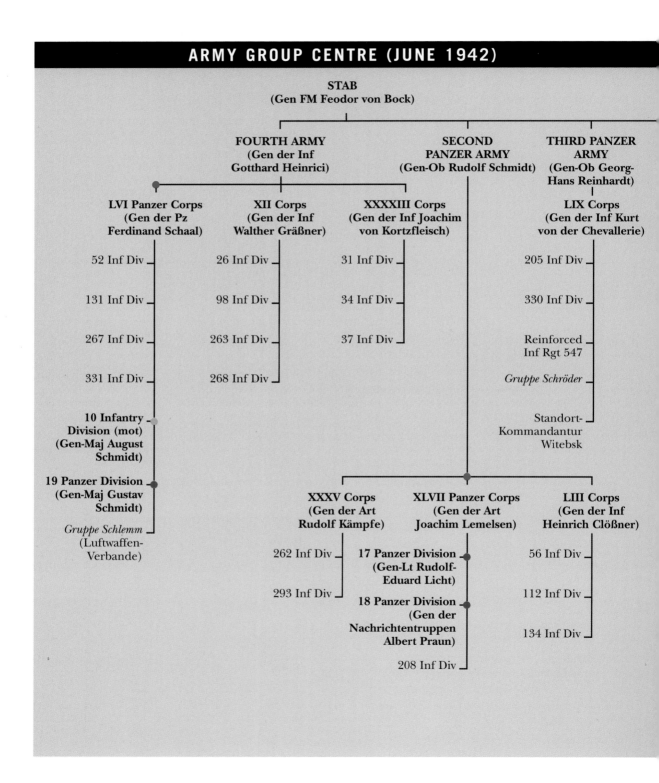

ARMY GROUP CENTRE (JUNE 1942)

STAB
(Gen FM Feodor von Bock)

FOURTH ARMY
(Gen der Inf
Gotthard Heinrici)

SECOND
PANZER ARMY
(Gen-Ob Rudolf Schmidt)

THIRD PANZER
ARMY
(Gen-Ob Georg-
Hans Reinhardt)

LVI Panzer Corps
(Gen der Pz
Ferdinand Schaal)

XII Corps
(Gen der Inf
Walther Gräßner)

XXXXIII Corps
(Gen der Inf Joachim
von Kortzfleisch)

LIX Corps
(Gen der Inf Kurt
von der Chevallerie)

52 Inf Div

26 Inf Div

31 Inf Div

205 Inf Div

131 Inf Div

98 Inf Div

34 Inf Div

330 Inf Div

267 Inf Div

263 Inf Div

37 Inf Div

Reinforced
Inf Rgt 547

331 Inf Div

268 Inf Div

Gruppe Schröder

Standort-
Kommandantur
Witebsk

10 Infantry
Division (mot)
(Gen-Maj August
Schmidt)

19 Panzer Division
(Gen-Maj Gustav
Schmidt)

XXXV Corps
(Gen der Art
Rudolf Kämpfe)

XLVII Panzer Corps
(Gen der Art
Joachim Lemelsen)

LIII Corps
(Gen der Inf
Heinrich Clößner)

Gruppe Schlemm
(Luftwaffen-
Verbande)

262 Inf Div

17 Panzer Division
(Gen-Lt Rudolf-
Eduard Licht)

56 Inf Div

293 Inf Div

18 Panzer Division
(Gen der
Nachrichtentruppen
Albert Praun)

112 Inf Div

134 Inf Div

208 Inf Div

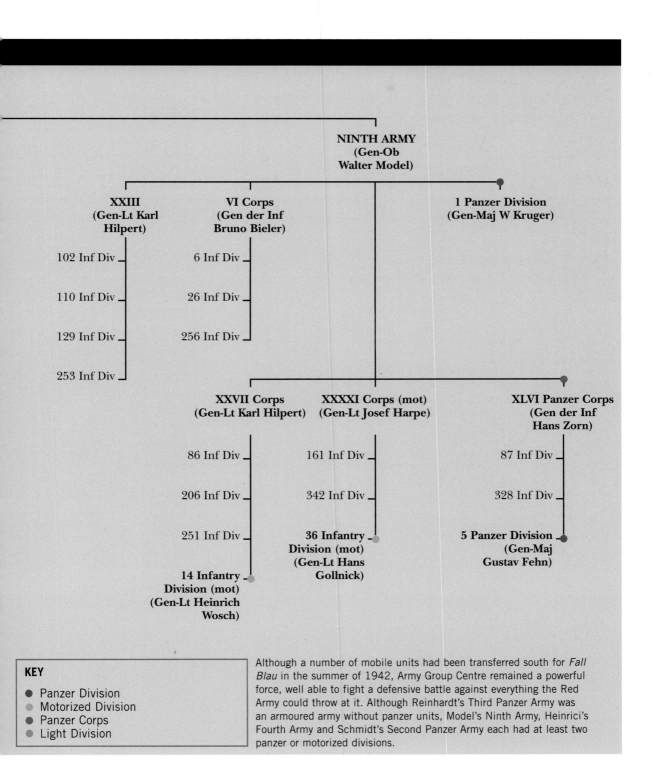

NINTH ARMY
(Gen-Ob
Walter Model)

XXIII
(Gen-Lt Karl
Hilpert)

VI Corps
(Gen der Inf
Bruno Bieler)

1 Panzer Division
(Gen-Maj W Kruger)

102 Inf Div

6 Inf Div

110 Inf Div

26 Inf Div

129 Inf Div

256 Inf Div

253 Inf Div

XXVII Corps
(Gen-Lt Karl Hilpert)

XXXXI Corps (mot)
(Gen-Lt Josef Harpe)

XLVI Panzer Corps
(Gen der Inf
Hans Zorn)

86 Inf Div

161 Inf Div

87 Inf Div

206 Inf Div

342 Inf Div

328 Inf Div

251 Inf Div

36 Infantry
Division (mot)
(Gen-Lt Hans
Gollnick)

5 Panzer Division
(Gen-Maj
Gustav Fehn)

14 Infantry
Division (mot)
(Gen-Lt Heinrich
Wosch)

KEY

● Panzer Division
● Motorized Division
● Panzer Corps
● Light Division

Although a number of mobile units had been transferred south for *Fall Blau* in the summer of 1942, Army Group Centre remained a powerful force, well able to fight a defensive battle against everything the Red Army could throw at it. Although Reinhardt's Third Panzer Army was an armoured army without panzer units, Model's Ninth Army, Heinrici's Fourth Army and Schmidt's Second Panzer Army each had at least two panzer or motorized divisions.

Southern Front: *Fall Blau*

Anticipating that 1942 would bring the victory over the Soviet Union that he confidently expected, Adolf Hitler moved his headquarters to Vinnitsa in Ukraine to oversee the opening stages of the campaign in the south.

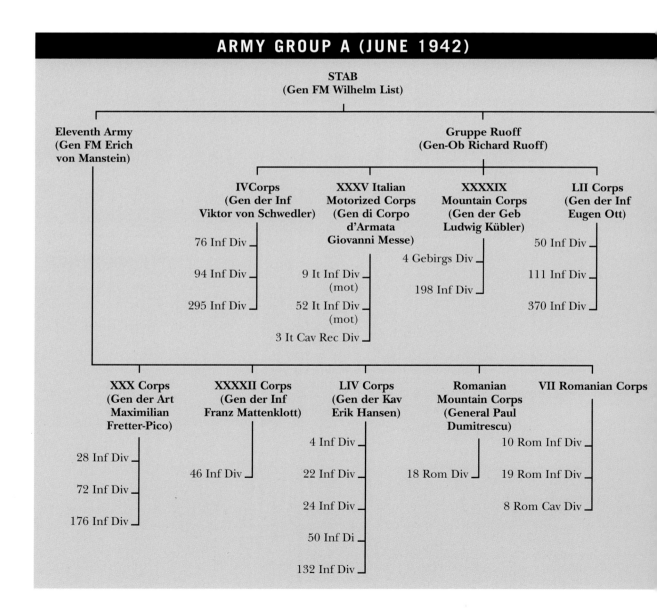

ARMY GROUP A (JUNE 1942)

STAB
(Gen FM Wilhelm List)

Eleventh Army
(Gen FM Erich von Manstein)

Gruppe Ruoff
(Gen-Ob Richard Ruoff)

IVCorps
(Gen der Inf Viktor von Schwedler)

76 Inf Div
94 Inf Div
295 Inf Div

XXXV Italian Motorized Corps
(Gen di Corpo d'Armata Giovanni Messe)

9 It Inf Div (mot)
52 It Inf Div (mot)
3 It Cav Rec Div

XXXXIX Mountain Corps
(Gen der Geb Ludwig Kübler)

4 Gebirgs Div
198 Inf Div

LII Corps
(Gen der Inf Eugen Ott)

50 Inf Div
111 Inf Div
370 Inf Div

XXX Corps
(Gen der Art Maximilian Fretter-Pico)

28 Inf Div
72 Inf Div
176 Inf Div

XXXXII Corps
(Gen der Inf Franz Mattenklott)

46 Inf Div

LIV Corps
(Gen der Kav Erik Hansen)

4 Inf Div
22 Inf Div
24 Inf Div
50 Inf Di
132 Inf Div

Romanian Mountain Corps
(General Paul Dumitrescu)

18 Rom Div

VII Romanian Corps

10 Rom Inf Div
19 Rom Inf Div
8 Rom Cav Div

Army Group South, renamed Army Group B, included the Second and Sixth Armies, Fourth Panzer Army and Third Hungarian Army. It was to advance into the bend of the Don River then on to the Volga at Stalingrad.

Army Group A

The other claw in a gigantic pincer movement would be a new formation, Army Group A, comprising Kleist's powerful First Panzer Army, the Seventeeth Army and the Third Romanian army. This would link up with Army Group B somewhere on the steppe west of the Volga, hopefully trapping another vast haul of Soviet prisoners in the process.

Having gutted the Soviet armies again, Army Group A would then lunge southeast to over-run the Soviet oilfields in the Caucasus.

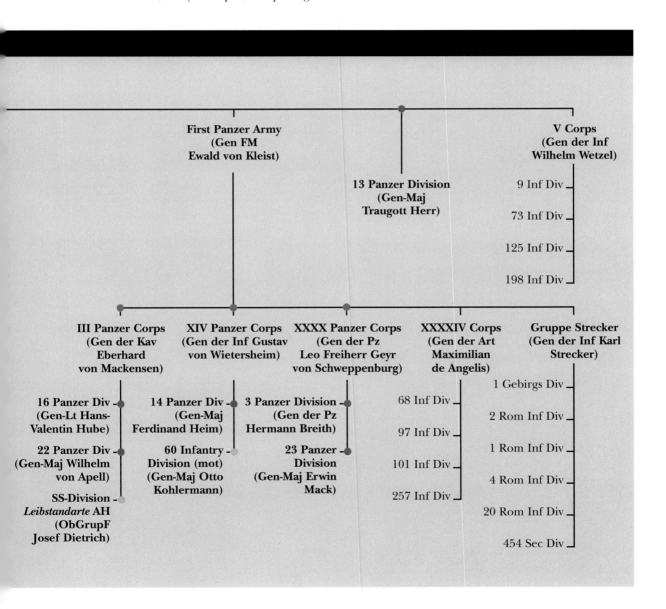

First Panzer Army
(Gen FM Ewald von Kleist)

V Corps
(Gen der Inf Wilhelm Wetzel)

13 Panzer Division
(Gen-Maj Traugott Herr)

9 Inf Div

73 Inf Div

125 Inf Div

198 Inf Div

III Panzer Corps
(Gen der Kav Eberhard von Mackensen)

XIV Panzer Corps
(Gen der Inf Gustav von Wietersheim)

XXXX Panzer Corps
(Gen der Pz Leo Freiherr Geyr von Schweppenburg)

XXXXIV Corps
(Gen der Art Maximilian de Angelis)

Gruppe Strecker
(Gen der Inf Karl Strecker)

16 Panzer Div
(Gen-Lt Hans-Valentin Hube)

14 Panzer Div
(Gen-Maj Ferdinand Heim)

3 Panzer Division
(Gen der Pz Hermann Breith)

68 Inf Div

1 Gebirgs Div

22 Panzer Div
(Gen-Maj Wilhelm von Apell)

60 Infantry Division (mot)
(Gen-Maj Otto Kohlermann)

23 Panzer Division
(Gen-Maj Erwin Mack)

97 Inf Div

2 Rom Inf Div

SS-Division
Leibstandarte AH
(ObGrupF Josef Dietrich)

101 Inf Div

1 Rom Inf Div

257 Inf Div

4 Rom Inf Div

20 Rom Inf Div

454 Sec Div

On 28 June, the great summer offensive began. Army Group B, under Field Marshal Feodor von Bock, attacked on a 150km (93-mile) front.

The spearhead was General Hoth's Fourth Panzer Army. Paulus's Sixth Army extended the front a further 80km (49 miles) to the south. Two days later, Army Group A under Siegmund List burst over the Donets bend and drove southwards to Proletarskaya and the Caucasus.

The attacks were resoundingly successful. Hoth was in Voronezh by 3 July, though progress was not fast enough to satisfy Hitler, who replaced von Bock with Baron Maximilian Von Weichs.

Army Group B then poured down the Donets corridor to link up with Von Kleist's armour pushing on Rostov.

Days of victory

It seemed that the days of easy victory had returned. The Soviet forces were contemptuously swept aside.

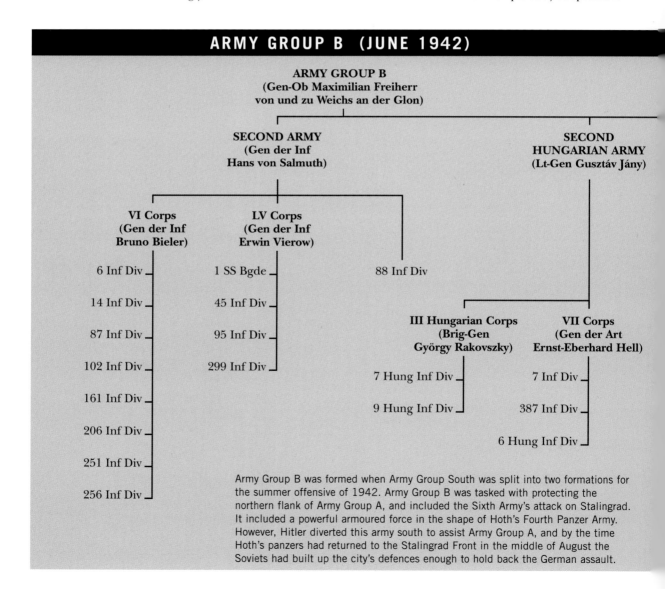

ARMY GROUP B (JUNE 1942)

ARMY GROUP B
(Gen-Ob Maximilian Freiherr von und zu Weichs an der Glon)

SECOND ARMY
(Gen der Inf Hans von Salmuth)

SECOND HUNGARIAN ARMY
(Lt-Gen Gusztáv Jány)

VI Corps
(Gen der Inf Bruno Bieler)

LV Corps
(Gen der Inf Erwin Vierow)

6 Inf Div

14 Inf Div

87 Inf Div

102 Inf Div

161 Inf Div

206 Inf Div

251 Inf Div

256 Inf Div

1 SS Bgde

45 Inf Div

95 Inf Div

299 Inf Div

88 Inf Div

III Hungarian Corps
(Brig-Gen György Rakovszky)

7 Hung Inf Div

9 Hung Inf Div

VII Corps
(Gen der Art Ernst-Eberhard Hell)

7 Inf Div

387 Inf Div

6 Hung Inf Div

Army Group B was formed when Army Group South was split into two formations for the summer offensive of 1942. Army Group B was tasked with protecting the northern flank of Army Group A, and included the Sixth Army's attack on Stalingrad. It included a powerful armoured force in the shape of Hoth's Fourth Panzer Army. However, Hitler diverted this army south to assist Army Group A, and by the time Hoth's panzers had returned to the Stalingrad Front in the middle of August the Soviets had built up the city's defences enough to hold back the German assault.

For the first time in many months, the ground favoured the large-scale sweeping manoeuvres.

Hundreds of miles of open rolling corn and steppe grass offered perfect country for the massed legions of German armour. Their advance was visible for miles: smoke from burning villages and dust kicked up by thousands of heavy vehicles signalled the irresistable onrush of a perfectly functioning war machine.

However, the commander-in-chief, Hitler, became too ambitious. He believed that the Red Army was finished and just needed one more devastating victory to bring the Soviet edifice low.

Panzer encirclement

On 13 July, aiming at another vast encirclement, Hitler detached Hoth's armour, ordering it to swing southeast to link up with Army Group A's tanks, whose forces were now committed to an intense battle in the

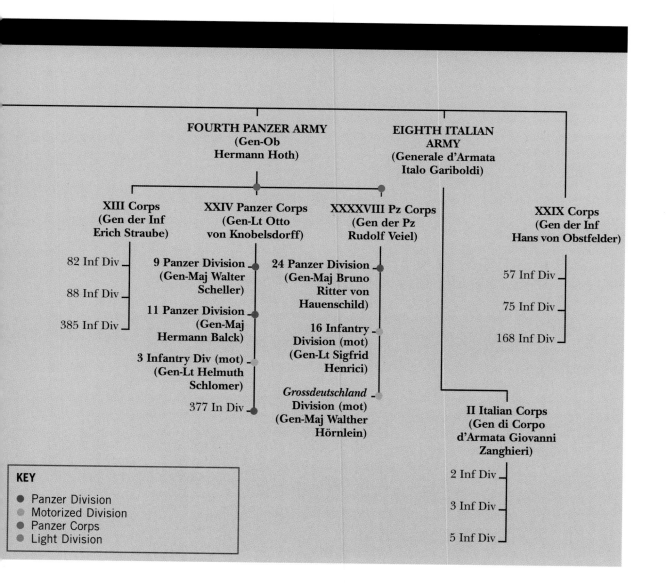

FOURTH PANZER ARMY
(Gen-Ob
Hermann Hoth)

EIGHTH ITALIAN
ARMY
(Generale d'Armata
Italo Gariboldi)

XIII Corps
(Gen der Inf
Erich Straube)

XXIV Panzer Corps
(Gen-Lt Otto
von Knobelsdorff)

XXXXVIII Pz Corps
(Gen der Pz
Rudolf Veiel)

XXIX Corps
(Gen der Inf
Hans von Obstfelder)

82 Inf Div

88 Inf Div

385 Inf Div

9 Panzer Division
(Gen-Maj Walter
Scheller)

11 Panzer Division
(Gen-Maj
Hermann Balck)

3 Infantry Div (mot)
(Gen-Lt Helmuth
Schlomer)

377 In Div

24 Panzer Division
(Gen-Maj Bruno
Ritter von
Hauenschild)

16 Infantry
Division (mot)
(Gen-Lt Sigfrid
Henrici)

Grossdeutschland
Division (mot)
(Gen-Maj Walther
Hörnlein)

57 Inf Div

75 Inf Div

168 Inf Div

II Italian Corps
(Gen di Corpo
d'Armata Giovanni
Zanghieri)

2 Inf Div

3 Inf Div

5 Inf Div

KEY
- Panzer Division
- Motorized Division
- Panzer Corps
- Light Division

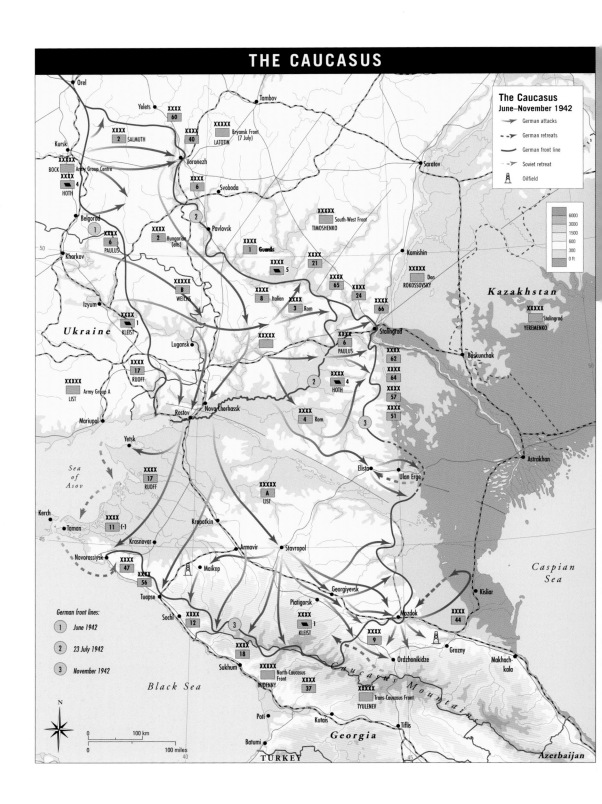

THE CAUCASUS

The Caucasus
June–November 1942

→ German attacks
⇢ German retreats
— German front line
⇠ Soviet retreat
⚑ Oilfield

6000
3000
1500
600
300
0 ft

Orel

Yelets
XXXX
60

Tambov

Saratov

Kursk
XXXX
2 SALMUTH

XXXX
40

Bryansk Front
(7 July)
LATOTIN

XXXXX
BOCK Army Group Centre
XXXX
4
HOTH

Voronezh

Belgorod
1

XXXX
6
PAULUS

XXXX
2
Hungarian
(elts)

Pavlovsk
2

XXXXX
South-West Front
TIMOSHENKO

Kamishin

Kharkov

Svoboda
XXXX
6

XXXX
1 Guards

XXXX
21

XXXXX
Don
ROKOSSOVSKY

Kazakhstan

Izyum

XXXXX
B
WEICHS

XXXX
8 Italian

XXXX
5

XXXX
65

XXXX
24

XXXXX
Stalingrad
YEREMENKO

Ukraine
XXXX
1
KLEIST

XXXX
3 Rom

XXXX
66

Lugansk

XXXXX

XXXX
6
PAULUS

Stalingrad

XXXX
62

XXXX
17
RUOFF

XXXXX
Army Group A
LIST

2

XXXX
4
HOTH

XXXX
64

XXXX
57

Rostov Novo-Cherkassk

XXXX
4 Rom

3

XXXX
51

Mariupol

Yetsk

Sea
of
Asov

XXXX
17
RUOFF

XXXXX
A
LIST

Elista

Ulan Erge

Astrakhan

Kerch

Taman

XXXX
11 (-)

Krasnovar

Kropatkin

Armavir

Stavropol

Caspian
Sea

Novorossiysk
XXXX
47

XXXX
56

Maikop

Georgiyevsk

Mozdok

Kisliar

XXXX
44

Tuapse

Sochi
XXXX
12

3

Piatigorsk

XXXX
1
KLEIST

XXXX
9

Grozny

Makhach-
kala

German front lines:

1　June 1942

2　23 July 1942

3　November 1942

N

XXXX
18

Sukhum

XXXXX
North-Caucasus
Front
BUDENNY

XXXX
37

XXXXX
Trans-Caucasus Front
TYULENEV

Ordzhonikidze

Caucasus Mountains

Black Sea

Poti

Kutais

Tiflis

Georgia

0　100 km
0　100 miles

Batumi

TURKEY

Azerbaijan

June–November 1942

At the start of *Fall Blau*, everything seemed to be going Hitler's way. The headlong advance across open country to the Volga was spearheaded by the Sixth Army, which cut a swathe of destruction across southern Russia as it smashed its way east.

But then Hitler compounded the decision to divide his forces by making ruinous reductions in the forces available to the operations in the south. The strategic reserve was sent to the four winds: 9th and 11th Panzer Divisions were assigned to General Von Kluge, the *Grossdeutschland* Division was sent to Army Group Centre, *Leibstandarte*-SS *Adolf Hitler* was ordered to France to be restored to strength, and the rested Eleventh Army was held back from taking part in the Caucasus drive.

streets of Rostov. Stalin had finally learned the lesson of trading space for time, and he allowed his marshals to pull their forces back, rather than letting them be fatally surrounded.

Divided objectives

On the same day, Hitler gave a directive that arguably cost him the war on the Eastern Front, and with it sealed the fate of the Third Reich. Totally underestimating the opposing forces, he changed the plans for his two Army Groups. Rather than capture Stalingrad first and then attack the Caucasus, he opted to move on both objectives simultaneously, and in doing so, seriously weaken both attacks. The debacle at Stalingrad the ensuing Red Army offensive was to turn the course of the war.

Into the Caucasus: Army Group A

The newly formed Army Group A, under the command of Field Marshal Sismund List, was tasked with capturing the vital oil resources of the Soviet Caucasus region. It was led by the experienced panzer crews of von Kleist's First Panzer Army.

Army Group A had been making excellent progress. Six months after they had endured winter temperatures of -30°C (-22°F), German soldiers found themselves on the Kuban steppe, where the thermometer topped 50°C (122°F) in the shade. Inside the tanks of First Panzer Army, the heat was simply unbearable.

List's major worries were about supplies. It was impossible to satisfy the needs of 26 advancing divisions. Jerricans of petrol dropped from Ju 52 transports had to be brought up to the panzers by camel transport.

The terrain slowed up fighting troops as well as supplies. Roads were rivers of dust, and the rivers were wide with unpredictable currents. Nevertheless, SS-*Wiking* Division forced the River Kuban in the face of intense resistance early in August. On 9 August, *Gruppe Ruoff* occupied simultaneously the port of Yeysk on the Sea of Azov, Krasnodar on the Kuban and the blazing

FIRST PANZER ARMY – PANZER STRENGTH (JUNE 1942)					
Tank type	Pz II	Pz III	Pz 38(t)	Pz IV	Pz Bef
3RD PANZER DIVISION					
6th Pz Rgt	25	106	0	33	4
14TH PANZER DIVISION					
36th Pz Rgt	14	60	0	24	4
16TH PANZER DIVISION					
2nd Pz Rgt	13	58	0	27	3
22ND PANZER DIVISION					
204th Pz Rgt	28	12	114	22	0
23RD PANZER DIVISION					
201st Pz Rgt	27	84	0	17	10

wreckage of the oil town of Maikop. Shimmering in the distance like a layer of cloud, the Caucasus mountains could be seen from over 100km (62 miles) away. On 9 August, First *Panzerarmee* took Pyatigorsk in the first foothills of the Caucasus. On 21 August, a detachment of the elite 1st and 4th *Gebirgsjager* Mountain Regiments planted the Swastika flag on the 5642m (17,920ft) summit of Mt Elbrus. Meanwhile, on the eastern side of the mountains, the River Terek was the last obstacle facing *Panzergruppe Kleist* on its breakneck advance.

Stalingrad: Army Group B

Hitler's decision to divide his forces seemed at first to have been successful, since both Army Groups in the southern Soviet Union made excellent initial progress. However, Army Group B in particular was much weaker than had orginally been planned.

Field Marshal von Weichs, who had replaced Field Marshal von Bock soon after the launch of *Fall Blau,* had been left only with the Sixth Army to break through the Soviet forces barring the way to Stalingrad.

He was forced to delay to await the arrival of the Italian Eighth Army, and lack of fuel stopped him employing all of his armour at any one time. For once, Hitler listened to one of his generals, and agreed to provide the Army Group with panzer reinforcements.

Sensing that Hoth's panzers were doing more harm than good in the overcrowded roads south of the Don, he returned the forces to Army Group B on 30 July. But, by that stage, Hoth was already 140km (87 miles) south

of Tsimlyansk and strong Soviet forces were preventing a link up with Paulus. As Hoth's panzers fought their way north, they were slowly being ground down.

At the Volga
Nevertheless, Sixth Army reached the banks of the Volga on 23 August. In spite of furious Soviet counterattacks, a defensive line was established upstream of Stalingrad. That night, Stalingrad was subjected to an air raid reminiscent of the heaviest London blitz. The bulk of the bombs dropped were incendiaries, and the wooden buildings of the city burned in a spectacular holocaust. Acres of Stalingrad had been reduced to charred ashes and it was evident to the thoroughly satisfied German observers that only the main factories and stone-built offices remained for the attention of the German artillery.

His left flank secured, Von Paulus finally managed to link up his panzer reinforcement on 2 September. An assault on the city was now planned. But it was to prove an infinitely more difficult task, now that Stalingrad's defenders had had time to prepare its defences.

Stalin's response
With hindsight, it seems that Hitler may have been attempting the impossible, but Stalin was sufficiently alarmed by the series of reverses since the fall of Kerch to issue a famous order of the day on 28 July:

'Every inch of territory we concede strengthens the enemy and weakens the defence of our country. If we do not stop

SIXTH ARMY – PANZER STRENGTH (SEPT 1942)					
Tank type	Pz II	Pz III (kz)	Pz III (lg)	Pz IV (kz)	Pz Bef
14TH PANZER DIVISION					
36th Pz Rgt	14	41	19	24	4
Tank type	Pz IV	StuG	Pz Bef		
16TH PANZER DIVISION					
2nd Pz Rgt	98	42	12		
Tank type	Pz II	PzIII(5kz)	PzIII (5lg)	PzIV (kz)	Pz Bef
24TH PANZER DIVISION					
24th Pz Rgt	32	54	36	32	7

the retreat we shall be left with no grain, fuel, metal, workshops, factories or railways. Therefore the moment has come to stop the retreat: not another step back! Cowards and panic mongers will be executed on the spot. Henceforth every commander, soldier and political officer must be subject to iron discipline. Not a step back unless ordered by the supreme commander.'

In the city

In Stalingrad, the order achieved desired effect. The city had half a million inhabitants, and much of the civilian population had been marched out to dig trenches and anti-tank ditches. But that was not the only German worry. German intelligence had not warned the units taking part that Stalingrad sprawled for more than 30km (19 miles) along the Volga and that, in places, the

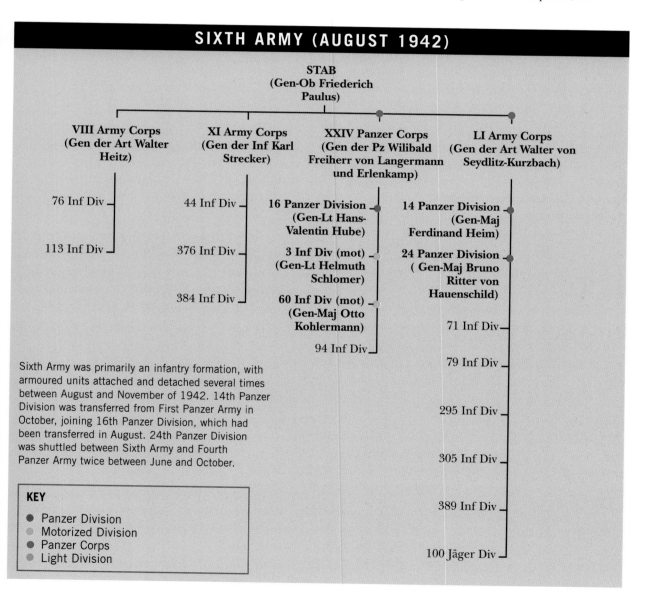

SIXTH ARMY (AUGUST 1942)

STAB
(Gen-Ob Friederich Paulus)

VIII Army Corps
(Gen der Art Walter Heitz)

XI Army Corps
(Gen der Inf Karl Strecker)

XXIV Panzer Corps
(Gen der Pz Wilibald Freiherr von Langermann und Erlenkamp)

LI Army Corps
(Gen der Art Walter von Seydlitz-Kurzbach)

76 Inf Div

113 Inf Div

44 Inf Div

376 Inf Div

384 Inf Div

16 Panzer Division
(Gen-Lt Hans-Valentin Hube)

3 Inf Div (mot)
(Gen-Lt Helmuth Schlomer)

60 Inf Div (mot)
(Gen-Maj Otto Kohlermann)

94 Inf Div

14 Panzer Division
(Gen-Maj Ferdinand Heim)

24 Panzer Division
(Gen-Maj Bruno Ritter von Hauenschild)

71 Inf Div

79 Inf Div

295 Inf Div

305 Inf Div

389 Inf Div

100 Jäger Div

Sixth Army was primarily an infantry formation, with armoured units attached and detached several times between August and November of 1942. 14th Panzer Division was transferred from First Panzer Army in October, joining 16th Panzer Division, which had been transferred in August. 24th Panzer Division was shuttled between Sixth Army and Fourth Panzer Army twice between June and October.

KEY

- Panzer Division
- Motorized Division
- Panzer Corps
- Light Division

western edge of the city was more than 8km (5 miles) from the bank of the river.

The time for taking the city by *coup de main* had passed. Von Paulus's makeshift attack could have succeeded only if it had met an enemy who was not only beaten, but whose morale was also extremely low.

From the very first engagements in the increasingly bitter street fighting in Stalingrad, it was clear to the Germans on the front line that the Soviets had recovered beyond anyone's expectations, and that the Russian slogan 'The Volga has only one bank' was no empty boast.

On 16 September, *Luftwaffe Generaloberst* Wolfram von Richtofen, commander of *Luftflotte* IV, complained of the lack of spirit in the Sixth Army. He wrote in his diary: 'With a little effort, the town should have fallen in just two days.'

Less than a week later, he noted, with a more realistic assessment: 'September the 2nd. In the town itself progress is desperately slow. The 6th Army will never finish the job at this rate. Above all because it is threatened from the North by the Russians and because reinforcements arrive only in dribs and drabs. We have to fight endless engagements, taking one cellar after another in order to gain any ground at all.'

Street fighting

The Soviet soldiers, spurred on by patriotic propaganda, were now fighting in circumstances in which their own natural abilities were an advantage, and their lack of armour and mobility did not matter. They fought from holes burrowed in rubble, from the blackened caverns of burned-out offices, from behind parapets of gaunt towering blocks; they fought for every yard of every street and every alleyway in the city.

Here, all the panzers could do was to creep over the wasteland of a city devastated by their own efforts. Unable to see the hidden enemy, their fate was to be blasted by liquid fire, or have their tracks blown off by grenades and mines. Armoured vehicles are virtually defenceless once immobilized. And once the tanks were stopped, German infantry were mown down by machine-gun fire as they sought protection behind their vehicles.

In Berlin, Hitler was already proclaiming the victory in Stalingrad, and poured as many reinforcements as

possible into the inferno. By contrast, the Soviets fed in just enough troops to keep the Germans occupied, and to resist their best efforts. In the meantime, the mass of men and arms accumulating in reserve were being held back for a different purpose.

The Red Army strikes

The Soviet plan was finally revealed on 19 November. The most recent of six major attacks by the Sixth Army finally to take the small sectors of the city that were still in Soviet hands had been repulsed, and the weary German troops were licking their wounds.

Surprise was near total when the Soviets unleashed massive barrages north and south of Stalingrad. The Red Army had finally learned the lessons of *Blitzkrieg*. This time, their attacks would be launched at the weakest part of the German line: von Paulus's thinly held flanks, protected only by Romanian and Italian formations.

The battle for Stalingrad had entered a new and desperate phase. Soviet forces attacked in unbelievable strength from their bridgeheads over the Don.

The next day, the Red Army attacked in the south, with equal effect. By 23 November, the encirclement was complete. Some 300,000 Axis soldiers were trapped in the Stalingrad pocket.

Manstein failed to relieve the trapped army. He sent *Generaloberst* Hermann Hoth's Fourth Panzer Army to blast a way through the Soviet lines on 12 December,

29 January – 20 February 1943

Within days of the fall of Stalingrad, Soviet tank battalions were racing across the open steppe west of the River Donets, overtaking scattered groups of retreating Germans. On 26 January, they recovered Voronezh; by 8 February, they were through Kursk and driving for the railway at Suzemka. Ahead lay the Dniepr crossings and the giant hydroelectric plant at Zaporezhe; north and, about to be surrounded, lay the industrial city of Kharkov. On 14 February, the latter was abandoned by its SS garrison, who ignored Hitler's orders to hold fast.

Kharkhov was the first major Soviet city to be liberated. Eighteen months of Nazi occupation had reduced its population by 25 per cent: some 100,000 young men and women had been deported to Germany as slave labourers.

and in a week of desperate fighting, his panzer corps got close enough to see the horizon lit up at night, flares rising and falling over the pocket.

The last stand of the Sixth Army delayed a general Soviet offensive long enough to allow other German forces to retreat and regroup. The reduction and final destruction of the Stalingrad pocket occupied seven Soviet armies until the last day of January 1943 – armies that would otherwise have joined their comrades in a massive drive west.

But the blow to German prestige was severe. The fierce winter still gripped the land when Paulus surrendered, on 30 January 1943. Of the 300,000 men in the pocket, 91,000 survived to surrender, of whom half would be dead before spring. Only 5000 would ever return from Soviet captivity.

SOVIET BREAKTHROUGH

Third Battle of Kharkov
29 January–20 February 1943

- Soviet front line 29 January
- Soviet front line 9 February
- Soviet front line 20 February
- Soviet advance to 9 February
- Soviet advance to 20 February
- Soviet withdrawal
- German counterattack
- German withdrawal

Army Group Don

Following the encirclement of the Sixth Army at Stalingrad, Field Marshal Erich von Manstein was given command of a new formation known as Army Group Don, which was intended to protect the gap that had opened between Army Groups A and B.

WALTHER MODEL (1891–1945)

The son of a music teacher, Model joined the army in 1910 and remained in the *Reichswehr* after 1918.

• Model was a supporter of Hitler. He served in staff positions in Poland and France before commanding the 3rd Panzer Division in the invasion of the Soviet Union.

• Model commanded XLI Panzer Corps in 1941–42. He devised effective defensive tactics using small, mobile *Kampfgruppen* to counter Soviet breakthroughs. A master of defensive warfare, he became known as 'the Führer's Fireman'.

• Promoted to *Feldmarschall* in March 1944, he was sent to France in August 1944. Trapped in the Ruhr pocket in 1945, he shot himself in a wood near Duisburg and died on 21 April.

Manstein's orders were simple: to relieve the troops at Stalingrad. On 12 December, Manstein launched his attack towards Stalingrad with 13 divisions. The Soviets countered by attacking the Italian Eighth Army and the Romanian armies along the river Chir, northwest of Stalingrad. The threat Manstein had feared – of his offensive simply adding to the German casualty lists – was fast becoming a reality.

Manstein sent Generaloberst Hermann Hoth to blast a way through the Soviet lines, and in a week of desperate fighting, his Fourth Panzer Army got close enough to see flares rising and falling over the pocket. However, another great breakthrough by the Red Army forced Hoth's relief force to turn away and meet the new threat.

Relief effort fails

By 19 December, with Army Group Don's progress grinding to a halt, Manstein suggested that Paulus should attempt an immediate breakout; Paulus refused without specific orders from Hitler – which did not come. On 23 December, the relieving force was stopped at the Myshkova River; the troops in Stalingrad could hear the sound of the guns of Hoth's Fourth Panzer Army, but relief would come no closer.

The Soviets had launched Operation Little Saturn on 16 December, designed to cut off and destroy the German relief force. By Christmas 1942, Manstein's forces were in full retreat and the Red Army was advancing. Retreating from the Caucasus, Army Group A had, by the end of January, been squeezed into a small bridgehead on the Black Sea coast opposite the Kerch peninsula. However, Soviet progress was stopped by Manstein's victory at Kharkov.

Army Group Don existed only until February 1943, when it was combined with Army Group B and was renamed as the new Army Group South.

ARMY GROUP DON (JAN–FEB 1943)

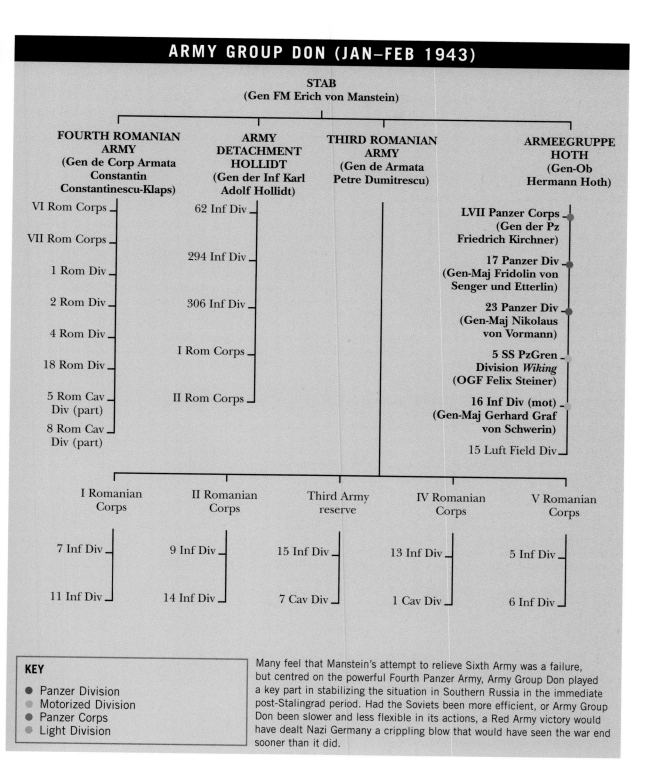

STAB
(Gen FM Erich von Manstein)

FOURTH ROMANIAN ARMY
(Gen de Corp Armata Constantin Constantinescu-Klaps)

ARMY DETACHMENT HOLLIDT
(Gen der Inf Karl Adolf Hollidt)

THIRD ROMANIAN ARMY
(Gen de Armata Petre Dumitrescu)

ARMEEGRUPPE HOTH
(Gen-Ob Hermann Hoth)

VI Rom Corps

VII Rom Corps

1 Rom Div

2 Rom Div

4 Rom Div

18 Rom Div

5 Rom Cav Div (part)

8 Rom Cav Div (part)

62 Inf Div

294 Inf Div

306 Inf Div

I Rom Corps

II Rom Corps

LVII Panzer Corps
(Gen der Pz Friedrich Kirchner)

17 Panzer Div
(Gen-Maj Fridolin von Senger und Etterlin)

23 Panzer Div
(Gen-Maj Nikolaus von Vormann)

5 SS PzGren Division *Wiking*
(OGF Felix Steiner)

16 Inf Div (mot)
(Gen-Maj Gerhard Graf von Schwerin)

15 Luft Field Div

I Romanian Corps

7 Inf Div

11 Inf Div

II Romanian Corps

9 Inf Div

14 Inf Div

Third Army reserve

15 Inf Div

7 Cav Div

IV Romanian Corps

13 Inf Div

1 Cav Div

V Romanian Corps

5 Inf Div

6 Inf Div

KEY

● Panzer Division
○ Motorized Division
● Panzer Corps
○ Light Division

Many feel that Manstein's attempt to relieve Sixth Army was a failure, but centred on the powerful Fourth Panzer Army, Army Group Don played a key part in stabilizing the situation in Southern Russia in the immediate post-Stalingrad period. Had the Soviets been more efficient, or Army Group Don been slower and less flexible in its actions, a Red Army victory would have dealt Nazi Germany a crippling blow that would have seen the war end sooner than it did.

Soviet Union: 1943

The catastrophe at Stalingrad was the worst disaster to befall Hitler's *Wehrmacht* in its war of conquest. Even so, the German armies on the Eastern Front were far from down and out, and 1943 would see some of the largest German operations of the war.

The ordinary soldiers of the Sixth Army trapped in Stalingrad believed, against mounting evidence to the contrary, that Hitler would get them out. Hitler insisted that 'Festung Stalingrad' hold out until relieved, but the the troops had no proper fortifications, just holes in the frozen ground, which they had managed to excavate with their remaining explosives.

Stalingrad abandoned

Manstein failed to relieve the trapped army. He sent *Generaloberst* Hermann Hoth to blast a way through the Soviet lines on 12 December, and in a week of desperate

fighting, his panzer corps got close enough to see flares rising and falling over the pocket. But the Soviets attacked the Italian and Romanian armies along the River Chir, northwest of Stalingrad. Another great breakthrough was achieved, and Hoth's relief force was compelled to turn away and meet the new threat.

Stalin ordered the pocket crushed in January, and a Soviet *blitzkrieg* broke into the perimeter west of the city. Hitler promoted Paulus to full General and then to Field Marshal, on the understanding that no German Field Marshal had ever been taken alive. But Paulus refused to kill himself, and surrendered on 30 January.

TYPE 43 PANZER COMPANY

Introduced in September 1943, the Type 43 Panzer Division table of organization saw panzer divisions being equipped with a single panzer *Abteilung* or battalion. The battalion comprised a staff company, three panzer companies and a panzer maintenance company. Each panzer company was authorized 17 tanks rather than the 22 that had been standard earlier in the war.

As the *Panzerkampfwagen* V Panther entered service, the divisions formed a second battalion equipped with panthers, but until the end of the war most panzer regiments continued to operate with the Panzer IV, as seen here. By the end of 1943, the Panzer IVs in service had been upgraded with long-barrel, 7.5-cm guns, and most carried side skirts to protect the hull and turret from shaped-charge weapons.

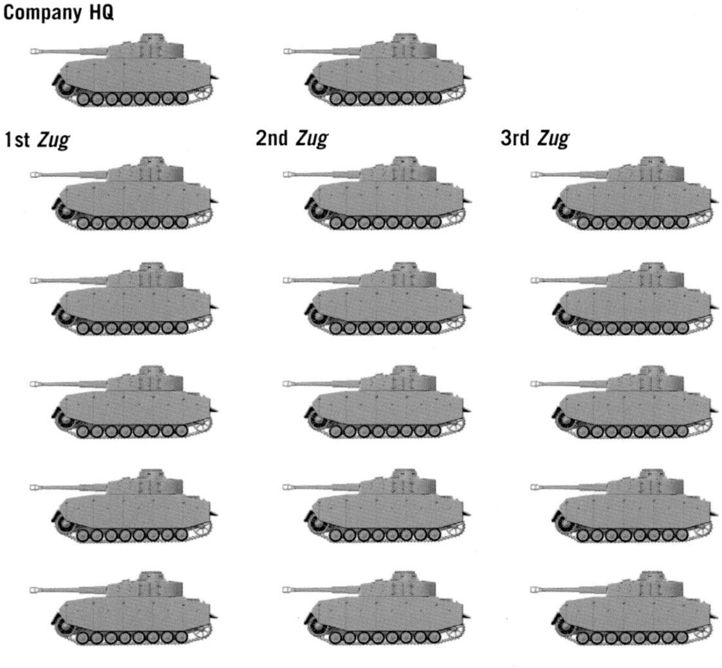

Company HQ

1st *Zug*   **2nd *Zug***   **3rd *Zug***

Northern Front

By the beginning of 1943, the siege of Leningrad had been under way for more than a year. The first German attempts to take the city by storm had failed, and by now the Wehrmacht was attempting to starve the city into submission.

A series of heavy Soviet offensives were mounted, but Army Group North managed to blunt all attempts to break through. A bare minimum of supplies were getting through to Leningrad, but there was only enough to allow the defenders to keep on fighting, and mass starvation remained an ever present threat. The previous winter, which had been particularly cold, the city's food rations reached an all time low of only 125 grams of bread per person per day. In just two months, January and February of 1942, 200,000 people had died of cold and starvation. By 1943, however, the population of the city had decreased after several hundred thousand civilians were evacuated across Lake Ladoga, and food supplies stretched a little further.

March 1943

In March 1943, the *Wehrmacht* was still reeling from the disaster at Stalingrad, and on the southern front the Red Army was advancing westwards at a headlong pace. However, the Soviet lines of communications were extended, and spearhead units were rapidly coming to the end of their resources. German divisions were, however, regrouping, slowing the Soviet advance and allowing time for a counterstrike to be prepared.

To the North, Army Group Centre had stopped a series of Soviet attacks around the Rzhev salient, inflicting a stinging reverse on Marshal Georgii Zhukov, and was now retiring to prepared defensive positions. Army Group Nortn was still investing Leningrad, managing to blunt most Soviet attempts to break through to the city, although it could not cut the tenuous supply lines that ensured the city's survival.

EASTERN FRONT

Eastern Front
Beginning of
March 1943

1500
1000
500
200
100
0 m

0   100 km
0   100 miles

Leningrad
Leningrad Front
XXXX 18
Army Group North
Volkhov Front
XXXX 16
North-West Front
XXXX 3
Velikiye Luki
Kalinin Front
Army Group Centre
West Front
MOSCOW
Smolensk
R u s s i a
B e l o r u s s i a
XXXX 4
Bryansk Front
Bryansk
XXXX 2
Orel
U   S   S   R
XXXX 9
Kursk
Voronezh
Voronezh Front
XXXX 2
Kiev
U k r a i n e
Kharkov
XXXX 4
South-West Front
Army Group South
Dnepropetrovsk
XXXX 8
XXXX 1
XXXX 6
Southern Front
Sea of Azov
North Caucasus Front
Army Group A
Black Sea
Crimea
XXXX 17
Sevastopol
Novorossiysk

ARMY GROUP NORTH (JANUARY 1943)

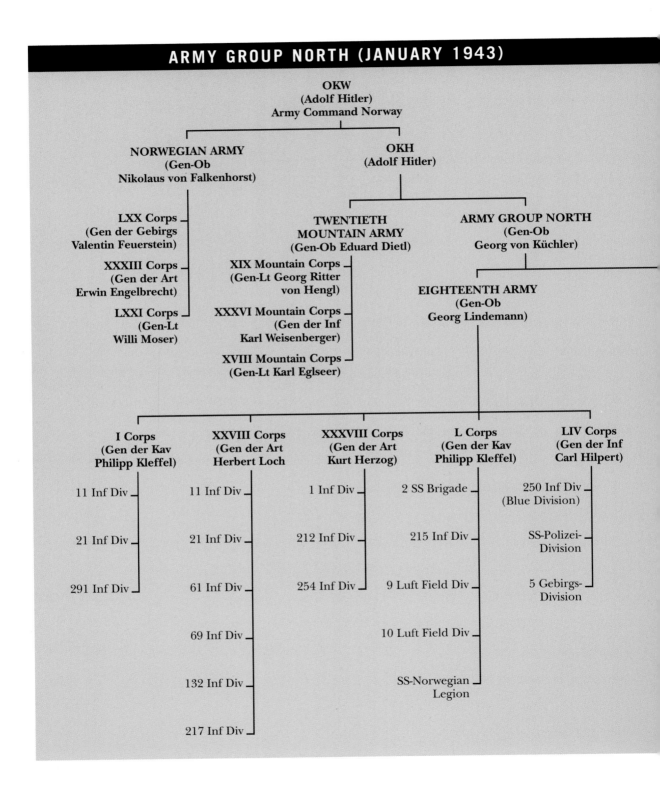

OKW
(Adolf Hitler)
Army Command Norway

NORWEGIAN ARMY
(Gen-Ob
Nikolaus von Falkenhorst)

OKH
(Adolf Hitler)

LXX Corps
(Gen der Gebirgs
Valentin Feuerstein)

XXXIII Corps
(Gen der Art
Erwin Engelbrecht)

LXXI Corps
(Gen-Lt
Willi Moser)

**TWENTIETH
MOUNTAIN ARMY**
(Gen-Ob Eduard Dietl)

XIX Mountain Corps
(Gen-Lt Georg Ritter
von Hengl)

XXXVI Mountain Corps
(Gen der Inf
Karl Weisenberger)

XVIII Mountain Corps
(Gen-Lt Karl Eglseer)

ARMY GROUP NORTH
(Gen-Ob
Georg von Küchler)

EIGHTEENTH ARMY
(Gen-Ob
Georg Lindemann)

I Corps
(Gen der Kav
Philipp Kleffel)

11 Inf Div

21 Inf Div

291 Inf Div

XXVIII Corps
(Gen der Art
Herbert Loch)

11 Inf Div

21 Inf Div

61 Inf Div

69 Inf Div

132 Inf Div

217 Inf Div

XXXVIII Corps
(Gen der Art
Kurt Herzog)

1 Inf Div

212 Inf Div

254 Inf Div

L Corps
(Gen der Kav
Philipp Kleffel)

2 SS Brigade

215 Inf Div

9 Luft Field Div

10 Luft Field Div

SS-Norwegian
Legion

LIV Corps
(Gen der Inf
Carl Hilpert)

250 Inf Div
(Blue Division)

SS-Polizei-
Division

5 Gebirgs-
Division

KEY

- ● Panzer Division
- ○ Motorized Division
- ● Panzer Corps
- ● Light Division

In January 1943, Army Group North, which was continuing to besiege Leningrad, was an almost exclusively infantry formation. The German Army was suffering from manpower shortages at the time, and several *Luftwaffe* Field Divisions were deployed to serve on the Leningrad Front, as was the Spanish volunteer 'Blue' Division. Eighteenth Army also controlled numerous independent police and security battalions, as well as a number of Soviet volunteer formations, the so-called *Ost Bataillonen*.

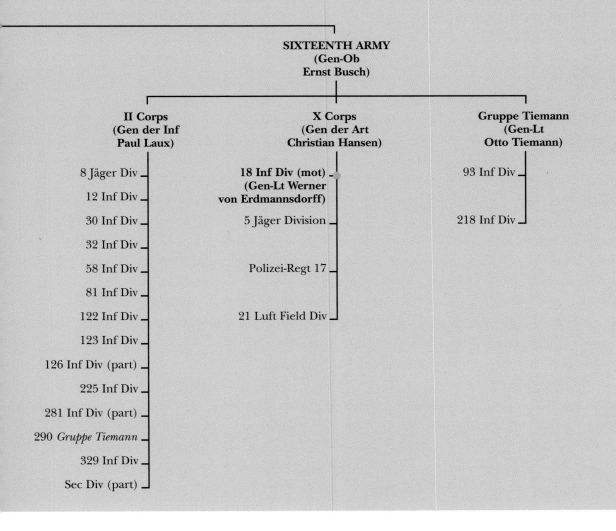

SIXTEENTH ARMY
(Gen-Ob
Ernst Busch)

II Corps
(Gen der Inf
Paul Laux)

8 Jäger Div
12 Inf Div
30 Inf Div
32 Inf Div
58 Inf Div
81 Inf Div
122 Inf Div
123 Inf Div
126 Inf Div (part)
225 Inf Div
281 Inf Div (part)
290 *Gruppe Tiemann*
329 Inf Div
Sec Div (part)

X Corps
(Gen der Art
Christian Hansen)

18 Inf Div (mot)
(Gen-Lt Werner
von Erdmannsdorff)
5 Jäger Division

Polizei-Regt 17

21 Luft Field Div

Gruppe Tiemann
(Gen-Lt
Otto Tiemann)

93 Inf Div

218 Inf Div

Central Front

Although much of the world's attention was on the southern sector of the Eastern Front, where German and Soviet armies fought battles of annihiliation at Stalingrad and Kursk, Army Group Centre fought its own fierce war in 1943.

The spring thaw of 1942 had halted operations. The *raspuditza,* or thaw, turned the steel-hard ground into impenetrable rivers of mud. Nothing could move, and the Germans were given the chance to breathe again. With the *Wehrmacht* less than 300km (186 miles) from Moscow – a distance the panzer divisions could cover in a week – the Soviets concentrated their forces around the capital. It was the obvious military strategy, and it was wrong.

War of attrition

The *Wehrmacht*'s High Command calculated that over the entire Eastern Front the Germans had lost 376,000 men killed and wounded during the Soviet winter offensive.

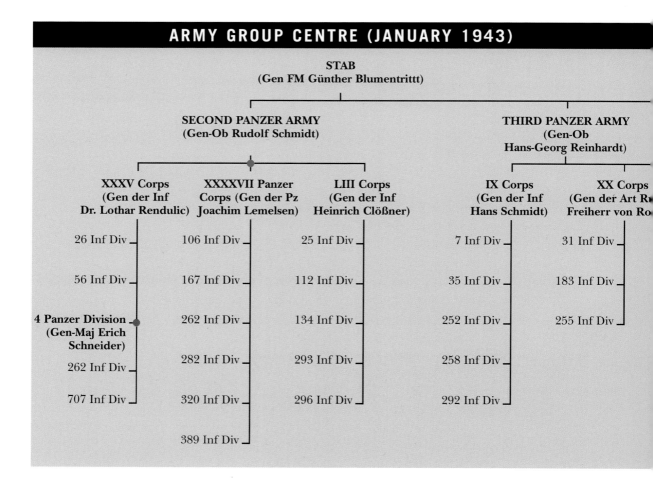

ARMY GROUP CENTRE (JANUARY 1943)

STAB
(Gen FM Günther Blumentrittt)

SECOND PANZER ARMY (Gen-Ob Rudolf Schmidt)			THIRD PANZER ARMY (Gen-Ob Hans-Georg Reinhardt)	
XXXV Corps (Gen der Inf Dr. Lothar Rendulic)	XXXXVII Panzer Corps (Gen der Pz Joachim Lemelsen)	LIII Corps (Gen der Inf Heinrich Clößner)	IX Corps (Gen der Inf Hans Schmidt)	XX Corps (Gen der Art R◆ Freiherr von Ro◆
26 Inf Div	106 Inf Div	25 Inf Div	7 Inf Div	31 Inf Div
56 Inf Div	167 Inf Div	112 Inf Div	35 Inf Div	183 Inf Div
4 Panzer Division (Gen-Maj Erich Schneider)	262 Inf Div	134 Inf Div	252 Inf Div	255 Inf Div
262 Inf Div	282 Inf Div	293 Inf Div	258 Inf Div	
707 Inf Div	320 Inf Div	296 Inf Div	292 Inf Div	
	389 Inf Div			

Nearly double that number had been lost from frostbite and sickness. At the beginning of April 1942, the armies on the Eastern Front were 625,000 men under strength.

However, they had inflicted more than 400,000 casualties on their enemies, and many soldiers puzzled over the Red Army's ability to take such punishment. Göbbels damned them as mindless automata. But in its counteroffensive, the Red Army learned the true nature of its opponents. The ordinary Soviet soldier discovered that the most outlandish tales of atrocity fed to them by the commissars were not so incredible after all.

The Soviet counteroffensive over the winter of 1941–42 forced the Germans back from the gates of Moscow. When the Soviet offensive ran out of steam in the spring of 1942, much of Army Group Centre found

ARMY GROUP CENTRE – PANZER STRENGTH (1943)					
Tank type	Pz III	Pz III(75)	Pz IV (kz)	Pz IV (lg)	Pz Bef
4TH PANZER DIVISION					
35th Pz Rgt	15	0	1	79	6
5TH PANZER DIVISION					
31st Pz Rgt	0	17	0	76	9

itself occupying a huge salient penetrating Soviet-held territory around the city of Rzhev. Elsewhere on the front the Germans were forced back, but the Rzhev salient held, and would continue to hold into 1943.

It was the scene of heavy fighting during the Red Army's Moscow counteroffensive in the winter of 1941–42, during Red Army offensives from July to

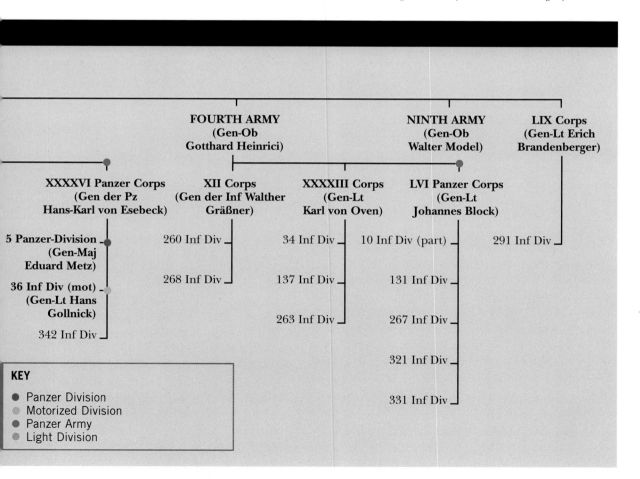

FOURTH ARMY
(Gen-Ob
Gotthard Heinrici)

NINTH ARMY
(Gen-Ob
Walter Model)

LIX Corps
(Gen-Lt Erich
Brandenberger)

XXXXVI Panzer Corps
(Gen der Pz
Hans-Karl von Esebeck)

XII Corps
(Gen der Inf Walther
Gräßner)

XXXXIII Corps
(Gen-Lt
Karl von Oven)

LVI Panzer Corps
(Gen-Lt
Johannes Block)

5 Panzer-Division
(Gen-Maj
Eduard Metz)

36 Inf Div (mot)
(Gen-Lt Hans
Gollnick)

342 Inf Div

260 Inf Div

268 Inf Div

34 Inf Div

137 Inf Div

263 Inf Div

10 Inf Div (part)

131 Inf Div

267 Inf Div

321 Inf Div

331 Inf Div

291 Inf Div

KEY
- Panzer Division
- Motorized Division
- Panzer Army
- Light Division

PANZERJAGERKOMPANIE NASHORN, 1943

Introduced in 1943, the *Nashorn* (or 'Rhinoceros') was a powerful self-propelled tank-hunter mounting the PaK variant of the 8.8cm FlaK gun onto a modified Panzer IV. The *Nashorns* were issued to independent *schwere Panzerjäger abteilungen*, attached to formations at corps or army level. Typically, a heavy *panzerjäger* battalion would include a staff battery with three *Nashorns* and three *Flakvierling* quad 20mm air defence guns, and three *panzerjäger* companies arranged as seen here.

Company HQ

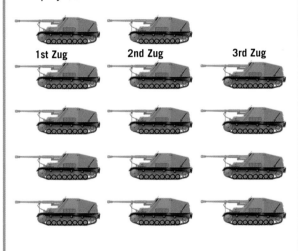

1st Zug   **2nd Zug**   **3rd Zug**

early September 1942, and in the major attempt by the Red Army to pinch out the salient in November and December 1942. Codenamed Operation Mars, this was as bloody as the first attempts to pinch off the salient and destroy Army Group Centre. It failed in its aims, but the Soviets had tied down German forces that may otherwise have been used to try to relieve the Stalingrad garrison, which was fighting for its life.

Soviet pressure on Rzhev

Although Army Group Centre had held the massive Soviet offensive at the end of 1942, losses in Southern Russia and the general advance of the Red Army across Ukraine might have left German forces in central Russia dangerously exposed. Following the success of their Stalingrad and Voronezh counteroffensives, the Soviets planned another attack on Army Group Centre for February 1943. The plan was for a coordinated assault by Soviet forces in the Kursk and northern Army Group Centre areas to encircle and first destroy the German forces at Orel and then the Rzhev Salient, with Soviet units ultimately to meet at Smolensk in a grand encirclement of Army Group Centre.

Withdrawal from Rzhev

The Germans forestalled this offensive by carrying out Operation *Buffel*, or 'Buffalo'. This was the long-planned evacuation of the Rzhev salient, to which Hitler had given his reluctant approval. The withdrawal was intended to shorten the German lines. When Soviet attacks from Kursk towards Orel failed to make progress, the offensive was called off.

In July and August 1943, the Soviets succeeded in stopping the German offensive Operation Citadel penetrating into the Kursk Salient. Army Group Centre provided the northern prong of the giant pincer movement designed to eliminate Soviet forces around Kursk, but Model's Ninth Army could make little progress against the strongly prepared Soviet defences.

Pressure on Smolensk

Following the Kursk battles, Soviet armies counterattacked towards Orel and Kharkov. In tandem with the offensive into Ukraine, another offensive, the Smolensk Operation (Operation *Suvarov*), was launched against Army Group Centre between August and October 1943. The attacks made slow progress but were successful in recapturing Smolensk and the important rail junction at Nevel, forcing the German line back on a broad front. However, the attack foundered on the strong German defensive works in the Vitebsk-Orsha-Mogilev area (the Ostwall defensive line).

Further Soviet offensives against Army Group Centre – the Gomel and Orsha Operations in November 1943 and the Vitebsk Operation in February 1944 – were unsuccessful against the strong Ostwall defences.

Ostwall defences

The Ostwall was built after the battle of Kursk.

Beginning in the south at Melitopol, the wall was intended to run due north to the Dnieper, then on to Kiev and the Desna River to Chernigov. From there, it was to take a line almost due north to the southern tip of Pskov Lake, then run along the west shores of Peipus Lake, to be anchored on the Gulf of Finland at Narva.

Orel bulge

Elsewhere, the Soviets continued to put pressure on Army Group Centre. The withdrawal from the Rzev salient in the spring of 1943 left a bulge in the German lines around the city of Orel. Even as the battle of Kursk was winding down, on 15 July, Rokossovsky's Central Front struck at the Orel bulge. A strategic decision was made to abandon Orel, which was retaken by the Red Army on 5 August 1943, and fall back to the partly completed Hagen line near Bryansk.

August 1943 saw Army Group Centre pushed slowly back from the Hagen line, ceding comparatively little territory, but the loss of Bryansk and, more importantly, Smolensk on 25 September cost the *Wehrmacht* the keystone of the entire German defensive system. The Fourth and Ninth Armies and Third Panzer Army still held their own east of the upper Dnieper, stifling Soviet attempts to reach Vitebsk.

It has been estimated that as many as 55 German divisions were committed to countering the Smolensk Operation – divisions that would have been critical to preventing Soviet troops from crossing the Dnieper in the south.

Southern Front

The southern sector of the Eastern Front was where the main German offensive of 1942 had taken place, and it remained the scene of key battles all through 1943. However, after the Battle of Kursk, the *Wehrmacht* was never to regain the initiative.

Two weeks after the liberation of Kharkov, the Red Army was at Pavlograd, only 40km (25 miles) from the Dnieper – and quite close to Hitler, who was paying a flying visit to Zaporozhye.

German counterstroke

Field Marshal von Manstein had a clear plan for stabilizing the desperate situation in the East, and he persuaded the Führer to let him conduct the battle his way, instead of conducting the rigid defence that Hitler usually favoured. The result was a tactical masterstroke that is still studied in military academies today.

Manstein's plans took into account the iron laws of logistics now hampering the Soviets. The leading Red Army formations were separated by miles of devastated country from their bases. Red Army staff officers lacked experience of feeding huge, rapidly advancing armies. Worst of all, the Germans were now reorganized and well supplied, poised to cut them to pieces.

Manstein let the Soviet advance continue while he assembled a powerful striking force on its flanks, consisting of SS panzergrenadier divisions *Leibstandarte*, *Das Reich* and *Totenkopf* combined with five army panzer divisions and the *Grossdeutschland* division.

Manstein sprang his first trap on 20 February. On the day that the forward Soviet patrols reached Pavlograd,

XLVI PANZER CORPS – PANZER STRENGTH (JUNE 1943)					
Tank type	Pz II	Pz III	Pz IV	Pz Bef	Pz 38(t)
2ND PANZER DIVISION					
3rd Pz Rgt	12	40	60	6	0
9TH PANZER DIVISION					
33rd Pz Rgt	1	38	38	6	0
20TH PANZER DIVISION					
21st Pz Rgt	0	17	49	7	9

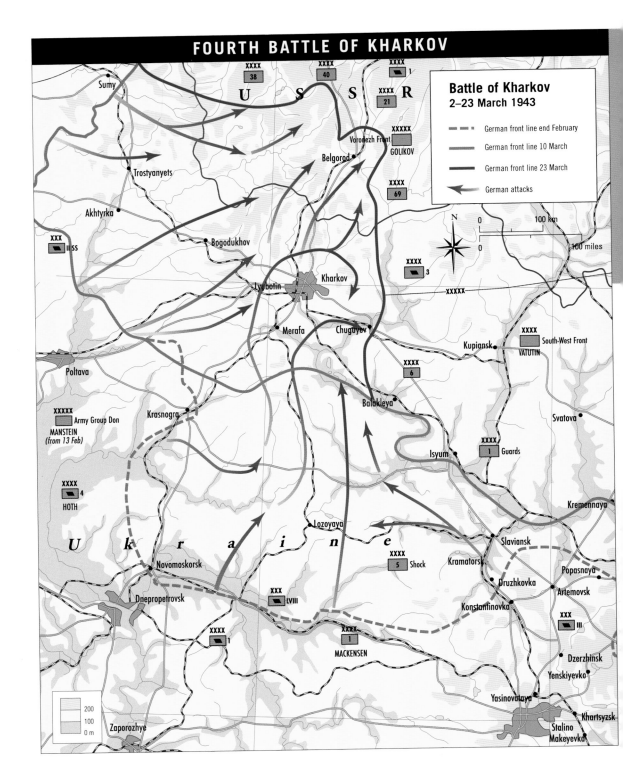

FOURTH BATTLE OF KHARKOV

Battle of Kharkov
2–23 March 1943

- – – – German front line end February
- ——— German front line 10 March
- ——— German front line 23 March
- ← German attacks

XXXX 38

XXXX 40

XXXX 1

XXXX 21

Sumy

U S S R

Trostyanyets

XXXXX
GOLIKOV
Voronezh Front

Belgorod

XXXX 69

Akhtyrka

XXX II SS

Bogodukhov

N

0   100 km

0   100 miles

XXXX 3

Kharkov

Lyubotin

XXXXX

Merafa

Chugayev

Kupiansk

XXXX
VATUTIN
South-West Front

XXXX 6

Poltava

XXXXX
Army Group Don
MANSTEIN
(from 13 Feb)

Krasnograd

Balakleya

Svatova

Isyum

XXXX 1 Guards

XXXX 4
HOTH

U   k   r   a   i   n   e

Lozoyaya

Kremennaya

Slaviansk

XXXX 5 Shock

Kramatorsk

Popasnaya

Novomoskorsk

XXX LVIII

Druzhkovka

Artemovsk

Konstantinovka

XXX III

Dnepropetrovsk

XXXX 1

XXXX 1
MACKENSEN

Dzerzhinsk

Yenskiyevko

200
100
0 m

Zaporozhye

Yasinovataya

Stalino
Makeyevka

Khartsyzsk

2–23 March 1943

Kharkov had fallen to the Soviets in February 1943, following the Red Army's offensive at Stalingrad. However, led by Field Marshal Erich von Manstein, the Germans counterattacked and, after destroying Soviet spearheads in a classic battle of manoeuvre, retook the city after a period of costly street fighting. Tank spearheads from Hoth's Fourth Panzer Army and Army Detachment *Kempf* cut off large portions of the Soviet Southwest Front and, by 9 March, the *Wehrmacht* had inflicted a heavy defeat on the Soviets at Krasnograd and Barvenkovo. The II SS Panzer Corps was attached to Manstein's counter-thrust, which destroyed the Soviet spearheads and saved Army Group South. The *Leibstandarte* Division then retook Kharkov, for which Hitler renamed the central square *Leibstandarteplatz*. The battle was the last successful German offensive on the Eastern Front.

panzers were driving up the west bank of the Donets behind them. Their aim was to smash into the flank of the Third Soviet Tank Army and destroy it. In what he dubbed his 'backhand blow', Manstein drove east to cut off all the Soviet forces that had broken over the Donets.

By 3 March, the Soviets had been forced to abandon nearly 15,540km² (6000 square miles) of their recent gains. The SS panzer corps stormed Kharkov in mid-March, and Belgorod was retaken. By the end of the month, the four Soviet tank corps strung out between the Donets and Zaporezhe were annihilated.

The Battle of Kharkov improved the German position just as the spring thaw imposed its annual halt on military operations. The startling recovery of the German Army after the Stalingrad disaster unsettled Stalin, who made a tentative approach to Hitler via Swedish diplomats. But the Führer was still set on decisive victory and the extermination of what he still regarded as the Jewish-Bolshevik threat.

Hitler's army was outnumbered 2:1 in men and 5:1 in tanks and guns, but the *Wehrmacht* knew that its training and tactical leadership were far superior to that of the Red Army. Though the odds did not favour a third successive large-scale summer offensive in 1943, the German Army High Command was still determined to attack.

Battle of Kursk

The last major German offensive on the Eastern Front took place in the summer of 1943, when a large proportion of the panzer strengths of Army Groups Centre and South were thrown against the huge Soviet-held salient around Kursk.

Following Kharkov, the front line had stabilized – running from just west of Rostov in the south, up to Velikiye-Luki west of Moscow, then on to Leningrad. However, a huge Soviet salient protruded 80km (50 miles) westwards in front of Kursk, from just north of Belgorod up to the line of Ponyri. The salient was about 200km (124 miles) wide at its base, and positively invited attack.

Operation Citadel

Initial orders for the offensive, code-named Operation Citadel, were issued by OKH – the German Army High Command – on 13 March 1943. Army Group Centre would attack from the north with a massively reinforced

III PANZER CORPS – PANZER STRENGTH (JUNE 1943)					
Tank type	**Pz II**	**Pz III**	**Pz IV**	**Pz Bef**	**Flmmpz**
6TH PANZER DIVISION					
11th Pz Rgt	13	52	32	6	14
Tank type	**Pz II**	**PzIII (50)**	**PzIII (75)**	**Pz IV**	**Pz Bef**
7TH PANZER DIVISION					
25th Pz Rgt	12	43	12	38	5
19TH PANZER DIVISION					
27th Pz Rgt	2	27	11	38	14

panzer group, while Army Group South would strike northwards from the opposite side of the salient with even stronger forces.

The panzers had to break through little more than 100km (62 miles) to cut off all Soviet units in the salient. Further exploitation might take them back to the Don at Voronezh. Elimination of the Kursk bulge would also bring the *Wehrmacht* into a position to threaten Moscow. Kursk was such an obvious objective that the Soviets began fortifying it almost as soon as the Germans decided to attack it. Hitler postponed his attack several times in order to bring his forces up to

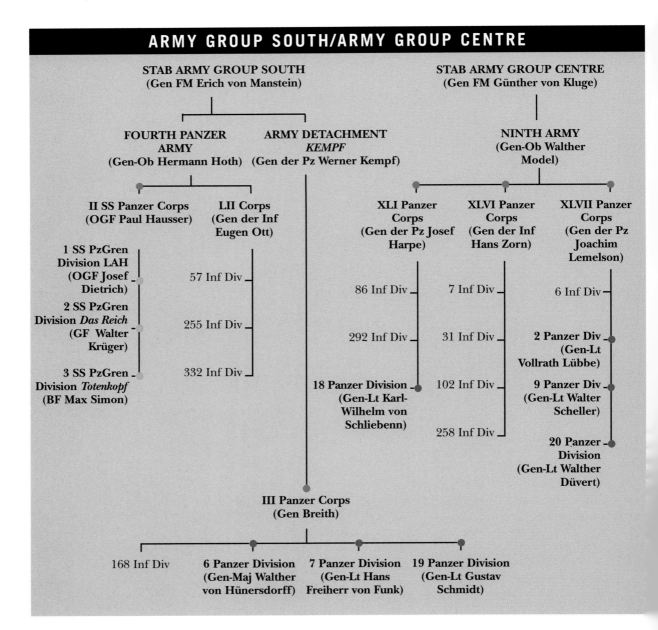

ARMY GROUP SOUTH/ARMY GROUP CENTRE

STAB ARMY GROUP SOUTH
(Gen FM Erich von Manstein)

STAB ARMY GROUP CENTRE
(Gen FM Günther von Kluge)

FOURTH PANZER ARMY
(Gen-Ob Hermann Hoth)

ARMY DETACHMENT KEMPF
(Gen der Pz Werner Kempf)

NINTH ARMY
(Gen-Ob Walther Model)

II SS Panzer Corps
(OGF Paul Hausser)

LII Corps
(Gen der Inf Eugen Ott)

XLI Panzer Corps
(Gen der Pz Josef Harpe)

XLVI Panzer Corps
(Gen der Inf Hans Zorn)

XLVII Panzer Corps
(Gen der Pz Joachim Lemelson)

1 SS PzGren Division LAH
(OGF Josef Dietrich)

2 SS PzGren Division *Das Reich*
(GF Walter Krüger)

3 SS PzGren Division *Totenkopf*
(BF Max Simon)

57 Inf Div

255 Inf Div

332 Inf Div

86 Inf Div

292 Inf Div

18 Panzer Division
(Gen-Lt Karl-Wilhelm von Schliebenn)

7 Inf Div

31 Inf Div

102 Inf Div

258 Inf Div

6 Inf Div

2 Panzer Div
(Gen-Lt Vollrath Lübbe)

9 Panzer Div
(Gen-Lt Walter Scheller)

20 Panzer Division
(Gen-Lt Walther Düvert)

III Panzer Corps
(Gen Breith)

168 Inf Div

6 Panzer Division
(Gen-Maj Walther von Hünersdorff)

7 Panzer Division
(Gen-Lt Hans Freiherr von Funk)

19 Panzer Division
(Gen-Lt Gustav Schmidt)

OPERATION *ZITADEL*

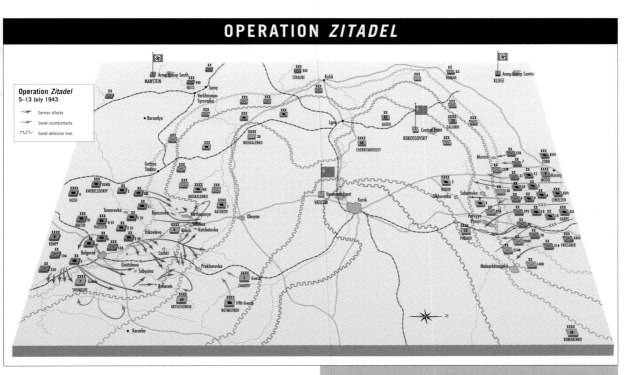

Operation *Zitadel*
5–13 July 1943

➤ German attacks
➤ Soviet counterattacks
ᏗᏗᏗ Soviet defensive lines

maximum strength, and to employ the latest heavy tanks
now in production.

Offensive begins

When Operation Citadel finally opened on 5 July, 1800
tanks and 900 assault guns spearheaded the ground
battle. Heavy strike power was provided by 147 Tigers,
200 Panthers and 89 Elefants, but the bulk of the panzer
battalions were still using Panzer IIIs and IVs.

At 2 a.m. on 5 July – an hour before the *Wehrmacht's*
opening barrage was due to launch the great offensive –
hundreds of Soviet guns opened up. Soviet artillery
blanketed the German assembly areas, killing
hundreds of waiting troops and wrecking important
communication networks. They destroyed quite a few
guns and panzers in the process, and made it
abundantly clear that the Red Army knew far too much
about German preparations for comfort.

The Soviets had also made excellent use of the
repeated German delays. Soviet infantry had dug deep
into the black earth of central Russia. Networks of
underground bunkers connected by trenches were

5–13 July 1943

The ambitious German plan to attack the huge Soviet
salient around Kursk promised a return to the
overwhelming German successes of the summer of
1941. Not only would the removal of the Kursk Salient
flatten the line of the front, but it would provide a
sound strategic base for a drive deep into Russia,
which would show the world that the German Army was
still the most powerful military machine in the world.

defended by clusters of concealed anti-tank guns. The
defences were designed first to channel the panzer
formations into killing grounds, and then demolish
them. Over 3000 mines were laid per kilometre of
fronts. By nightfall on the first day, 200 panzers had
been knocked out – and the days that followed
increased the cost proportionately.

The German Ninth Army, commanded by the
determined *Generaloberst* Model, made little headway
into the northern shoulder of the salient. His forces ran
headlong into the Soviet Thirteenth Army with the
Forty-Eighth and Seventieth Armies on each side. In
savage fighting that barely let up over the short summer

BATTLE OF PROKHOROVKA

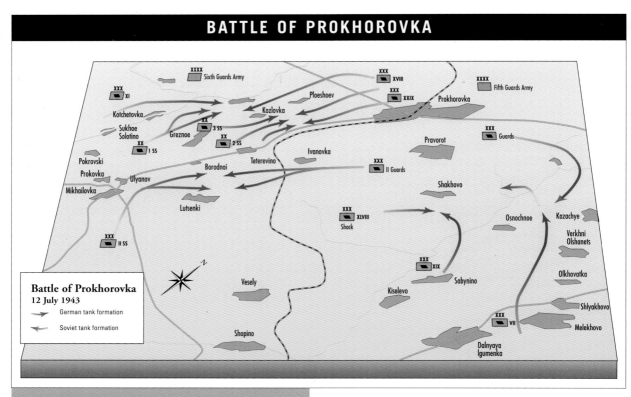

Battle of Prokhorovka
12 July 1943

→ German tank formation

← Soviet tank formation

12 July 1943: Prokhorovka

The tank battles fought through the duration of Operation Citadel culminated in the celebrated action near the small town of Prokhorovka. On 10 July, the SS vanguard, led by *Totenkopf*, tore through the Soviet First Tank Army, over-running the 71st Guards Rifle Division. Stalin sat at his desk in the Kremlin day and night, demanding hourly situation reports. He consented to the release of the Fifth Guards Tank Army and the Fifth Guards Army from the reserve: they moved up, ready to counterattack. Here, they encountered the Germans in the largest and most bloody tank action of the whole battle, which can best be described as a tactical loss but an operational draw for the Soviets. The Fifth Guards Tank Army did not achieve its mission of destroying the SS panzers, but they did stop the German advance.

nights, his men advanced barely 10km (6 miles). Operation Citadel was more successful in the south. Hoth's panzers and Kempf's motorized infantry faced the Sixth Guards Army and the Seventh Guards Army.

At the beginning, the SS panzer corps smashed through each line of defence. The tank battles reached their climax at the village of Prokhorovka.

Even as the Kursk battles were reaching their climax, the attention of the German High Command was drawn to what was happening thousands of miles away, in Sicily, where Anglo–American forces had landed on 9 July.

On 12 July, Army Group Centre was attacked by Soviet forces. The ground won at such terrible cost had to be abandoned as Ninth Army pulled back to defend its own flank. As the Soviets counterattacked at Prokhorovka, Hitler summoned Field Marshals Manstein and Kluge to Rastenburg. Kluge reported that Army Group Centre could not maintain the offensive: Ninth Army had suffered 20,000 casualties in a week and the Soviets counteroffensive was so powerful that Orel might be lost. Manstein pleaded that if he committed his reserves to one more effort, he might break through to Kursk. Hitler was not convinced. He called off Operation Citadel and ordered that they go over to the defensive and contain the Soviet drive on Orel.

Army Group A: the Crimea

Following Stalingrad, Army Group A mounted an expertly conducted fighting retreat from the Caucasus, where it was in danger of being cut off by the advancing Soviets, back to the Don and the Crimea.

Although the German assault on the Caucasus in 1942 had originally gone well, offensive operations of First Panzer Army and Seventeenth Army had bogged down at the end of impossibly long supply lines. After the Soviets trapped Paulus's German Sixth Army in Stalingrad, the Soviet general staff planned an ambitious winter campaign of codenamed Saturn.

Late in December, after Manstein's Army Group Don was unable to break the siege of Stalingrad, it became clear that Army Group A would have to retreat from the North Caucasus.

On 28 December, Manstein had to order his forces back from the front to avoid encirclement himself. The Soviets smashed the Hungarians on the Don River on 16 January, opening a 322km (200-mile) gap in the German lines. This allowed the Soviets to threaten Army Group A and the remains of Army Group Don.

Ordered to withdraw

Hitler finally had to admit that serious withdrawals had to be ordered in order to save his forces. Units of Army Group Don held open Rostov to allow Army Group A to retreat.

Kleist's northern flank – over 1000km (621 miles) long – was still protected by the desperate resistance of the encircled Sixth Army. Kleist's forces were making their way back across the Don at Rostov when Paulus at last surrendered. Had Paulus surrendered three weeks earlier, Kleist's escape would have been impossible.

Soviet attack

In January, two Soviet armies under Generals Vatutin and Golikov had crossed the Don upstream from Serafimovich and were thrusting southwestwards to the Donets between Kamensk and Kharkov: Vatutin's forces, having crossed the Donets at Izyum, took Lozovaya Junction on 11 February; Golikov's took Kharkov five

days later. Further to the north, a third Soviet army, under General Ivan Danilovich Chernyakhovsky, had initiated a drive westwards from Voronezh on 2 February and had retaken Kursk on 8 February. Thus, the Germans had to retreat from all the territory that they had taken in their great summer offensive of 1942. The Caucasus returned to Soviet hands.

Germans escape

A sudden thaw supervened to hamper the Red Army's transport of supplies and reinforcements across the swollen rivers. With Soviet momentum slowed, the Germans made good their retreat to the Dniepr along the Black Sea coast and were able, in February 1943, to mount a counteroffensive of their own at Kharkov.

One formation that did not retreat was the Seventeenth Army. Crammed into a small pocket opposite the Kerch peninsula, the army was ordered to hold the Kuban Bridgehead.

By October 1943, the Seventeenth Army had been forced to retreat from the Kuban Bridgehead across the Kerch Strait to Crimea. The Red Army pushed back the *Wehrmacht* in southern Ukraine, eventually cutting off the land-based connection of Seventeenth Army through the Perekop Isthmus in November 1943.

Last stand in the Crimea

The Soviets began landing troops in Kerch Strait by the end of 1943 and, together with an attack at the Perekop Isthmus, forced Seventeenth Army to fall back to Sevastopol by 10 April 1944. The OKW intended to hold Sevastopol as a fortress, as the Red Army had done during the first battle for the Crimea in 1941–42.

The rapid movement of the Red Army, together with inadequate preparation of the defences of Sevastopol, made this impossible, and on 9 May 1944, not even one month after the start of the battle, Sevastopol fell.

Eastern Front: 1943–44

1944 was a year of retreat for the German armies in the Soviet Union. The Red Army had learned some harsh lessons at the hands of the *Wehrmacht*, and from the Winter of 1942, Soviet forces began pushing the Germans back from the Black Sea to Leningrad.

By mid-September 1943, the whole Soviet front from Smolensk down to the Black Sea was on the move. Within days, Central Front had swept through Sevsk as far as Konotop, Voronezh Front was through Piryatin, and Steppe Front had reached Poltava. Southwest and Southern Fronts between them had cleared all enemy forces from the Donets Basin and were within striking distance of the Dnieper at Zaporozhe.

Kiev retaken

By the end of September, the Red Army had reached the Dnieper north and south of Kiev. On 6 November, Kiev was once more in Soviet hands. The Soviets in the south then paused, while the Red Army retook some key towns held by Army Group Centre to the north.

The front continued to roll westwards during November as the Red Army recaptured Zhitomir and Korosten. Manstein managed to ignore Hitler's demands for immediate action. The Soviets became overextended as their mechanized units outran their supply columns. Their air support diminished because it took time to repair captured airfields. When Manstein did counterattack, he retook both towns and re-established the direct rail link with Army Group Centre.

However, a Soviet breakthrough at Cherkassy, combined with Hitler's refusal to retreat from the one stretch of the Dnieper still under German control, left a dangerously exposed salient jutting into Soviet territory by the end of a momentous year.

New offensives

January 1944 brought no respite for Hitler's hard-pressed Eastern legions. Since the Battle of Kursk the previous summer, the Red Army had been inexorably driving westwards, all along the thousands of kilometres of front. Apart from a few local counterattacks, there was little that the German Army could do but fall back.

It was outnumbered and outgunned. All it could hope for was that their long supply lines would eventually force the Soviets to halt and regroup. When that time came, the *Wehrmacht* might be able to use its superior skill to change the situation.

Rejuvenated Soviet Army

But German advantages in training had been worn away by the long, hard battles of 1943. The Red Army of 1944 was vastly more capable than it had been the year before, and its commanders showed little inclination to stop fighting just to suit the *Wehrmacht* High Command.

GERMAN AND SOVIET FIGHTING VEHICLES (1941–45)			
Date	Battle	German	Soviet
June 1941	*Barbarossa*	3600	15,000+
October 1941	Typhoon	1700	1000
January 1942	Central Front	1450	2000
August 1942	*Fall Blau*	3000	1250
November 1942	Rzhev	1200	3375
March 1943	Kharkov	350	200
July 1943	Kursk	2700	3600
January 1944	Ukraine	2200	2000
June 1944	*Bagration*	553	4080
September 1944	Narva	60	450
Feb–March 1945	Vistula	1150	4529
April 1945	Berlin	c.1000	6250

PANZER REGIMENT, TYPE 44 PANZER DIVISION

On 1 August 1944, *Wehrmacht* panzer divisions underwent a complete reorganization into the so-called 'Type 44 Panzer Division'. On paper, a panzer division of the period included one panzer regiment of two battalions; the first battalion included four companies of 17–22 PzKpfw V Panther tanks each, while the second battalion possessed four companies of 17–22 PzKpfw IVs. However, these were nominal strengths: since the beginning of 1942, the German Army had never been capable of replenishing the personnel losses sustained on the Eastern Front. The mobility of its support units, which had always been limited by a shortage of vehicles, was now severely reduced by the attrition of five years of warfare. Additionally, combat units were persistently short of manpower, weapons and munitions.

Company HQ (sample company)

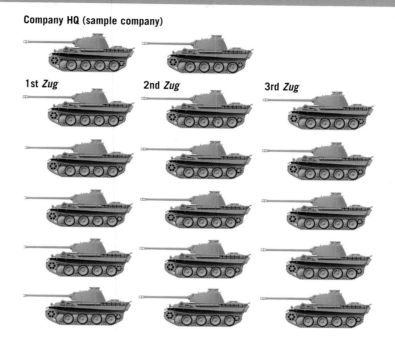

1st *Zug* 2nd *Zug* 3rd *Zug*

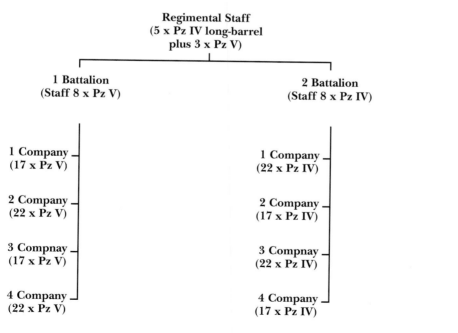

Regimental Staff
(5 x Pz IV long-barrel
plus 3 x Pz V)

1 Battalion
(Staff 8 x Pz V)

2 Battalion
(Staff 8 x Pz IV)

1 Company
(17 x Pz V)

2 Company
(22 x Pz V)

3 Compnay
(17 x Pz V)

4 Company
(22 x Pz V)

1 Company
(22 x Pz IV)

2 Company
(17 x Pz IV)

3 Compnay
(22 x Pz IV)

4 Company
(17 x Pz IV)

Army Group North: 1944

Forced to retreat from Leningrad in February 1944, Army Group North fell back to prepared defences in Estonia known as the Panther Line. It lost contact with Army Group Centre after the Soviet summer offensive of 1944, Operation *Bagration*.

On Army Group North's front, there was barely any fighting at all until January 1944, when out of nowhere Volkhov and Second Baltic Fronts struck. In a lightning campaign, Leningrad was liberated and Novgorod was recaptured; by February, the Red Army had reached the borders of Estonia after a 121km (75-mile) advance.

The Soviet offensive was met by SS-*Obergruppenfüher* Felix Steiner's III (Germanic) SS-Panzer Corps. Soon, Army Group North was falling back to new positions around the Narva River in Estonia. The Narva provided a natural chokepoint between the Northern end of Lake Peipus and the Baltic.

Defending the Narva crossings

This position, known as the Panther Line, was where Army Group North's commander, Georg von Küchler, wanted to set up his defence. Hitler refused, and replaced von Küchler with *Generalfeldmarschall* Walter Model as commander of Army Group North.

Model agreed with von Küchler; however, being one of Hitler's favourites, he also was allowed more freedom. Using this to his advantage, Model managed to fall back and begin establishing a line along the River Narwa, with a strong bridgehead on the eastern bank. This appeased Hitler, and also followed the German standard operating procedure for defending a river line.

Battle of the European SS

The Battle of the Narva, in which the European volunteer units serving with the SS played a major part, lasted until July 1944. Outnumbered, the Germans held off everything that the Soviets could throw at them until the launch of Operation *Bagration* against Army Group Centre in June threatened to cut off the entire Army Group.

By July 1944, Army Group North began withdrawing from Narva to a secondary defensive lines 25km

(15.5 miles) due west of the River Narva, known as the Tannenberg Positions. The Tannenberg defensive lines were anchored by a series of three hills, running west to east. In heavy fighting, the SS and Army troops were able to hold out against overwhelming odds. However, the sheer numbers of Soviet troops began to tell and, eventually, the battered German formations were over-run.

By September, the III (Germanic) SS-Armored Corps had withdrawn from Estonia and started defensive positions in Latvia. There, it fought desperate battles for the defense of the Latvian capital, Riga.

Trapped in the Courland

By now, the Soviet destruction of Army Group Centre had left the Red Army free to drive for the Baltic. By 12 October, Riga had been taken, and Army Group North had been forced into defensive positions on the Courland peninsula.

January–October 1944

The Soviets partially raised the siege of Leningrad with Operation *Iskra* (Spark) in January 1943. However, Army Group North remained in position to threaten the city for another year, until the launch of the Soviet Army's Leningrad-Novgorod Operation in January and February 1944. On the night of 13 January, General Govarov's Leningrad Front struck at the German forces around the city. On 20 January, the Volkhov Front took Novgorod after flank attacks to the south across the frozen waters of Lake Ilmen. Over the next nine months, Army Group North fought a series of delaying actions, most notably on the River Narva when a vastly inferior German force held up the Soviets until Army Group North could fall back to the Tannenburg Line. On 14 September, a huge offensive was launched by the Soviet 1st, 2nd and 3rd Baltic Fronts, isolating the bulk of Army Group North in the Courland.

LENINGRAD AND THE KARELIAN FRONT

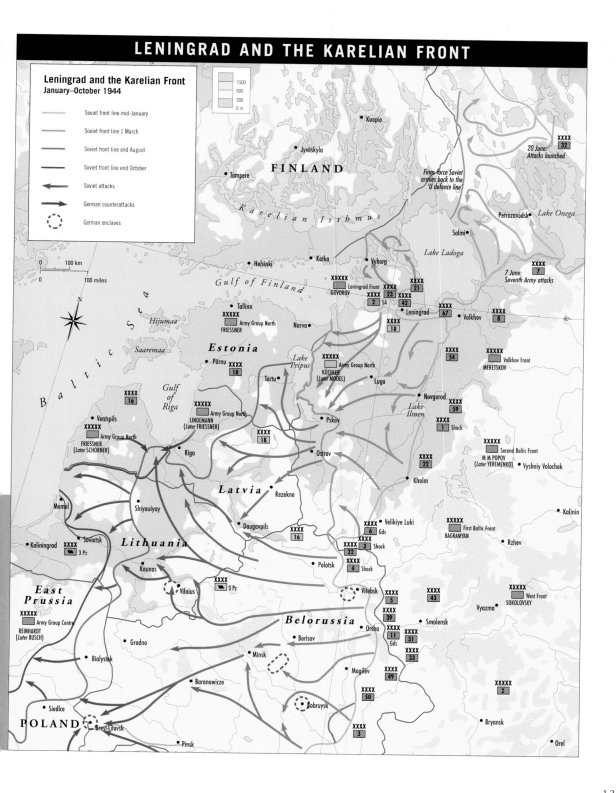

Leningrad and the Karelian Front
January–October 1944

1500
600
300
0 m

——— Soviet front line mid-January

——— Soviet front line 1 March

——— Soviet front line end August

——— Soviet front line end October

→ Soviet attacks

→ German counterattacks

⭘ German enclaves

100 km

0

100 miles

0

FINLAND

Kuopio

Jyväskylä

Tampere

Karelian Isthmus

20 June:
Attacks launched

XXXX
32

Finns force Soviet
armies back to the
'U' defence line

Petrozavodsk • *Lake Onega*

Salmi •

7 June:
Seventh Army attacks

XXXX
7

Helsinki •   Kotka •   Vyborg •

Lake Ladoga

Gulf of Finland

XXXXX Leningrad Front
GOVOROV

XXXX
23

XXXX
21

XXXX 2 SA

XXXX
42

Leningrad

XXXX
67

• Volkhov

XXXX
8

• Tallinn

XXXXX Army Group North
FRIESSNER

Narva •

XXXX
18

Baltic Sea

Hijumaa

Saaremaa

Estonia

• Pärnu

XXXX
18

Tartu •

*Lake
Peipus*

XXXXX Army Group North
KÜCHLER
(*Later* MODEL)

• Luga

XXXX
54

XXXXX Volkhov Front
MERETSKOV

*Gulf
of
Riga*

XXXX
16

XXXXX Army Group North
LINDEMANN
(*Later* FRIESSNER)

• Pskov

• Novgorod

*Lake
Ilmen*

XXXX
59

XXXX
1 Shock

• Ventspils

XXXXX Army Group North
FRIESSNER
(*Later* SCHÖRNER)

• Riga

XXXX
18

• Ostrov

XXXX
22

XXXXX Second Baltic Front
M M POPOV
(*Later* YEREMENKO)

• Vyshniy Volochek

Latvia • Rezekne

• Kholm

Memel •

• Shiyauiyay

Daugavpils •

XXXX
16

XXXX Velikiye Luki
6 Gds

XXXXX First Baltic Front
BAGRAMYAN

• Kalinin

• Rzhev

• Kaliningrad

XXXX
3 Pz

Sovietsk

Lithuania

Kaunas •

• Polotsk

XXXX 3 Shock
22

XXXX
4 Shock

XXXX
3 Pz

• Vilnius

• Vitebsk

XXXX
5

XXXX
43

XXXXX West Front
SOKOLOVSKY

Vyazma •

*East
Prussia*

XXXXX Army Group Centre
REINHARDT
(*Later* BUSCH)

• Grodno

• Bialystok

• Minsk

Belorussia

• Borisov

Orsha •

XXXX
39

XXXX 11
Gds

XXXX
31

• Smolensk

XXXX
33

Mogilёv •

XXXX
49

XXXXX
2

• Baranowicze

• Bobruysk

• Bryansk

• Siedlce

POLAND • Brest-Litovsk

XXXX
50

XXXX
3

• Pinsk

• Orel

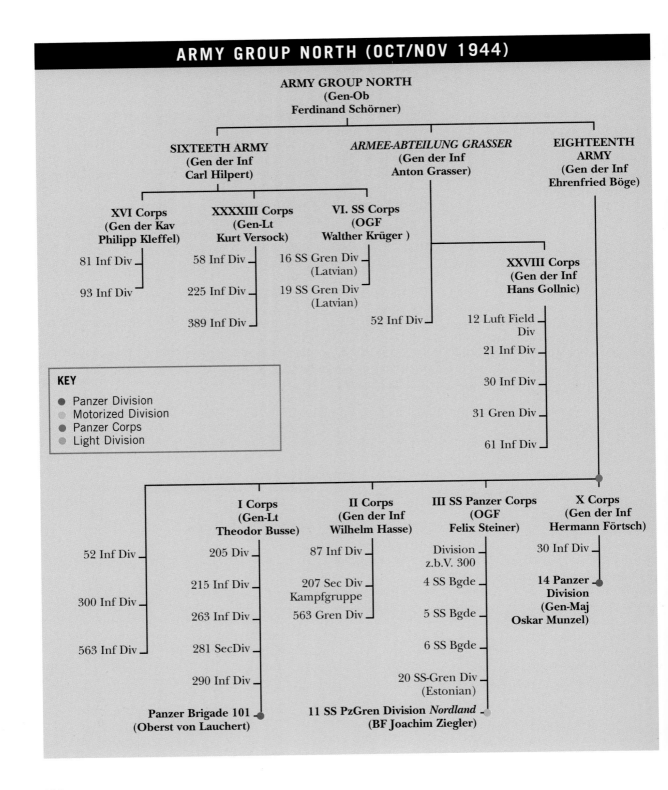

ARMY GROUP NORTH (OCT/NOV 1944)

ARMY GROUP NORTH
(Gen-Ob
Ferdinand Schörner)

SIXTEETH ARMY
(Gen der Inf
Carl Hilpert)

ARMEE-ABTEILUNG GRASSER
(Gen der Inf
Anton Grasser)

EIGHTEENTH
ARMY
(Gen der Inf
Ehrenfried Böge)

XVI Corps
(Gen der Kav
Philipp Kleffel)

XXXXIII Corps
(Gen-Lt
Kurt Versock)

VI. SS Corps
(OGF
Walther Krüger)

XXVIII Corps
(Gen der Inf
Hans Gollnic)

81 Inf Div

93 Inf Div

58 Inf Div

225 Inf Div

389 Inf Div

16 SS Gren Div
(Latvian)

19 SS Gren Div
(Latvian)

52 Inf Div

12 Luft Field
Div

21 Inf Div

30 Inf Div

31 Gren Div

61 Inf Div

KEY
- Panzer Division
- Motorized Division
- Panzer Corps
- Light Division

I Corps
(Gen-Lt
Theodor Busse)

II Corps
(Gen der Inf
Wilhelm Hasse)

III SS Panzer Corps
(OGF
Felix Steiner)

X Corps
(Gen der Inf
Hermann Förtsch)

52 Inf Div

300 Inf Div

563 Inf Div

205 Div

215 Inf Div

263 Inf Div

281 SecDiv

290 Inf Div

87 Inf Div

207 Sec Div
Kampfgruppe

563 Gren Div

Division
z.b.V. 300

4 SS Bgde

5 SS Bgde

6 SS Bgde

20 SS-Gren Div
(Estonian)

30 Inf Div

14 Panzer
Division
(Gen-Maj
Oskar Munzel)

Panzer Brigade 101
(Oberst von Lauchert)

11 SS PzGren Division *Nordland*
(BF Joachim Ziegler)

Army Group Centre

From 1942 to 1944, the Red Army made little progress in attacking the German Army Group Centre, forcing the Germans back slowly on a broad front at the cost of horrendous casualties. However, in the summer of 1944, that was about to change.

By the early summer of 1944, the Red Army was the biggest land force ever put into the field of battle. Close to 20 million Russian men and women were wearing service uniform, and although both the Red Air Force and the Red Navy were enormous by any standards, the bulk of the fighting forces were in the Red Army.

The Allied invasion of Normandy on 6 June 1944 brought about what the German generals had most feared – an all-out war of attrition on two fronts. However, although air units were sent westwards, the bulk of the German Army in the East remained, with about half of its strength being kept on the Ukrainian Front, where the heaviest attacks of the spring had occurred.

The largest concentration of German force in the east, Army Group Centre consisted of three infantry armies and one panzer army under Field Marshal Busch, who had replaced the injured Kluge in October 1943. He was a reasonably competent commander but had been promoted far beyond his ability and was a devoted follower of Hitler, who appreciated the General's brutality as well as his habit of obeying every one of the Führer's orders without question.

In the winter of 1943–44, Busch had managed to hold the line in Army Group Centre. He even mounted some reasonably successful local counterattacks. But he had neither the force nor the strength of will to do what was necessary when the full force of the Red Army was thrown at him in June.

Operation *Bagration*

They were in the wrong place. On 22 June 1944, three years to the day after *Barbarossa* had been launched, the great Soviet Summer Offensive opened – in the centre of the front, not in the south.

From Velikie Luki in the north around a huge arc to Kovel below the Pripet Marshes, the artillery of four Red Army fronts – 15 armies – crashed out, while the aircraft

OPERATION *BAGRATION* (JUNE 1944)		
	Soviet Strength	**German Strength**
Troops	1,700,000	800,000
Artillery	24,000	9500
Tanks	4080	553
Aircraft	6334	839

of four air armies flew overhead. Infantry and tanks – increased to more than 60 per cent more than their normal establishment – moved out of their concentration areas into the attack. Their objective was simple: to obliterate Army Group Centre.

Slaughter of Army Group Centre

The Red Army aimed to smash through the German Army and all of its defences. By destroying the centre, they would also force the German and Finnish Armies to the north and the German, Romanian and Hungarian Armies to the south to withdraw.

Within a week, the torrent of men and tanks had cut off, then captured, Germany's three main bastions in the east – Vitebsk, Mogilev and Bobruisk.

Vitebsk in the north was isolated by converging attacks from Bagramyan's First Baltic Front and Chernyakovsky's Third Belorussian Front. Mogilev was attacked by Zakharov's Secondnd Belorussian Front. Bobruisk was the target for Rokossovsky's First Belorussian Front.

Rokossovsky's forces had moved massively but secretly over countless small rivers and lakes at night, attacking out of marshy ground that their opponents had considered impassable. Parts of two panzer corps were cut off and bombed into disintegration, and then Rokossovsky's armies took Bobruisk and 24,000 prisoners. On 28 June, *Generaloberst* Busch was relieved of his command, and Model, the 'Führer's Fireman', was

ARMY GROUP CENTRE (JUNE 1944)

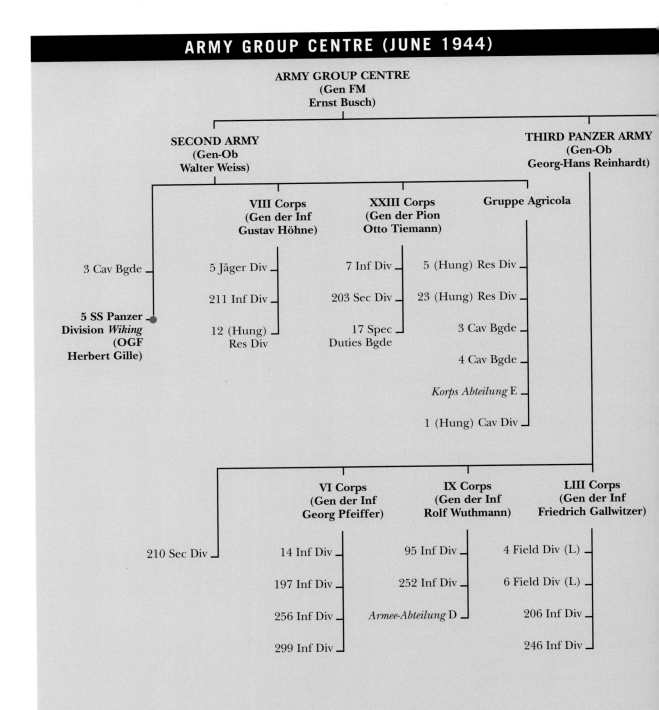

ARMY GROUP CENTRE
(Gen FM
Ernst Busch)

SECOND ARMY
(Gen-Ob
Walter Weiss)

THIRD PANZER ARMY
(Gen-Ob
Georg-Hans Reinhardt)

VIII Corps
(Gen der Inf
Gustav Höhne)

XXIII Corps
(Gen der Pion
Otto Tiemann)

Gruppe Agricola

3 Cav Bgde

5 SS Panzer
Division *Wiking*
(OGF
Herbert Gille)

5 Jäger Div

211 Inf Div

12 (Hung)
Res Div

7 Inf Div

203 Sec Div

17 Spec
Duties Bgde

5 (Hung) Res Div

23 (Hung) Res Div

3 Cav Bgde

4 Cav Bgde

Korps Abteilung E

1 (Hung) Cav Div

VI Corps
(Gen der Inf
Georg Pfeiffer)

IX Corps
(Gen der Inf
Rolf Wuthmann)

LIII Corps
(Gen der Inf
Friedrich Gallwitzer)

210 Sec Div

14 Inf Div

197 Inf Div

256 Inf Div

299 Inf Div

95 Inf Div

252 Inf Div

Armee-Abteilung D

4 Field Div (L)

6 Field Div (L)

206 Inf Div

246 Inf Div

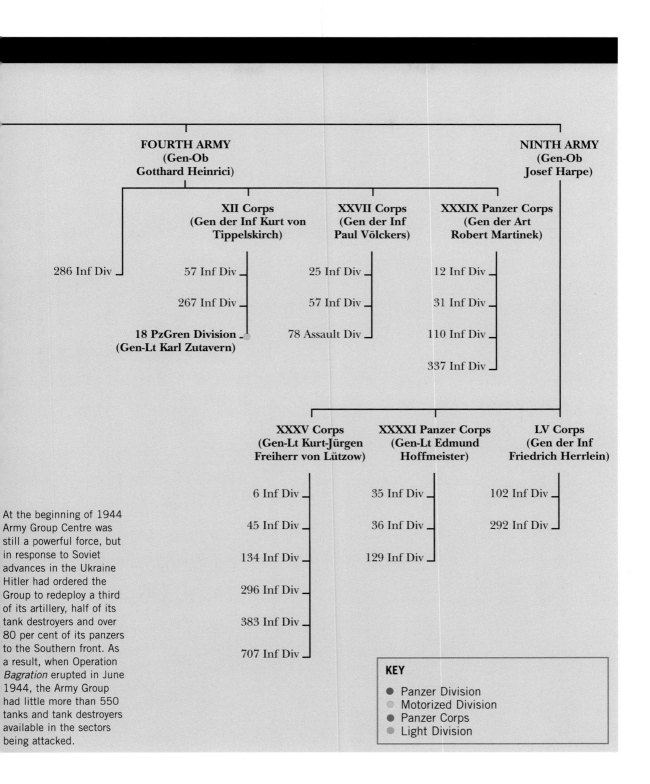

FOURTH ARMY
(Gen-Ob
Gotthard Heinrici)

NINTH ARMY
(Gen-Ob
Josef Harpe)

XII Corps
(Gen der Inf Kurt von
Tippelskirch)

XXVII Corps
(Gen der Inf
Paul Völckers)

XXXIX Panzer Corps
(Gen der Art
Robert Martinek)

286 Inf Div

57 Inf Div

267 Inf Div

18 PzGren Division
(Gen-Lt Karl Zutavern)

25 Inf Div

57 Inf Div

78 Assault Div

12 Inf Div

31 Inf Div

110 Inf Div

337 Inf Div

XXXV Corps
(Gen-Lt Kurt-Jürgen
Freiherr von Lützow)

XXXXI Panzer Corps
(Gen-Lt Edmund
Hoffmeister)

LV Corps
(Gen der Inf
Friedrich Herrlein)

6 Inf Div

45 Inf Div

134 Inf Div

296 Inf Div

383 Inf Div

707 Inf Div

35 Inf Div

36 Inf Div

129 Inf Div

102 Inf Div

292 Inf Div

At the beginning of 1944 Army Group Centre was still a powerful force, but in response to Soviet advances in the Ukraine Hitler had ordered the Group to redeploy a third of its artillery, half of its tank destroyers and over 80 per cent of its panzers to the Southern front. As a result, when Operation *Bagration* erupted in June 1944, the Army Group had little more than 550 tanks and tank destroyers available in the sectors being attacked.

KEY
- Panzer Division
- Motorized Division
- Panzer Corps
- Light Division

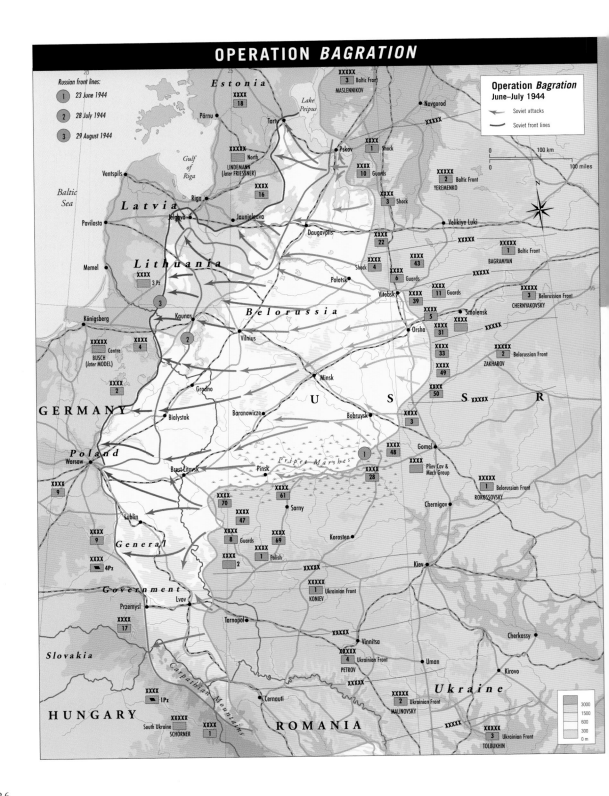

OPERATION *BAGRATION*

Russian front lines:

1 23 June 1944

2 28 July 1944

3 29 August 1944

Operation *Bagration*
June–July 1944

Soviet attacks

Soviet front lines

0   100 km
0   100 miles

Estonia

XXXXX 3 Baltic Front
MASLENNIKOV

Lake Peipus

Novgorod

XXXX 18

Pärnu

Tartu

XXXXX Baltic Front
YEREMENKO

Pskov

XXXX 1 Shock

XXXX 10 Guards

Ventspils

Gulf of Riga

XXXX 3 Shock

XXXXX 2 Baltic Front

Baltic Sea

Latvia

Riga

Jelgava

Jaunjelgava

Daugavpils

XXXX 22

Velikiye Luki

XXXXX 1 Baltic Front
BAGRAMYAN

Pavilosta

Memel

Lithuania

XXXX 3 Pz

Shock XXXX 4

XXXX 43

XXXX 6 Guards

Polotsk

Belorussia

Vitebsk

XXXX 39

XXXX 11 Guards

XXXXX 3 Belorussian Front
CHERNYAKOVSKY

Königsberg

Kaunas

Vilnius

Smolensk

XXXX 5

XXXX 31

Orsha

XXXXX Centre
BUSCH
(later MODEL)

XXXX 4

XXXX 33

XXXXX 2 Belorussian Front
ZAKHAROV

XXXX 2

Grodno

Minsk

XXXX 49

XXXX 50

GERMANY

Bialystok

Baranowicze

Bobruysk

U   S   S   R

XXXX 3

Poland

Warsaw

Brest-Litovsk

Pinsk

Pripet Marshes

XXXX 1

XXXX 48

Gomel

XXXX Pliev Cav & Mech Group

XXXX 9

XXXX 28

XXXX 70

XXXX 61

Sarny

Chernigov

XXXXX 1 Belorussian Front
ROKOSSOVSKY

Lublin

XXXX 9

General

XXXX 47

XXXX 8 Guards

XXXX 69

Korosten

XXXX 4Pz

XXXX 2

XXXX 1 Polish

Kiev

Government

Przemysl

Lvov

XXXXX 1 Ukrainian Front
KONIEV

Tarnopol

Cherkassy

XXXX 17

XXXXX Vinnitsa

XXXXX 4 Ukrainian Front
PETROV

Uman

Slovakia

Kirovo

XXXXX 2 Ukrainian Front
MALINOVSKY

Ukraine

XXXX 1Pz

Cernauti

HUNGARY

XXXXX South Ukraine
SCHÖRNER

XXXX 1

ROMANIA

XXXXX 3 Ukrainian Front
TOLBUKHIN

3000
1500
600
300
0 m

June–July 1944

The Soviet summer offensive of 1944 was the most decisive campaign of World War II. Launched three years to the day after the German invasion, and three weeks after the Western Allies landed in Normandy, the largest military force in history, totalling more than 2.7 million men, smashed into the German front lines. More than 1 million men were thrown at Army Group Centre alone.

By the end of August, Soviet forces were in the Baltic States, across the Polish border and about to cross into Romania. Army Group Centre had been annihilated. From the 97 German divisions and 13 separate brigades that had been in place in Army Group Centre or which had been rushed into action as reinforcements throughout the two-month operation, 17 divisions and three brigades were destroyed completely. Another 50 divisions lost between 60 and 70 per cent of their manpower.

given command of Army Group Centre in addition to Army Group Ukraine. Model quickly realized that there was little hope of countering the massive Soviet drive at Minsk, as he had planned. Instead, he used what

remaining strength he had to hold open escape routes to the west.

By 4 July, both Zakharov's men and Chernyakovsky's had driven forwards more than 200km (124 miles), leaving only one pocket of German resistance behind, which surrendered on 11 July 1944.

The momentum never flagged. Everywhere, the Germans were in full retreat, though they turned and struck back ferociously at times. Nevertheless, armies of the First Baltic Front forced the River Dvina crossing and took Polotsk within days.

It was Germany's worst disaster of the war – worse than Stalingrad. Twenty-eight divisions had been totally destroyed, and more than 350,000 men had been killed or captured.

Forced out of the Soviet Union

Brest-Litovsk fell to Rokossovsky on 28 July, and soon afterwards his forces had reached the River Bug north of Warsaw. On his left, Chuikov's Eighth Guards Army had stormed out of Kovel, capturing Lublin and reaching the River Vistula, which they crossed on 2 August. The Red Army was now fighting on Polish soil.

Army Group North Ukraine

Soviet deception measures meant that the Germans had no inkling that the main Soviet offensive of 1944 would be against Army Group Centre: the German High Command had expected the Red Army to attack further to the south.

Marshal Koniev's armies on the Ukrainian Front had not been involved at the start of the *Bagration* offensive. On 13 July, they drove forwards against very strong resistance from Army Group North Ukraine. This was where the *Wehrmacht* had expected the Soviet onslaught.

Model had been transferred from command of Army Group North Ukraine to Normandy and had been replaced by *Generaloberst* Josef Harpe.

German strength

On the face of it, Harpe commanded a powerful force.

Army Group North Ukraine included two panzer armies, the First and the Fourth. Attached to the First Panzer Army was the Hungarian Hungarian First Army.

However, Harpe could muster fewer than 500 tanks and assault guns. He had released units in the previous weeks in an attempt to help stop the collapse of Army Group Centre. His Army Group comprised around 370,000 men, and the reliability of the Hungarian forces under his command was questionable. The only positive was the presence of the 700 aircraft of *Luftflotte* IV, including the veteran air units of VIII *Fliegerkorps*.

Soviet juggernaut

The Soviet forces under Konev outnumbered the Germans considerably. The 1st Ukrainian Front could muster over 1,200,000 men, 2050 tanks, 16,000 guns and mortars, and more than 3250 aircraft. Additionally, the morale of Konev's troops was extremely high. They had been on the offensive for almost a year, and were now witnessing the collapse of Army Group Centre to their north.

The Soviet attack was to have two points. The first, aiming towards Rawa Ruska, was to be led by Third Guards, First Guards Tank and Thirteenth Armies. The second pincer was aimed at Lvov itself, and was to be led by Sixtieth, Thirty-Eighth, Third Guards Tank and Fourth Tank Armies. The Soviets achieved a massive superiority against the Germans by limiting their attacks to a front of 26km (16 miles). Konev had set up approximately 240 guns and mortars per kilometre of front.

Brody Pocket

Forty thousand Germans were surrounded near Brody. Under continued Soviet attacks, Harpe ordered his forces to fall back, abandoning the trapped XIII Corps. Under constant artillery and aerial bombardment, the beleaguered forces attempted several breakout attempts,

ARMY GROUP NORTH UKRAINE (MARCH 1944)

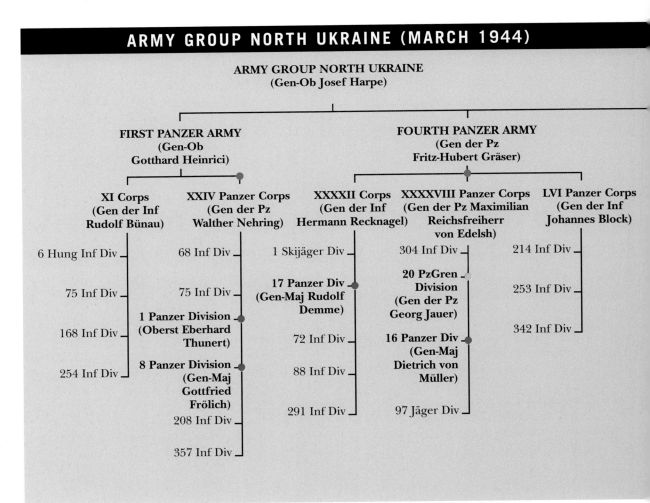

ARMY GROUP NORTH UKRAINE
(Gen-Ob Josef Harpe)

FIRST PANZER ARMY
(Gen-Ob
Gotthard Heinrici)

FOURTH PANZER ARMY
(Gen der Pz
Fritz-Hubert Gräser)

XI Corps
(Gen der Inf
Rudolf Bünau)

XXIV Panzer Corps
(Gen der Pz
Walther Nehring)

XXXXII Corps
(Gen der Inf
Hermann Recknagel)

XXXXVIII Panzer Corps
(Gen der Pz Maximilian
Reichsfreiherr
von Edelsh)

LVI Panzer Corps
(Gen der Inf
Johannes Block)

XI Corps	XXIV Panzer Corps	XXXXII Corps	XXXXVIII Panzer Corps	LVI Panzer Corps
6 Hung Inf Div	68 Inf Div	1 Skijäger Div	304 Inf Div	214 Inf Div
75 Inf Div	75 Inf Div	17 Panzer Div (Gen-Maj Rudolf Demme)	20 PzGren Division (Gen der Pz Georg Jauer)	253 Inf Div
168 Inf Div	1 Panzer Division (Oberst Eberhard Thunert)	72 Inf Div	16 Panzer Div (Gen-Maj Dietrich von Müller)	342 Inf Div
254 Inf Div	8 Panzer Division (Gen-Maj Gottfried Frölich)	88 Inf Div	97 Jäger Div	
	208 Inf Div	291 Inf Div		
	357 Inf Div			

but these were easily rebuffed by the Soviet armoured forces, and the Germans suffered heavy casualties.

On 22 July, a Soviet attack cut the pocket in two, and by nightfall almost all resistance had been eliminated. The scattered survivors broke up into small groups and attempted to break out. Few reached allied lines, but among them were 2000 Ukrainian volunteers of the SS *Galizien* Division. Before the battle, the division had numbered 15,000 men.

Retreat to Poland

Konev was elated at the unexpected success of the operation. Harpe's Army Group was falling back rapidly,

16TH PANZER DIVISION – PANZER STRENGTH (1944)					
Tank type	Pz IV	StuG	Pz V	Pz Bef	Pz IV/70
2nd Pz Rgt	7	37	10	1	10

Fourth Panzer Army to the River Vistula and First Panzer Army along with the First Hungarian Army to the area around Karpaty.

Rokossovsky's right-hand army drove straight to the Vistula, crossed it and formed a bridgehead at Sandomir. One tank army flanked Lvov to the north and another was thrown into a direct assault that led

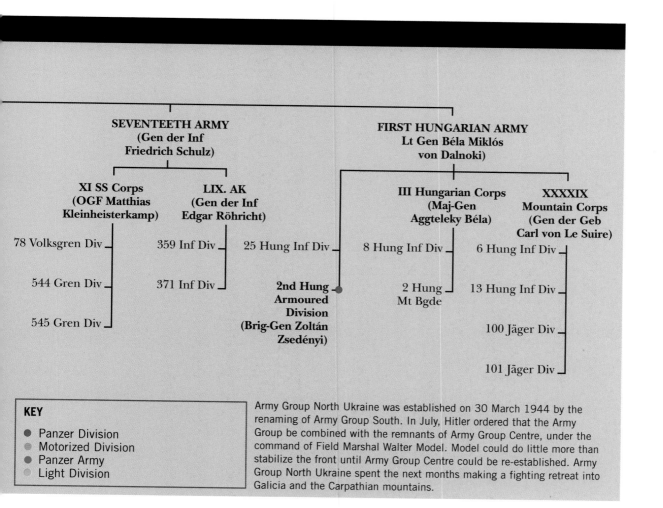

SEVENTEETH ARMY
(Gen der Inf Friedrich Schulz)

FIRST HUNGARIAN ARMY
Lt Gen Béla Miklós von Dalnoki)

XI SS Corps (OGF Matthias Kleinheisterkamp)

LIX. AK (Gen der Inf Edgar Röhricht)

III Hungarian Corps (Maj-Gen Aggteleky Béla)

XXXXIX Mountain Corps (Gen der Geb Carl von Le Suire)

78 Volksgren Div
359 Inf Div
25 Hung Inf Div
8 Hung Inf Div
6 Hung Inf Div

544 Gren Div
371 Inf Div
2nd Hung Armoured Division (Brig-Gen Zoltán Zsedényi)
2 Hung Mt Bgde
13 Hung Inf Div

545 Gren Div
100 Jäger Div

101 Jäger Div

KEY
- Panzer Division
- Motorized Division
- Panzer Army
- Light Division

Army Group North Ukraine was established on 30 March 1944 by the renaming of Army Group South. In July, Hitler ordered that the Army Group be combined with the remnants of Army Group Centre, under the command of Field Marshal Walter Model. Model could do little more than stabilize the front until Army Group Centre could be re-established. Army Group North Ukraine spent the next months making a fighting retreat into Galicia and the Carpathian mountains.

ARMY GROUP SOUTH UKRAINE (SEPTEMBER 1944)

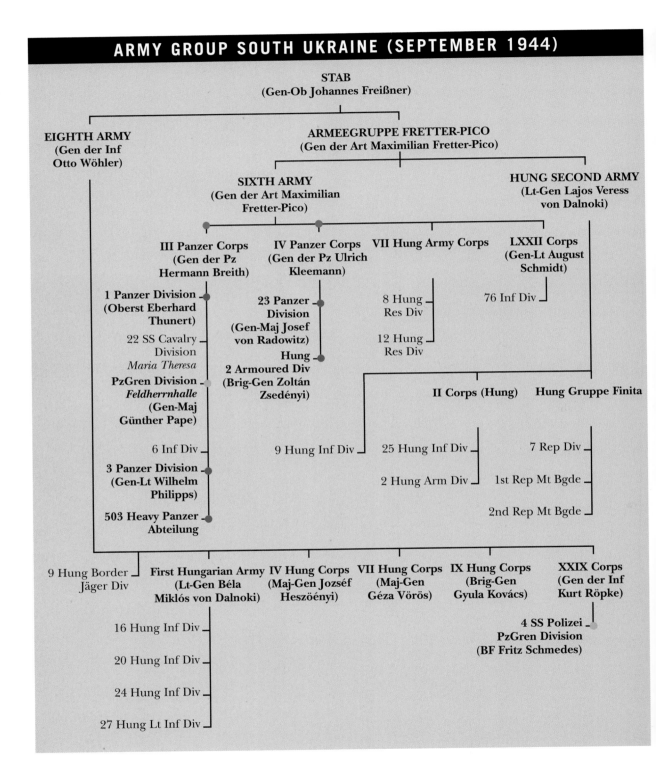

STAB
(Gen-Ob Johannes Freißner)

EIGHTH ARMY
(Gen der Inf
Otto Wöhler)

ARMEEGRUPPE FRETTER-PICO
(Gen der Art Maximilian Fretter-Pico)

SIXTH ARMY
(Gen der Art Maximilian
Fretter-Pico)

HUNG SECOND ARMY
(Lt-Gen Lajos Veress
von Dalnoki)

III Panzer Corps
(Gen der Pz
Hermann Breith)

IV Panzer Corps
(Gen der Pz Ulrich
Kleemann)

VII Hung Army Corps

LXXII Corps
(Gen-Lt August
Schmidt)

1 Panzer Division
(Oberst Eberhard
Thunert)

22 SS Cavalry
Division
Maria Theresa

PzGren Division
Feldherrnhalle
(Gen-Maj
Günther Pape)

6 Inf Div

3 Panzer Division
(Gen-Lt Wilhelm
Philipps)

503 Heavy Panzer
Abteilung

23 Panzer
Division
(Gen-Maj Josef
von Radowitz)

Hung
2 Armoured Div
(Brig-Gen Zoltán
Zsedényi)

9 Hung Inf Div

8 Hung
Res Div

12 Hung
Res Div

76 Inf Div

II Corps (Hung)

Hung Gruppe Finita

25 Hung Inf Div

2 Hung Arm Div

7 Rep Div

1st Rep Mt Bgde

2nd Rep Mt Bgde

9 Hung Border
Jäger Div

First Hungarian Army
(Lt-Gen Béla
Miklós von Dalnoki)

IV Hung Corps
(Maj-Gen Jozséf
Heszöényi)

VII Hung Corps
(Maj-Gen
Géza Vörös)

IX Hung Corps
(Brig-Gen
Gyula Kovács)

XXIX Corps
(Gen der Inf
Kurt Röpke)

4 SS Polizei
PzGren Division
(BF Fritz Schmedes)

16 Hung Inf Div

20 Hung Inf Div

24 Hung Inf Div

27 Hung Lt Inf Div

to the capture of the city on 27 July. German counterattacks were launched in an attempt to throw the Soviets back across the Vistula. Using the towns of Mielec and Tarnobrzeg on the eastern bank of the river as bases, these attacks caused heavy casualties to the Soviet forces. By mid-August, Konev's spearhead, the VI Guards Tank Corps had only 67 tanks remaining.

Panzers strike

The Germans launched a fierce counterattack with *Schwere Panzer Abteilung* 501 and 16th Panzer Division, totalling around 140 panzers, including 20 Tiger IIs. Despite being outnumbered, the Sixth Guards Army held the bridgehead, knocking out 10 Tiger IIs.

By 16 August, the German counterattacks were beginning to lose steam, and Rybalko, commander of the Bridgehead, was able to expand the Soviet controlled area by a depth of 120km (75 miles), capturing the city of Sandomierz. With both sides exhausted, the fighting died down.

The irreplaceable German losses in Belorussia and Ukraine, in conjunction with the Normandy landings and the attempt on Hitler's life on 20 July, spread despair throughout the upper ranks of the *Wehrmacht*'s command structure, and ensured that the Red Army would never be stopped.

Soviet advances

By the end of August, the Carpathians had been reached along their main length. The Red Army had now driven right through Poland and was closing on the prewar borders with Czechoslovakia and Hungary.

A *coup d'état* took place in Bucharest. Marshal Antonescu was overthrown. King Michael replaced him, the government sued for peace with the Allies, and two Romanian armies laid down their arms. Southern Bessarabia, the Danube delta and the Carpathian passes to the north lay open to the Soviet armies.

Romania and Bulgaria change sides

By the time Romania was in the process of being occupied by the Red Army, Bulgaria to the south was about to be invaded by one of Tolbukhin's armies driving down the Black Sea coast through Constanza.

Officers seized control in Sofia and welcomed the Red Army, which raced through the capital on 15 September. Collecting two Bulgarian armies, it pressed on to the Yugoslav border opposite Bor in the north and Skopje in the south.

In two months, the Soviet troops had advanced over 700km (435 miles), and the time had come to reorganize the supply lines. The advance had been costly – but had inflicted greater losses on the Germans.

Army Group A/Army Group South Ukraine

The campaigns in Belorussia and northern Ukraine had been catastrophic defeats for the *Wehrmacht*. However, to the south, another campaign was about to open, with perhaps more political motivation than military.

The Balkans were as great an attraction to Stalin as they had been for centuries to his imperial predecessors, the Romanovs. On 20 August, Malinovskys 2nd Ukrainian Front broke through the defences of Army Group Ukraine in the Pruth valley opposite Jassy. By 24 August, they were near Leovo, where they met two of Tolbukhin's mechanized corps, which had forced the lower Dniester into Bessarabia. They had isolated the German Sixth Army, reconstituted after Stalingrad, when political events intervened.

GERMAN AND RUSSIAN FIGHTING VEHICLES (1944–45)

Date	Sector	Formations German	Formations Russian	Tanks and Self-propelled Guns German	Tanks and Self-propelled Guns Russian
14 Jan 44	Leningrad	18 Army	Leningrad Fr.; Volkov Fr.	200	1200
30 Jan 44	Krivoi Rog/Nikopol	6 Army	3 Ukrainian Fr.; 4 Ukrainian Fr.	250	1400
4 Mar 44	River Pripet/Nikolaev	1 Pz Army; 4 Pz Army; 6 Army; 8 Army	1 Ukrainian Fr.; 2 Ukrainian Fr. 3 Uk Fr.	1300	6400
5 Mar 44	Uman/Kirovgrad	8 Army	2 Ukrainian Fr.	310	2400
8 April 44	Crimea	17 Army	4 Ukrainian Fr.; Ind. Cst. Army	70	900
22 Jun 44	Vitebsk/River Pripet	Army Group Centre	1 Baltic Fr.; 1 Byelo. Fr.; 2 Byelo. Fr.; 3 Byelo. Fr.	800	4100
12 July 44	Kovel/Tarnopol	A. Group N. Ukraine	1 Ukrainian Fr.	700	2040
18 July 44	Chelm/Rava Russkaya	4 Pz Army	3 Gds Army; 13 Army; 1 Gds Tk Army	174	550
19 July 44	Mariampol/Daugavpils	3 Pz Army	1 Baltic Fr.; 3 Byelo Fr. (parts)	95	1100
20 Aug 44	Bendory/Chernovitsy	Army Group S. Ukraine	2 Ukrainian Fr.; 3 Ukrainian Fr.	400	1880
14 Sep 44	Narva	Army Group North	Leningrad Fr.; 1 Baltic Fr.; 2 Baltic Fr.; 3 Baltic Fr.	400	3000
12 Jan 45	Warsaw/Tarnow	Army Group A	1 Byelo. Fr.; 1 Ukrainian Fr.	770	6460
13 Jan 45	East Prussia	Army Group Centre	2 Byelo. Fr.; 3 Byelo. Fr.	750	3300
1 Mar 45	Pomerania	3 Pz Army	1 Byelo. Fr. (part)	70	1600
16 Apr 45	Oder/Neisse confluence to Stettin	Army Group Vistula	1 Byelo. Fr.; 2 Byelo. Fr.	750	4100
26 Apr 45	River Neisse	4 Pz Army	1 Ukrainian Fr.	200	2150

By 8 September, Romania and Bulgaria had switched sides and Malinovsky's armies had joined Tolbukhin's. On 28 September, they moved forwards to link up with Marshal Tito's Partisans, while 2nd Ukrainian Front drove over the Romanian border north of the Danube.

Army Group South Ukraine

Army Group South Ukraine had been established in March 1944 by the renaming of the old Army Group A. In August and September 1944, it controlled Eighth Army and Army Group Fretter-Pico, which included the reconstituted Sixth Army and the Hungarian Second Army.

The Sixth Army had largely been destroyed in an encirclement during the Jassy-Kishinev Operation in September 1944, but this time the army HQ survived.

In October 1944, under the command of Maximilian Fretter-Pico, the Sixth Army returned the favour,

encircling and destroying three Soviet tank corps of Mobile Group Pliyev in the Battle of Debrecen.

The Soviets pushed on into Yugoslavia, but German Army Group F under Maximilian Weichs was holding open an escape route for both themselves and Army Group E under Field Marshal Alexander Löhr, rapidly retreating up through Greece.

The Germans put up such a stout resistance that it was 20 October before Belgrade was in Allied hands – and then only after the bulk of both German army groups had raced north through the gap.

They joined a hastily forming defence line in Hungary, where yet another attempt to desert the Axis had been foiled.

Meanwhile, Army Group South Ukraine had again been renamed, becoming Army Group South on 23 September 1944.

Army Group South

By 1944, Hungary was very much an unwilling ally of Germany. The Hungarian government was attempting to quit the war and was seen by Germany as reluctant to take sufficiently harsh measures against the Jews.

Germany needed Hungarian oil wells located around Lake Balaton. On 19 March 1944, the Germans launched Operation *Margarethe* and the German military entered Hungary. On 16 October 1944, the Germans, following an attempt by the Hungarian Regent Miklós Horthy to negotiate peace with the Allies, launched Operation *Panzerfaust* and forced Horthy to abdicate. Horthy and his government were replaced by members of the fascist Arrow Cross party.

The Soviets also knew the importance of the Lake Balaton oilfields, but their spearhead formations needed to recuperate after the headlong advances of the summer.

Hungarian battlefield

The autumn of 1944 found the troops of Marshal Malinowski's Second Ukranian Front sweeping through the Carpathian Mountains and onto the broad plains of Hungary. Behind them lay Romania and the wreckage of the German Sixth and Eighth Armies. Ahead of them lay Budapest and Vienna and the battered lines of German and Hungarian defenders. The men of the Red Army were confident of a quick and easy victory. Appearances were deceiving, however.

By the time Malinovksy's and Tolbukhin's armies had assembled for a drive up from the Lake Balaton area, not only were the Germans in some force throughout Hungary but Budapest in particular was strongly held and fortified.

German forces

The newly renamed Army Group South, which had retreated into Hungary, now consisted of the Sixth Army, the Third Hungarian Army and Army Group Wöhler, commanded by *General der Infanterie* Otto Wöhler. Wöhler's command included the Eighth German Army, First Hungarian Army, IX Hungarian Corps and the German XXIX Corps.

After the local defeat of Soviet armour by German panzer forces at the Battle of Debrecen, Marshal Malinovsky wished to regroup his men. Stalin, however, ordered him to capture the Hungarian capital immediately. This had a price: the siege of Budapest dragged on for months. The marshal, rightly fearing Stalin's wrath, justified the amount of time needed by claiming that the Hungarian component of the army defending the capital was much larger than was actually the case.

Budapest surrounded

By November, the Soviet armies were fighting their way north on each side of the Hungarian capital, slowly, implacably, but at great cost and with little of the energy and momentum of the previous months.

On 8 November, Red Army units reached Budapest. The city's defences held up the 3rd Ukrainian Front for six weeks, as the Sixth and Eighth Armies, backed by the retreating Army Groups E and F, fought hard.

On 25 December 1944, when divisions of the two Ukrainian fronts that had fought all the way from the Dniester met to the west of Budapest, it was decided that the 180,000 Germans and Hungarians encircled meant there was no chance of taking the city by storm.

Siege of Budapest

They therefore organized for a full-scale siege, calling up super-heavy artillery from hundreds of miles back in the Soviet Union, extra divisions from reserves, and supplies and food from wherever they could be found.

For the Germans, 1944 saw all hope of ultimate victory dashed. A few still believed in their Führer, but the Red Army had finally broken the once-proud German war machine. Everywhere, the Nazis were in retreat, crushed between the Allies in west and east. Defeat was inevitable – but the final assault did not come until 1945.

Sicily and Italy: 1943–45

Churchill described Italy as 'the soft underbelly of Europe', but the German forces that fought a stubborn defensive campaign up the Italian peninsula proved that the soft underbelly was, in fact, armoured in steel.

Sturmgeschutz assault guns move through Naples towards the Salerno invasion front in the autumn of 1943.

Hitler assumed that the Allies would follow up their victory in Tunisia with an immediate assault on his Italian ally. But the attack did not come, as the Allies debated at length over what to do next. The US Army wanted to land in western Europe; they and the Soviets demanded a 'second front' in 1943. Only the British insisted on attacking Italy. Eventually, the British view prevailed, and it was decided to mount an invasion of Sicily.

On paper, the Axis forces in Sicily appeared strong. The Italian Sixth Army could field 230,000 men and 1500 guns. However, the units were not motorized, and the difficult terrain and poor roads would hinder attempts by the defenders to concentrate their forces against any Allied thrust. However, the Italians were supported by two of the German Army's crack formations: the 15th Panzergrenadier Division and the *Hermann Göring* Division.

Hitler was confident of success. He felt that the Allies had virtually thrown away the war in the Mediterranean by neglecting to attack Sicily directly after their landings in North Africa.

Pessimistic generals

In stark contrast to the Führer's optimism, the prevailing view at German Army HQ was that it was only a matter of time before Sicily would have to be given up. There were too few German troops on the island, the Italian defenders were of extremely poor quality, and the *Luftwaffe* was in very poor shape.

On 10 July 1943, British and American forces invaded. The US Seventh Army, under General George S Patton, attacked through the west of Sicily. The British Eighth Army under General Bernard Montgomery was to drive up the east coast. It was the largest amphibious operation of the war to date. More than 160,000 men, 14,000 vehicles, 600 tanks and 1800 guns were landed from 2500 ships.

Resistance to the landings was mixed. Some Italian formations fought hard, but others melted away. The Germans, however, fought with exemplary professionalism. Divided into small *kampfgruppen* – battlegroups – German rearguards tenaciously held up vastly larger forces. Sharp counterattacks won local victories that kept the Allies off balance. German

ALBERT KESSELRING (1881–1960)

Born in Bavaria, he joined the German Army and served on the Western Front in World War I. A talented artillery and staff officer, he rose to the rank of *Generalmajor* under the *Reichswehr*. In 1933 he transferred to the clandestine German Air Force.

• He commanded *Luftflotte* 1 in Poland in 1939 and in Flanders in 1940. From December 1941 to March 1945, Kesselring was commander in chief of the Armed Forces in the Mediterranean area.

• Nicknamed 'Smiling Albert', Kesselring was a *Luftwaffe* Field Marshal who proved to be one of Germany's most capable land commanders. Under his command, the Germans held the Allies in a series of hard-fought defensive actions up the Italian peninsula.

On 6 May 1947, he was found guilty of ordering the execution of 335 Italian civilians, as a reprisal for an attack by Italian partisans, and condemned to death. The sentence was later commuted to life imprisonment and he was pardoned and released in 1952.

TENANT ARMY – PANZER STRENGTH (SEPT 1943)				
Tank type	Pz IV	StuG	Pz Bef	Flmmpz
16TH PANZER DIVISION				
2nd Pz Rgt	92	40	12	7
Tank type	PzKpfw III	Pz IV(kz)	Pz IV(ig)	Flmmpz
26TH PANZER DIVISION				
26th Pz Rgt	16	17	36	14
HERMANN GÖRING PANZER DIVISION				
Tank type	PzKpfw IV	JgPz IV	FlkPz 38	
HG Pz Rgt	64	31	8	

reinforcements also arrived, including Göring's elite
1st *Fallschirmjäger* division and the newly-formed
29th Panzergrenadier division.

While Montgomery's Eighth Army made slow progress
up the eastern side of the island, the dynamic General
Patton was sent on a roundabout route to the north
coast and then raced towards Messina.

Retreat from Sicily

Clearly, Sicily was lost, and Hitler conceded that only
a timely withdrawal would avoid a second Tunisia
debacle. Stubborn defensive fighting held the Allies
back until the beginning of August, when Kesselring
ordered the evacuation to begin. On 11 August, every
available vessel was employed to ferry the remaining
defenders to the mainland.

Despite ample warnings of German intentions, the
Allies failed to intervene; 40,000 German troops and

10 July–17 August 1943

The attack on Sicily took place on 10 July 1943,
on 26 beaches along 240km (150 miles) of Sicily's
southeastern coast. In place of the half-hearted resistance
expected, the Allied army faced fierce combat from the
German divisions on the island. As Montgomery's army
advanced north towards Messina, racing Patton's army,
which had burst through the centre of Sicily and was now
driving along the north coast, the Germans decided to
evacuate rather than make a last-ditch stand. Vigorous
German rearguards gave a foretaste of the bitter fighting
that was to come in Italy.

Invasion of Sicily
10 July–17 August 1943

- Allied landings with dates
- Axis counterattacks
- Allied front line 11 July
- Allied front line 15 July
- Allied front line 23 July
- Axis retreat line
- Axis retreat line
- Axis retreat line
- Axis retreat route
- Airfields constructed by Allies
- Allied airborne landings

INVASION OF SICILY

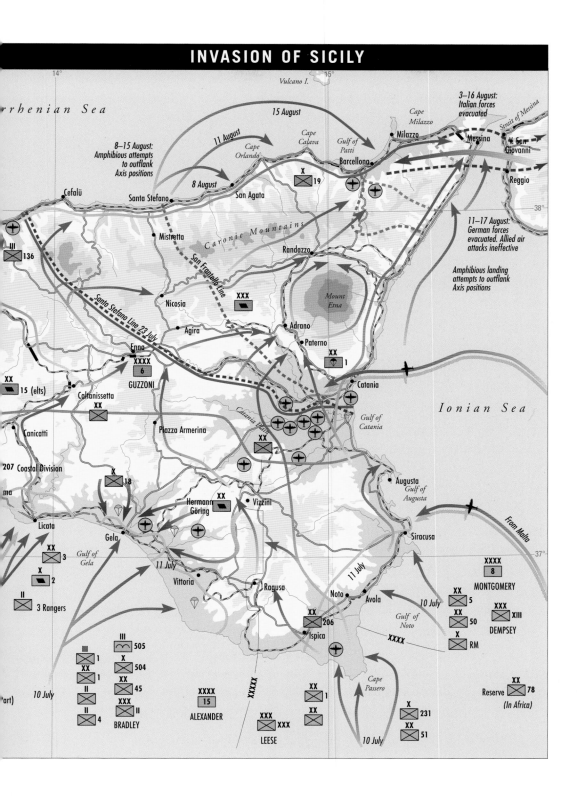

Tyrrhenian Sea

Vulcano I.

14°   15°

3–16 August:
Italian forces
evacuated

Cape
Milazzo

Strait of Messina

15 August

Cape
Calava

Gulf of
Patti

Milazzo

Messina

San
Giovanni

8–15 August:
Amphibious attempts
to outflank
Axis positions

11 August

Cape
Orlando

X 19

Barcellona

Reggio

8 August

San Agata

38°

Cefalü

Santa Stefano

11–17 August:
German forces
evacuated. Allied air
attacks ineffective

III 136

Mistretta

Caronic Mountains

Randazzo

Amphibious landing
attempts to outflank
Axis positions

San Frantello Line

Nicosia

XXX

Mount
Etna

Santo Stefano Line 23 July

Agira

Adrano

Paterno

XX 1

Enna

XXXX 6
GUZZONI

Catania

Ionian Sea

XX 15 (elts)

Caltanissetta

XX

Piazza Armerina

Catania Plain

XX

Canicatti

X 18

207 Coastal Division

Hermann
Göring

XX

Vizzini

Augusta
Gulf of
Augusta

ma

Licata

Gela

From Malta

XX 3

Gulf of
Gela

11 July

37°

X 2

Vittoria

Ragusa

Noto

11 July

Avola

10 July

Siracusa

XXXX 8
MONTGOMERY

II 3 Rangers

Cape
Passero

Gulf of
Noto

XX 5

XX 50

XXX XIII
DEMPSEY

X RM

XXXX

III 505

XX 206

Ispica

III 1

X 504

XX 1

XX 45

XXXX 15
ALEXANDER

XXXXX

XX 1

XXXX
Reserve XX 78

(In Africa)

XXX II

BRADLEY

X 231

II 4

10 July
(art)

XXX XXX

LEESE

XX 51

10 July

137

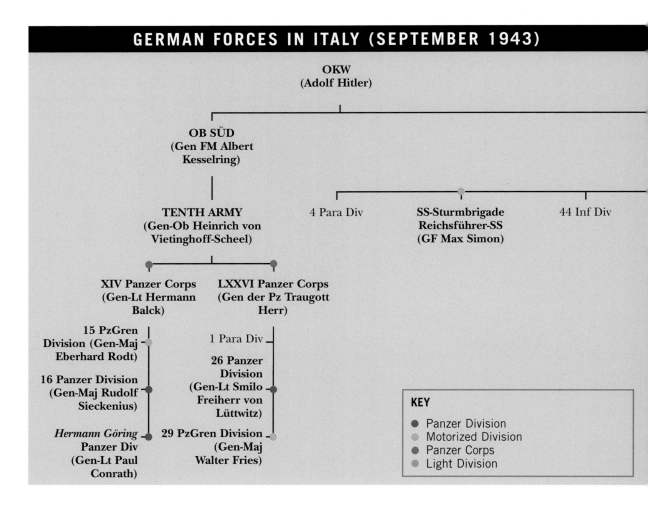

GERMAN FORCES IN ITALY (SEPTEMBER 1943)

OKW
(Adolf Hitler)

OB SÜD
(Gen FM Albert
Kesselring)

TENTH ARMY
(Gen-Ob Heinrich von
Vietinghoff-Scheel)

4 Para Div

SS-Sturmbrigade
Reichsführer-SS
(GF Max Simon)

44 Inf Div

XIV Panzer Corps
(Gen-Lt Hermann
Balck)

LXXVI Panzer Corps
(Gen der Pz Traugott
Herr)

15 PzGren
Division (Gen-Maj
Eberhard Rodt)

16 Panzer Division
(Gen-Maj Rudolf
Sieckenius)

Hermann Göring
Panzer Div
(Gen-Lt Paul
Conrath)

1 Para Div

26 Panzer
Division
(Gen-Lt Smilo
Freiherr von
Lüttwitz)

29 PzGren Division
(Gen-Maj
Walter Fries)

KEY
- Panzer Division
- Motorized Division
- Panzer Corps
- Light Division

their equipment got clean away. Some 60,000 Italian troops were also returned to the mainland, but their role in the war was almost over.

Germans take control
The Italian people had lost all enthusiasm for the war. Mussolini was overthrown, and the new Italian government sought an armistice. Some Italian troops were able to surrender to the Allies, but although their leaders slipped away to comfortable exile, the surrender was a disaster for most ordinary soldiers. Across Italy, the Balkans and Greece, German garrisons now turned on their erstwhile allies. Italian units were disarmed and hauled off to Germany for use as slave labour.

Salerno
In an attempt to bypass German forces in the south, Allied armies landed at Salerno near Naples on 9 September. The landings semed to go well at first, but the 16th Panzer Division held up any Allied advance. Within a week of the landing, the Germans had six panzer or panzergrenadier divisions opposing four Allied infantry divisions.

On 12 September, the Germans commenced an all-out attack and pushed the Allies so hard that General Mark Clark prepared orders for evacuation.

Eventually, the Allied beachhead was relieved by the British Eighth Army advance from the south of Italy, but the Germans witdrew in good order to the massive prepared defences of the Gustav Line, south of Rome.

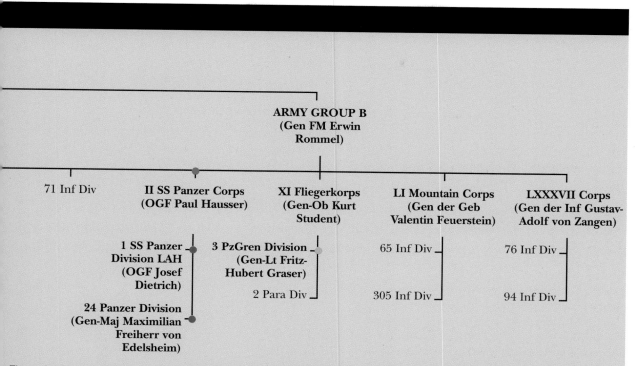

The major German command in the Mediterranean was *Oberbfehlshaber Süd*, which was nominally under the Italian *Comando Supremo*. Under *Luftwaffe* Field Marshal Albert Kesselring, German forces defended Sicily and southern Italy. In November 1943, after the Italian armistice and the German takeover of the peninsula, troops reporting to *OB Süd* were reorganized into Army Group C, comprising Tenth Army and Fourteenth Army. Meanwhile, a new formation, Army Group B, was established in northern Italy under Field Marshal Erwin Rommel in 1943, to defend against a possible Allied attack there, and was subsequently moved to northern France to defend against the D-Day landings in 1944.

Army Group B

Doubts over Italian loyalty to the Axis and fear of an Allied assault across the Channel had already left Hitler anxious over his planned summer offensive in the Soviet Union, even before the Allied landings in Sicily.

The Führer was all too aware that Italian public opinion was turning against the Fascists and that Mussolini might well be ousted. In such an event, the German armies were poised to disarm the Italian Army and occupy the whole of the mainland. However, the troops available to *Oberbefehlshaber Süd* were deployed in the south, where they would soon be in combat with the British and the Americans. To guard against any unpleasant surprises south of the Alps, Hitler sent Field Marshal Erwin Rommel to Italy, where he was tasked with contingency planning in case of Italian defection.

Rommel was given command of a new formation known as Army Group B, which was deployed in Northern Italy. Among the units sent to the area was the II SS Panzer Corps, though the 1st SS Panzergrenadier Division *Leibstandarte SS Adolf Hitler* was the only SS division on its strength. Not for the first time, Rommel disagreed with his nominal superiors. He felt that southern Italy should be abandoned, in direct opposition to Kesselring, who felt that a defence line south of Rome could be successful. In January 1944, the command structure of Army Group B was transferred to Western Europe, and by May 1944, it was in position on the Channel Coast, preparing for the expected Allied invasion.

Army Group C

Set up as the operational headquarters for *Oberbefehlshaber Süd*, Army Group C was established on 23 November 1943. Its main components were the Tenth Army and the newly formed Fourteenth Army, which had last been existence in Poland in 1939.

Following the failure of the Salerno counterattack, the Germans pulled back north of Naples, which rose in revolt on 27 September even before the Allies entered the city. The city was occupied on 1 October, as was the important airfield of Foggia. This would bring Allied bombers within range of the Balkans, Northern Italy and the southern flank of the Reich.

However, the prospect of taking Rome before winter had disappeared. Field Marshal Kesselring toured the likely front line in person, impressing on every man the necessity of holding the Allies as far south as possible. The terrain lent itself to defence, with towering mountain ranges dominating narrow valleys. The Germans demonstrated time and again the ease with which narrow mountain passes could be defended.

On one occasion, three divisions of the Fifth Army were pitched against a bottleneck that was held by three battalions. The Allies were unable to overcome their weaker opponents, who retired in good order.

Preparing the Gustav Line
Demolition of roads and bridges was painstakingly carried out as Kesselring's troops withdrew to the Volturno. They reached it by 16 October, and then made another fighting withdrawal, 24km (15 miles) further north. The time purchased by these rearguard actions allowed Kesselring to prepare his main defences.

From the east to the west coasts of Italy, the Germans dug in, building an awesome barrier known as the Gustav Line. It utilized some of the most powerful defensive features that nature could supply, and created a major obstacle to the Allied armies driving north through Italy in the winter of 1943.

Monte Cassino
In only one place was there even a remote chance of breaking through, and that was at Cassino in the Liri valley. Even here the town was protected by an artificially swollen river and by numerous fortified positions. It was overlooked by a hill crowned by an ancient Benedictine monastery, which formed a natural observation post overlooking the country for many miles around. Such was the strength of the Gustav Line that even this best chance of Allied success was a veritable fortress for the defence. If the strength of the defences was not enough, the Allies also had to attack in the middle of the Italian winter. Winter in central Italy is a cold season of rains and poor visibility, so the Allies had also to contend with the elements. Additionally, they were hampered by a long supply line. It extended across a large number of temporary river crossings over which supplies had to be moved on improvised bridging. The Italian campaign was, in fact, as much an engineer's war as it was an infantryman's.

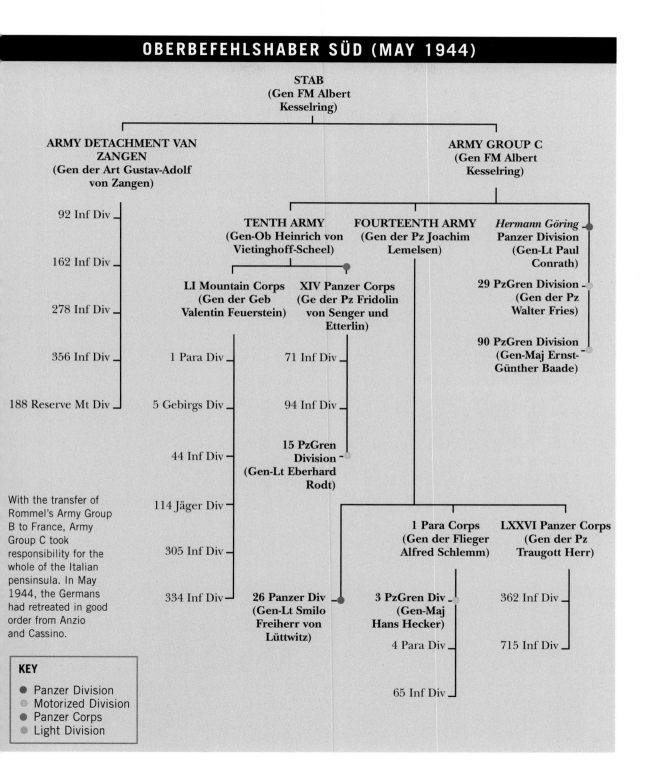

OBERBEFEHLSHABER SÜD (MAY 1944)

STAB
(Gen FM Albert Kesselring)

ARMY DETACHMENT VAN ZANGEN
(Gen der Art Gustav-Adolf von Zangen)

ARMY GROUP C
(Gen FM Albert Kesselring)

92 Inf Div

162 Inf Div

278 Inf Div

356 Inf Div

188 Reserve Mt Div

TENTH ARMY
(Gen-Ob Heinrich von Vietinghoff-Scheel)

FOURTEENTH ARMY
(Gen der Pz Joachim Lemelsen)

Hermann Göring **Panzer Division**
(Gen-Lt Paul Conrath)

29 PzGren Division
(Gen der Pz Walter Fries)

90 PzGren Division
(Gen-Maj Ernst-Günther Baade)

LI Mountain Corps
(Gen der Geb Valentin Feuerstein)

XIV Panzer Corps
(Ge der Pz Fridolin von Senger und Etterlin)

1 Para Div

5 Gebirgs Div

44 Inf Div

114 Jäger Div

305 Inf Div

334 Inf Div

71 Inf Div

94 Inf Div

15 PzGren Division
(Gen-Lt Eberhard Rodt)

26 Panzer Div
(Gen-Lt Smilo Freiherr von Lüttwitz)

1 Para Corps
(Gen der Flieger Alfred Schlemm)

LXXVI Panzer Corps
(Gen der Pz Traugott Herr)

3 PzGren Div
(Gen-Maj Hans Hecker)

4 Para Div

65 Inf Div

362 Inf Div

715 Inf Div

With the transfer of Rommel's Army Group B to France, Army Group C took responsibility for the whole of the Italian pensinsula. In May 1944, the Germans had retreated in good order from Anzio and Cassino.

KEY

● Panzer Division
● Motorized Division
● Panzer Corps
● Light Division

Gustav line defences

The Gustav Line was held by a variety of formations, including two panzer divisions. Their powerful tanks could do little to influence the fighting directly – the terrain was just as hostile to them as it was to the Allies – so they were frequently used as pillboxes, often placed in strong buildings to provide added protection. The Germans also used a new ploy in the form of simplified Panther tank turrets set into steel boxes dug into specially chosen defensive positions. The Allies soon learned that making headway would be difficult where either of these types of obstacle was situated.

Hard fighting

The first attacks were launched in January and February 1944. The Allies found themselves attempting to advance directly into a well-organized and stubborn defence. A direct frontal attack across the Liri by an American force in brigade strength turned into a major military disaster, and even when they managed to cross elsewhere the Allies found themselves faced with an almost sheer climb to the crest of Monte Cassino.

While the attack on Cassino stalled, General Clark attempted to outflank the German defences through an amphibious assault on the bay of Anzio. He bargained that if surprise could be achieved and time given for a really powerful force to be landed to the rear of the German lines, the Allies would be able to break out rapidly and smash their way clean across the western half of the peninsula. There was the further consideration that even if the Anzio operation stalled, it would at least draw German troops from the Gustav Line and so ease the passage for the troops attacking there.

Anzio landings

On the afternoon of 21 January 1943, 243 ships of all sizes sailed from the Bay of Naples and under clear skies made for the beaches on each side of Anzio and neighbouring Nettuno. Allied aircraft had pounded German airfields for days, keeping the *Luftwaffe* on the ground, while naval gunfire kept Kesselring's attention and those of his subordinate commanders elsewhere. By midnight, the first ships were off the beaches, and the landing craft were loaded and moving in. To everybody's astonishment, there was no sign of German opposition.

By the evening of 22 January, 90 per cent of the assault force – 45,000 men and 3000 vehicles – was ashore.

German response

Very quickly, panzer and panzergrenadier divisions were moved into place to put a band of steel around the beach-head. Within a week, eight German divisions had been concentrated at Anzio, and their artillery was shelling the entire area. The stage was set for one of the most bloody battles of the war.

Something of a lull began in early March, but for the the rest of that month, through April and most of May, a grim war of attrition was fought out. In no way can the Anzio landings be presented as an Allied success.

Bombing the abbey

Back at the Gustav Line, the Germans found themselves the subject of renewed interest. The town of Cassino was now mostly defended by paratroopers, who were in the thick of the fighting during the Second Battle, which opened in mid-February, starting with a controversial attack on the monastery itself.

3 September–15 December 1943

Following the conquest of Sicily, part of Montgomery's Eighth Army crossed the Straits of Messina, while other elements landed at Taranto. In an effort to outflank the German and Italian defenders, General Mark Clark's Fifth Army made an amphibious landing at Salerno – the most northerly point that could be covered by Allied fighters. German troops based in the ring of hills surrounding Salerno struck the Allied beachhead hard, almost forcing the British and American troops back into the sea. Only after six days of bitter fighting did the Allies manage to stabilize the beachhead.

The Eighth Army's advance northwards began to swing the tide in favour of the Allies, and the German Tenth Army withdrew northwards. Slowly and with great skill, the Germans slowed the Allied advance to a crawl. At the same time, the Germans were preparing a powerful line of defences anchored on the ancient Benedictine abbey of Monte Cassino. The formidable defences of the Gustav Line were so powerful that the Allied advance ground to a halt as 1944 approached.

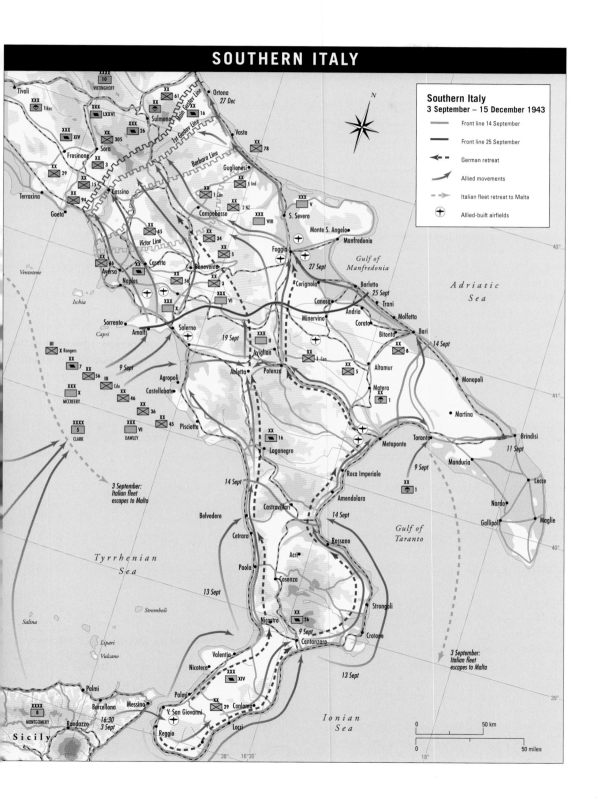

SOUTHERN ITALY

Southern Italy
3 September – 15 December 1943

Front line 14 September
Front line 25 September
German retreat
Allied movements
Italian fleet retreat to Malta
Allied-built airfields

Tivoli
1 Res
VIETINGHOFF
10
61
Ortona
27 Dec
Sulmona
16
LXXVI
Min Gustav Line
XIV
305
26
Sora
Frosinone
3
Vasto
78
29
15
Barbara Line
Guglianesi
1 Ind
Cassino
94
Terracina
1 Can
Gaeta
45
Campobasso
2 NZ
34
S. Severo
V
Victor Line
5
Monte S. Angelo
Caserta
VIII
Foggia
Manfredonia
46
Aversa
Benevento
27 Sept
Gulf of
Manfredonia
Naples
56
3
Cerignola
Barletta
25 Sept
VI
Canosa
Trani
X
Minervino
Andria
Molfetta
Sorrento
Corato
Adriatic
Sea
Capri
Amalfi
Salerno
Bitonta
Bari
19 Sept
II
Aviglian
8
14 Sept
X Rangers
1 Can
Altamur
Monopoli
7
56
III
Abletta
Potenza
5
Matera
Martina
X
Cdo
Agropoli
1
46
McCREERY
Castellabate
36
5
VI
45
Pisciotta
Brindisi
DAWLEY
16
Metaponte
Taranto
11 Sept
CLARK
Lagonegro
Manduria
9 Sept
Roca Imperiale
1
Lecce
3 September:
Italian fleet
escapes to Malta
14 Sept
Amendolara
Nardo
Castrovillari
14 Sept
Gulf of
Taranto
Gallipol
Maglie
Belvedere
Rossano
Tyrrhenian
Sea
Cetrara
Stromboli
Acri
Paola
Strongoli
Salina
Cosenza
13 Sept
3 September:
Italian fleet
escapes to Malta
Lipari
26
Crotone
Vulcano
Nicastro
9 Sept
Cantanzaro
Valentia
13 Sept
Nicotera
XIV
Ionian
Sea
Palmi
Canloma
29
Barcellona
Messina
V. San Giovanni
MONTGOMERY
8
16:30
3 Sept
Randazzo
Reggio
Locri
Sicily

Gustav Line to Gothic Line

Built along the Rivers Garigliano and Rapido, the Gustav Line was fortified with gun pits, concrete bunkers, turreted machine-gun emplacements, barbed wire and minefields, and was held by 15 German divisions.

On 18 May 1944, Allied troops led by the Polish Corps and the French Corps broke through the Line, which opened a corridor for Allied troops, who reached Anzio on 24 May. The German defence now disintegrated and General Mark Clark was able to liberate Rome on 4 June.

The Allies had suffered badly in a year of hard campaigning that had pitted them against the twin evils of the Italian weather and the tactical brilliance of the German defenders. Kesselring decided to make a stand on the Gothic Line in the northern Apennines, but he needed time to prepare his positions. The Allies must be stalled till the autumn, he told his commanders.

Italy lent itself to defensive fighting and the Germans fought a series of masterful withdrawals. The country was a narrow peninsula with steep mountains, narrow winding roads, deep river valleys and grim winter weather that produced ribald jokes about 'Sunny Italy'.

On the Gothic Line

At dawn on 25 August 1944, British, Canadian and Polish troops launched the first probing attacks on the Gothic Line. However, it was not until 12 September that the battle began in earnest. On that day, the US II and British

OB SÜD – PANZER STRENGTH (MARCH 1945)					
Tank type	PzIII (75)	PzIV (kz)	PzIV (lg)	Pz Bef	Flmmpz
26TH PANZER DIVISION					
26th Pz Rgt	16	17	36	9	14

XIII Corps were launched against the centre of the Gothic Line high on the Apennines. They were attacking at the junction between the German Tenth and Fourteenth Armies just east of the Giogo di Scarperia pass.

On the west coast, the US IV Corps kept the pressure on the Germans and prevented reinforcements moving to the mountains. On the coast, the British Eighth Army resumed its attacks on Cariano on the night of 12 September. A week's hard fighting followed and the Germans were finally forced back to the Rimini Line.

The next obstacle was the River Po about 100km (62 miles) to the north, but in between were no less than nine rivers to be assaulted before the Eighth Army reached this obstacle. The German Army had fought hard but, by 27 September, it appeared that the Allies were through the Gothic Line.

Northern Italy, 1944–45

Once through the Gothic Line in the autumn of 1944, the Allies felt that it would be relatively easy to roll up the German forces in Italy. However, the appaling weather in the mountains meant that the final offensive would have to wait until 1945.

By 7 October, the British Eighth Army began to attack towards the River Rubicon, and in five days they were across this symbolic barrier. At the end of October, the campaigning season in the central sector was over. In one month the Fifth Army had suffered 15,700 casualties, but it was still trapped in the mountains.

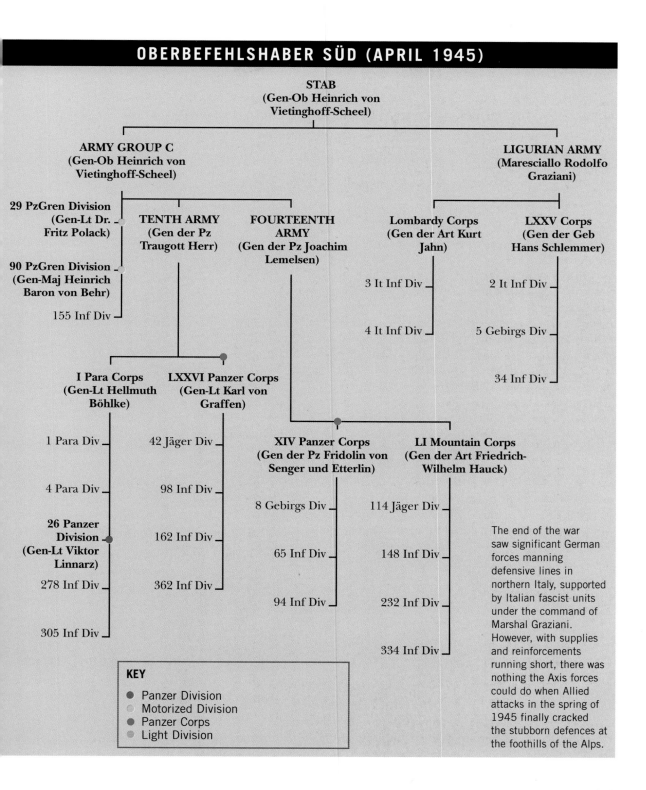

OBERBEFEHLSHABER SÜD (APRIL 1945)

STAB
(Gen-Ob Heinrich von Vietinghoff-Scheel)

ARMY GROUP C
(Gen-Ob Heinrich von Vietinghoff-Scheel)

LIGURIAN ARMY
(Maresciallo Rodolfo Graziani)

29 PzGren Division (Gen-Lt Dr. Fritz Polack)

TENTH ARMY (Gen der Pz Traugott Herr)

FOURTEENTH ARMY (Gen der Pz Joachim Lemelsen)

Lombardy Corps (Gen der Art Kurt Jahn)

LXXV Corps (Gen der Geb Hans Schlemmer)

90 PzGren Division (Gen-Maj Heinrich Baron von Behr)

3 It Inf Div

2 It Inf Div

155 Inf Div

4 It Inf Div

5 Gebirgs Div

34 Inf Div

I Para Corps (Gen-Lt Hellmuth Böhlke)

LXXVI Panzer Corps (Gen-Lt Karl von Graffen)

1 Para Div

42 Jäger Div

XIV Panzer Corps (Gen der Pz Fridolin von Senger und Etterlin)

LI Mountain Corps (Gen der Art Friedrich-Wilhelm Hauck)

4 Para Div

98 Inf Div

8 Gebirgs Div

114 Jäger Div

26 Panzer Division (Gen-Lt Viktor Linnarz)

162 Inf Div

65 Inf Div

148 Inf Div

278 Inf Div

362 Inf Div

94 Inf Div

232 Inf Div

305 Inf Div

334 Inf Div

KEY
- Panzer Division
- Motorized Division
- Panzer Corps
- Light Division

The end of the war saw significant German forces manning defensive lines in northern Italy, supported by Italian fascist units under the command of Marshal Graziani. However, with supplies and reinforcements running short, there was nothing the Axis forces could do when Allied attacks in the spring of 1945 finally cracked the stubborn defences at the foothills of the Alps.

On 24 November, General Mark Clark relinquished his command of the US Fifth Army. He was succeeded by General Lucien 'Old Gravel Guts' Truscott. Clark, in turn, took over from General Harold Alexander as commander-in-chief of the Fifteenth Army Group, thus giving him command of Allied ground forces in Italy. Alexander was promoted to Supreme Allied Commander in the Mediterranean.

On the coast, the advance continued. Canadian troops occupied Ravenna on 5 December. Fighting slowed down, but by 29 December the Eighth Army had reached the line of the River Senio south of Lake Comacchio.

Kesselring's plans

Kesselring had considered that the valleys of the Rivers Po and the Adige could be used as intermediate defence lines as his forces fell back to strong positions in the southern Alps. Both he and Alexander were aware of just how difficult it would be to dislodge German forces in the mountains. The British General knew that it was critical therefore to keep the pressure on the Germans.

At this point, Hitler issued one of his disastrous stand-fast orders. He refused Kesselring permission to withdraw into more defensible positions and insisted that Army Group C should stand and fight.

An uneasy stalemate now set in. With heavy frosts and snow, the struggle on both sides was against the elements and not each other. Allied supply routes were kept open only by the daily and unremitting efforts of thousands of civilians and all but those units in the most forward positions. While the Germans were forced to hoard their meagre stocks of petrol and ammunition, the Allies finally began to receive some of the specialized equipment that they had for so long been denied.

Final offensive

The Allied offensive was launched on 9 April. On the night of 1 April, in preparation for this, British commandos had attacked the spit running between Lake Comacchio and the Adriatic. On 4 and 5 April, the islands on the lake were seized. The fighting around the Lake area was intended to tie down the German flank to give the major assault a greater chance of success.

The first phase of the attack was by the 8th Army, with Indians and New Zealanders of V Corps attacking across the Senio towards Lugo. By 11 April, a bridgehead had been established over the Santerno and a day earlier an amphibious operation at Menate across Lake Comacchio had turned the German position in front of the Argenta Gap.

Battle for Bologna

On 14 April, Truscott's Fifth Army launched its attack, two days behind schedule because of bad weather. A day later, the Polish II Corps under General Anders began to cross the River Sillario and sat astride the excellent Route 9 drive northwest towards Bologna.

Despite tough fighting in mountainous terrain, Fifth Army broke through to the suburbs of Bologna on 20 April. General Vietinghoff, staring defeat in the face, ordered his troops to retreat across the Po. He succeeded by 23 April, but left most of his heavy equipment behind. On 25 April, the US Fifth Army, faced with little opposition, took Parma and Verona and a day later the Allies reached the River Adige. On the west coast, the US advance had been slower and it was not until 27 April that Genoa was liberated.

April–May 1945

The rapid Allied advances of September 1944 had forced a breach in the Gothic Line. The Germans fell back to hold the rugged terrain south of Bologna. The Allies were unable to make a decisive breakthrough until April 1945.

The Eighth Army advanced east of Bologna, while the Americans shattered the German defences further west. Outnumbered and lacking supplies, the German commander von Vietinghoff asked to retreat beyond the Po, but Hitler refused. Disobeying orders, Vietinghoff withdrew anyway.

However, at this stage in the war it was far too late. Allied armoured columns raced forwards, beating the retreating Germans to the river line, cutting them off. The Tenth Army had all but ceased to exist when Vietinghoff sought terms from the Allies, and on 2 May 1945 he surrendered his forces.

Now without his German allies to protect him, Mussolini was a hunted man. Caught by Partisans, he was executed on 28 April 1945.

On 29 April, the Germans signed an unconditional surrender at Caserta. It came into effect at 13.00 GMT on 2 May, just six days before Victory in Europe Day. In over 20 months of some of the most savage fighting of the war, the Germans had proved the lie to Churchill's famous maxim that Italy was the 'soft underbelly' of Europe.

THE END IN ITALY

The End in Italy
April–May 1945

→ Allied attacks
Allied front line
German defence lines

Normandy, France and the Low Countries: 1944

Although the larger part of Germany's armed forces remained on the Eastern Front, the High Command knew that it would have to face an invasion of Europe by the Western Allies some time in the spring or summer of 1944.

The war in northwest Europe saw the outnumbered and outgunned troops of the *Wehrmacht* pushed back to the German border. However, they were far from beaten, as the massive offensive in the Ardennes in December 1944 was to prove. Here, a Panzer V from the I SS Panzer Corps moves up to the front in preparation for the Ardennes Offensive.

BY THE AUTUMN OF 1943, the *Wehrmacht* still occupied huge swathes of territory in the East, as well as the western lands held since 1940. Italy had been occupied, and German armies were contesting the peninsula inch by inch. Hitler still had hopes for 1944, even though the year would almost certainly see the Western Allies return to the continent in force.

His generals were less confident. The one thing they had always feared was a two-front war, and now they were faced with the prospect of fighting on three fronts – in the Soviet Union, in Italy and in the west. But where would the western attack come? And when?

Even though the Red Army now held the initiative on the Eastern Front, Joseph Stalin doubted that he could defeat Hitler alone. He needed to weaken the powerful German armies on the Eastern Front. He demanded that the Western Allies establish a second front in 1944.

Invasion in the west

The ailing US President, Franklin Delano Roosevelt, was keen to aid Stalin. Winston Churchill, suspicious of the Soviet dictator, wanted the main Allied effort to be launched from the Mediterranean, through the 'soft underbelly' of Europe. Since the Americans had by now become the most powerful of the Western Allies, Roosevelt's wishes prevailed. At a conference in Tehran, the 'Big Three' decided upon an invasion of France, to be scheduled for the early summer of 1944. However, such an undertaking would not be easy.

Fortress Europe

Since his failure to bring Britain to terms in 1940, Hitler had been creating 'Fortress Europe'. He wanted to shield the western borders of the Reich by building massive defences in depth. Under the efficient leadership of Reich Armaments Minister Fritz Todt, the Germans began to turn the whole Atlantic coast, from Norway to the Pyrenees, into an impregnable barrier.

If the fortifications could be completed in time, the Allied invasion of France might well be thrown thrown back, and the liberation of Europe would be set back for months, or even years.

Army Groups B and G

Late in 1943, Hitler appointed Germany's most famous soldier, Field Marshal Erwin Rommel, to take charge of the possible invasion front. When he arrived in his new command from Italy, Rommel was shocked by the poor state of the defences.

Like most ordinary Germans, Rommel had believed in Goebbels' propaganda images of massive concrete redoubts, linked by bomb-proof shelters and protected by anti-personnel and anti-tank devices of every sort.

The reality was otherwise. The much vaunted 'Atlantic Wall' was little more than a thin defensive line, punctuated at intervals by strong bastions, which could simply be bypassed.

Army Group B

As commander of Army Group 'B' on the French coast, Rommel threw himself into the task of making the 'Atlantic Wall' a truly effective shield. Slave labour combined 1,444.159m^3 (51,000,000ft^3) of concrete with 1.5 million tons of iron to build a network of bunkers, pillboxes, observation towers and machine-gun nests. Anti-tank ditches were dug inland and steel girders were fixed at low water to impale incoming landing craft. Rommel worked feverishly through the winter of 1943 and spring of 1944 to make good the neglect.

But in the new age of mobile warfare, relying on static defence lines was doomed to failure. The defeat of any Allied landings would require all the guile and fighting experience of the German Army, combined with an all-out effort by the navy and the air force.

But in the invasion area in 1944, the *Luftwaffe* and the

D-DAY LANDINGS: PLANS AND OBJECTIVES

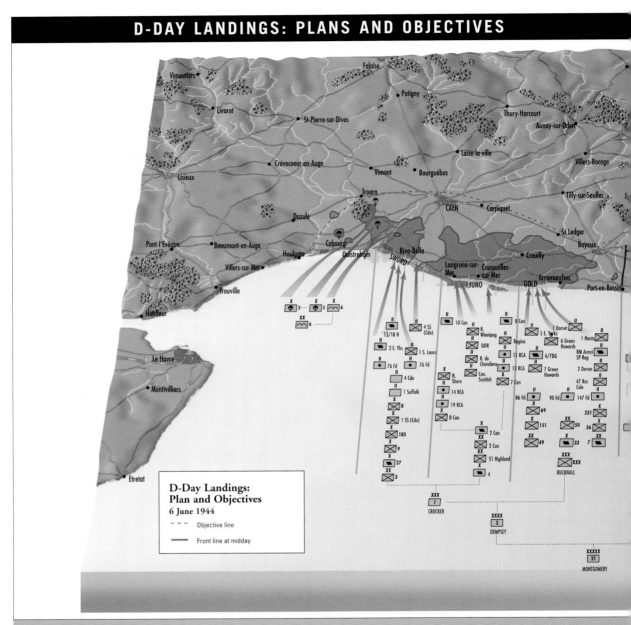

D-Day Landings:
Plan and Objectives
6 June 1944

- - - Objective line

──── Front line at midday

6 June 1944

The Allied landings took place on a 96.5km (60-mile) front, with five divisions assaulting from the sea and three by air. The airborne forces were the first into action. Two US airborne divisions were dropped at the foot of the Cotentin peninsula. At the Eastern end of the landing area, the British 6th Airborne Division was tasked with seizing a bridgehead between the River Orne and the Caen Canal, halfway between Caen and the coast. This would secure the eastern flank of the invasion force. British and Canadian forces landed on the three eastern beaches, codenamed Gold, Juno and Sword. The US Army divisions landed on Utah and Omaha beaches.

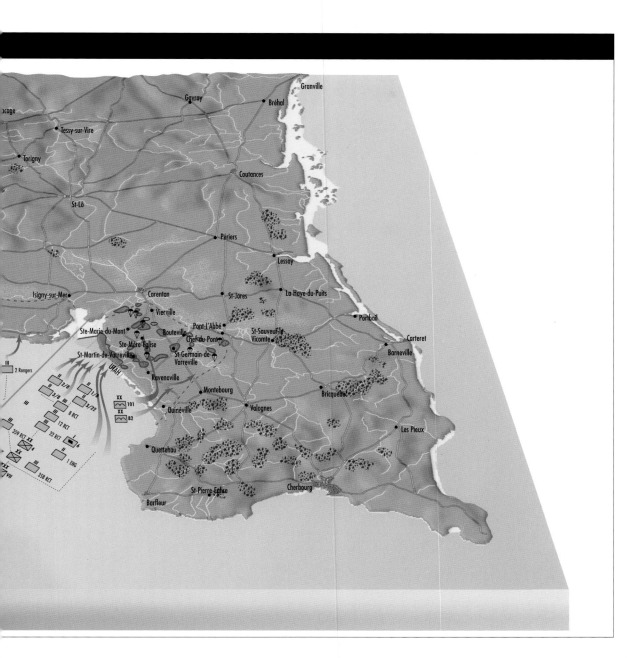

Kriegsmarine were even more badly off than the army. *Luftflotte* 3 had responsibility for defending France and the Low Countries. It had just 820 aircraft of all types, of which 170 were combat ready. By contrast, the Allies had more than 5000 operational aircraft available in June 1944.

Oberbefehlshaber West

Field Marshal Gerd von Rundstedt was the commander of German forces in the west. In addition to Rommel's Army Group B in Northern France, he also had Johannes Blaskowitz's Army Group G covering the south of France.

Rundstedt believed the invasion would take place in the Pas de Calais. Here, where the Channel is at its narrowest, the Germans would have less time to react once the invasion fleet had been detected. Once a beachhead had been secured, Rundstedt feared the enemy could use the good tank country inland to reach the Rhine in four days. Normandy he ruled out, because the hinterland was dominated by the bocage: narrow

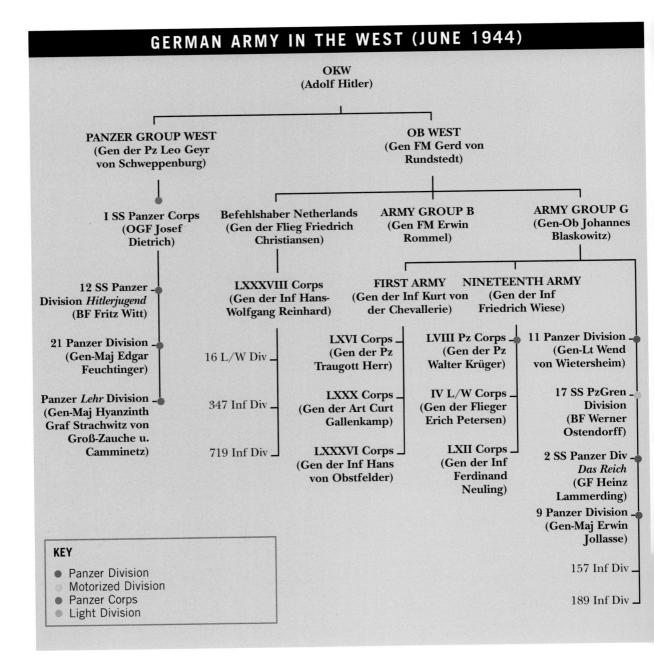

GERMAN ARMY IN THE WEST (JUNE 1944)

OKW
(Adolf Hitler)

PANZER GROUP WEST
(Gen der Pz Leo Geyr
von Schweppenburg)

OB WEST
(Gen FM Gerd von
Rundstedt)

I SS Panzer Corps
(OGF Josef
Dietrich)

Befehlshaber Netherlands
(Gen der Flieg Friedrich
Christiansen)

ARMY GROUP B
(Gen FM Erwin
Rommel)

ARMY GROUP G
(Gen-Ob Johannes
Blaskowitz)

**12 SS Panzer
Division** *Hitlerjugend*
(BF Fritz Witt)

LXXXVIII Corps
(Gen der Inf Hans-
Wolfgang Reinhard)

FIRST ARMY
(Gen der Inf Kurt von
der Chevallerie)

NINETEENTH ARMY
(Gen der Inf
Friedrich Wiese)

21 Panzer Division
(Gen-Maj Edgar
Feuchtinger)

16 L/W Div

LXVI Corps
(Gen der Pz
Traugott Herr)

LVIII Pz Corps
(Gen der Pz
Walter Krüger)

11 Panzer Division
(Gen-Lt Wend
von Wietersheim)

Panzer *Lehr* **Division**
(Gen-Maj Hyanzinth
Graf Strachwitz von
Groß-Zauche u.
Camminetz)

347 Inf Div

LXXX Corps
(Gen der Art Curt
Gallenkamp)

IV L/W Corps
(Gen der Flieger
Erich Petersen)

**17 SS PzGren
Division**
(BF Werner
Ostendorff)

719 Inf Div

LXXXVI Corps
(Gen der Inf Hans
von Obstfelder)

LXII Corps
(Gen der Inf
Ferdinand
Neuling)

2 SS Panzer Div
Das Reich
(GF Heinz
Lammerding)

9 Panzer Division
(Gen-Maj Erwin
Jollasse)

157 Inf Div

189 Inf Div

KEY
● Panzer Division
○ Motorized Division
● Panzer Corps
○ Light Division

lanes and high hedgerows ideal for defence. Furthermore, there were no major ports, which were assumed essential. The Allies' 'Mulberry' artificial harbours would come as a disagreeable surprise.

Runstedt's conclusion was reinforced by German intelligence. Hitler agreed with his commanders, and the Pas de Calais sector received the bulk of the new fortifications and the strongest concentration of troops.

Where to put the panzers

Rommel, who had bitter experience of fighting against superior air power, believed the Allies had to be destroyed on the beaches. Once a beachhead was established, he had little confidence that the German Army could throw the invaders back into the sea. He wanted panzer divisions positioned near enough to the coast to intervene within hours, not days.

Rundstedt, his immediate superior, disagreed. He planned a conventional defence assuming a successful Allied landing. Once he had identified the enemy's main thrust, the Germans would counterattack with a concentrated blow led by the panzer divisions.

Rundstedt accepted that daylight movement behind the lines would be vulnerable to air attack, but most divisions received additional anti-aircraft gun batteries. Since these guns would need to accompany the army, light and heavy flak pieces were mounted on any chassis that was available. These included half-tracks, obsolete tanks and trucks.

Many of the units in the west were second-line infantry divisions. Poorly equipped, their numbers were made up with semi-invalids and older men – a quarter of the German Army was in its mid-30s or older by 1944. Foreign troops of dubious loyalty were also used, with many divisions including a battalion of former Soviet troops. The infantry divisions had an impossibly long coastline to defend. In northeast France, divisional sectors averaged 80km (50 miles); along the Normandy coast, each division guarded 150km (93 miles), and divisions along the shores of the Atlantic and Mediterranean were expected to cover over 250km (155 miles) of coast.

Behind the brittle coastal formations, German hopes rested on 11 armoured and four airborne divisions, the latter serving as elite ground troops. But Rommel's

disagreement with von Rundstedt over how to fight the battle was never resolved. Hitler assigned some panzer divisions to Rommel, and others to Rundstedt's reserve, but decreed that none could move without his personal authorization.

Invasion

The timing of the attack took the Germans by surprise. The weather was unfavourable, but the Allies had the advantage in forecasting. German weather ships had

PANZER STRENGTHS: NORMANDY (JUNE 1944)			
Division	June	July	August
21st Panzer Division	117 Pz IV 12 FlakPz 38 4 Pz III	Fewer than 20 tanks	No tanks
12th SS Panzer Division *Hitlerjugend*	96 Pz IV 66 Pz V 12 FlakPz 38	(*KpfgpWunsch*) 18 Pz IV 13 Pz V	10 tanks
Panzer *Lehr* Division	101 Pz IV 89 Pz V 3 Pz VI 9 Stug 12 FlakPz 38	15 Pz IV 16 Pz V	about 10 Pz IV about 10 Pz V
2nd Panzer Division	99 Pz IV 79 Pz V 12 FlakPz 38 10 StuG	Not known	Destroyed at Falaise
2nd SS Panzer Division *Das Reich*	In Transit from South of France	78 Pz IV 79 Pz V 13 StuG	15 tanks
1st SS Panzer Division *Leibstandarte*-SS AH	Under reconstruction	98 Pz IV 89 Pz V 12 FlakPz 38	No tanks
9th SS Panzer Division *Hohenstaufen*	In transit	46 Pz IV 79 Pz V	No tanks
10th SS Panzer Division *Frundsberg*	In transit	39 Pz IV 38 StuG	25 tanks
116th Panzer Division	Forming	6 Pz III 73 Pz IV 79 Pz V 8 FlakPz IV(37)	600 men 12 tanks

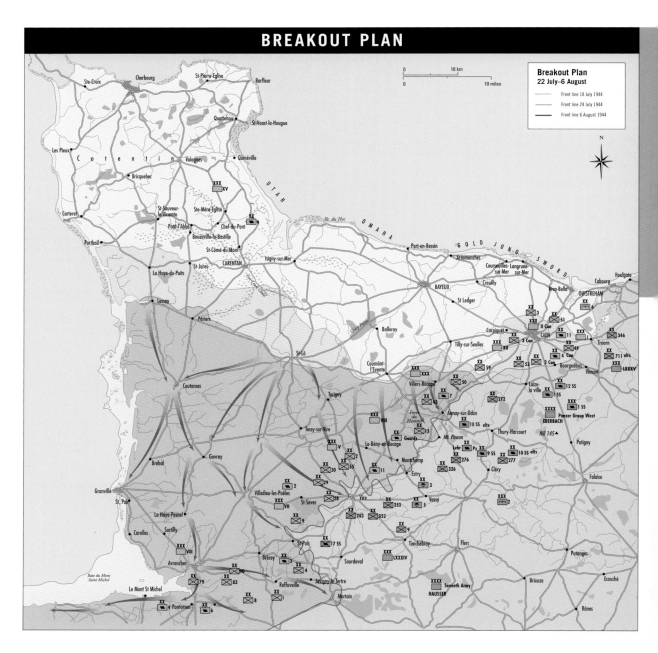

BREAKOUT PLAN

Breakout Plan
22 July–6 August

— Front line 18 July 1944
— Front line 24 July 1944
— Front line 6 August 1944

been swept from the Atlantic, but the Allies knew a break in the storms was on its way.

When the landings began on 6 June, Rommel was in Germany, visiting his wife. Many junior officers were away, ironically on an anti-invasion staff exercise – and Hitler was asleep.

Panzers paralyzed

Hitler was still asleep in the middle of the morning, by which time Rommel's staff had badgered Rundstedt to request the Führer's permission to commit the panzers. But no one at OKW dared wake him. Accordingly, it was not until the late afternoon of 6 June that the nearest

22 July–6 August 1944

The constant battering against the German right flank had been costly to the Anglo–Canadian forces. But the Germans had only finite reserves, and these were constantly short of fuel and ammunition. Meanwhile, at the other end of the line, the German defenders were even weaker.

Rommel had far more respect for the British as opponents than he had for the Americans. Accordingly, he and his staff opposed General Omar Bradley's powerful First US Army with 11 seriously under-strength divisions, only two of which were armoured.

The Americans, who were far from being the amateur incompetents Rommel imagined, were not going to pass up this opportunity. Operation Cobra, the plan to break out of the Normandy beachhead, was to be launched after an overwhelming air and naval bombardment.

armoured unit was given orders to intervene. Rommel's defensive strategy had collapsed before the battle had even begun.

The landings took place on a 96.5km (60-mile) front, with five divisions assaulting from the sea and three by air.

The 'Atlantic Wall' was pierced by a number of ingenious armoured assault vehicles: 'flail' tanks that beat paths through the minefields, bridgelayers and tanks fitted with 'bunker-busting' howitzers.

Only the belated intervention of the 21st Panzer Division prevented a complete disaster for the Germans. Once unleashed, the experienced unit reacted with characteristic aggression and skill. The 21st counter-attacked the Canadians, and was stopped short of the beach only by naval gunfire. The city of Caen, a key Allied objective for D-Day, was held by the Germans.

Northwest Europe: 1944

Curiously, Hitler welcomed the Allied landings in Normandy. He was sure that the *Wehrmacht* would inflict the same sort of carnage that the Canadians had suffered at Dieppe in 1942, and that the Allies would be driven back into the sea.

Hitler was convinced that if the Allies were defeated in this major landing, they would not attempt another. This would give the Germans greater strategic flexibility and the opportunity to fight the Soviet Union to a standstill.

In spite of 21st Panzer Division's counterattack, the British and Canadians had penetrated 8km (5 miles) inland by the end of the first day. At Omaha, the US V Corps were ashore after a bloody battle, and to the west at Utah the US VII Corps had crossed the flooded area close to the beach. By the end of the day, it had linked up with the 82nd and 101st Airborne Divisions.

Air superiority

Tactical air power was the major cause of German difficulties. Although reinforcements were getting through, Allied air superiority was making it difficult and costly. Squadrons of Typhoons, Spitfires, Mustangs

and Thunderbolts orbited continuously over the battlefield, on call at a moment's notice.

At the eastern end of the beachhead, British and Canadian divisions fought to reach Caen. The Germans held good defensive positions. They had concentrated the XXXXVII Corps and the I and II SS Panzer Corps opposite the Allied right flank. In all, 14 German divisions, six of which were armoured, faced the British and Canadians.

Stubborn defence

In spite of their best efforts, the British were unable to drive back the German defenders. Montgomery had even used heavy bombers to blast the German positions, but despite this, the attack ground to a halt with heavy losses in infantry and armour. Nevertheless, such intense effort eventually brought results, and in August the

FALAISE POCKET

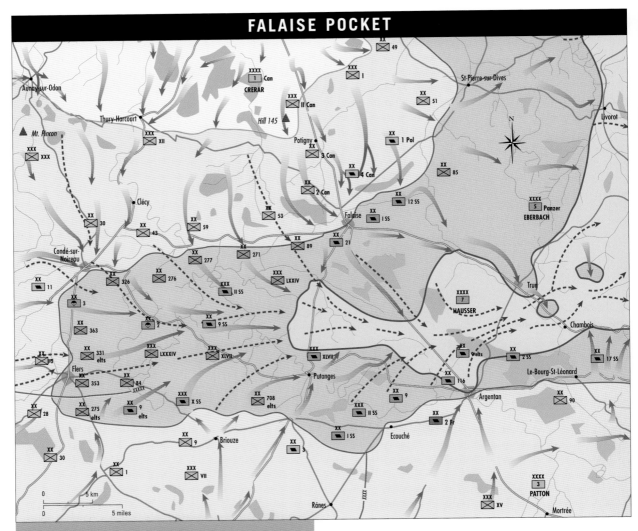

6–19 August 1944

Most of the German combat troops in Normandy were penned into an area just 65km (40 miles) long and 20km (12 miles) wide. As Allied ground forces closed in, aircraft cannon, machine-gun fire and rockets pulverized vehicles clogging the roads and river crossings.

The Polish tank crews serving with the British 4th Armoured Divsion became the cork in the bottle of the shrinking Falaise Pocket. On 19 August, they reached an isolated position at the village of St Lambert, and held it against German attacks from both east and west. The Canadians and Americans linked up with the Poles at the town of Chambois, and the trap was shut.

Falaise Pocket 6–19 August 1944	
	Front line 6 August
	Front line 16 August
	Front line 19 August

rubble that had been Caen finally fell.

At the end of July, in spite of bad weather, the Americans were ready to strike. General Omar Bradley readied six divisions of the First Army to punch through the German lines west of St Lô. Known as Operation Cobra, the breakout began on 24 July 1944.

On 25 July, the full weight of Cobra – 15 American divisions – fell on the men of the Panzer *Lehr* Division.

This elite force had been so ravaged by the intense fighting of the previous month that it could call on only 2200 men and 45 operational armoured vehicles.

Hitler ordered von Kluge, who had replaced the wounded Rommel, to launch an all-out effort to cut the Allied supply lines and drive the Americans into the sea. For this attack Hitler released the armoured divisions held in the Pas de Calais area. The counterattack would be against the narrow spearhead of the US advance from Avranches to Mortain.

Mortain attack

Four panzer divisions of General Paul Hausser's Seventh Army struck westwards, but the target of Avranches was not reached. The German attacks were finally stopped by artillery fire and by a devastating series of attacks by Allied fighter bombers.

Field Marshal Walther Model, 'The Führer's Fireman', had by now replaced von Kluge. The tough monocled general had a reputation for being able to reverse crises on the Eastern Front. However, on this occasion, all he could do was to call a halt to the attack at Mortain.

Even as the Americans continued pushing southeast, an attack by the Canadian First Army now threatened Falaise. It needed no great imagination to see what would happen if the pincers were to meet. Montgomery was playing it cool when he stated: 'If we can close the gap on the enemy, we shall put him in the most awkward predicament.'

The Germans were now in full flight. By 10 August, the US XX Corps had reached Nantes, and a day later Angers. Le Mans was liberated on 8 August, and Patton's troops reached Argentan on 13 August. The Canadians punched through to Falaise three days later.

As US and Anglo–Canadian forces pressed forwards from their positions in Normandy, the Fifth Panzer Army and the composite force designated *Panzergruppe Eberbach* were caught in a trap at Falaise: a pocket with a narrow exit to the east.

Massive losses

Some Germans did manage to slip through the Allied lines at night, in bad weather, but between 25,000 and 50,000 were taken prisoner, leaving another 10,000 dead behind them in the killing ground. In Normandy, the Germans had lost 1500 tanks, 3500 guns and 20,000 assorted vehicles. These were losses that they could never hope to replace.

Army Group B

Shattered in the two-and-a-half months of fighting in Normandy, Army Group B demonstrated the incredible ability of the German Army to re-create itself as the *Wehrmacht* stopped three major Allied offensives in northwest Europe.

Having broken their opponents in Normandy, the Allied armies were racing across France. The Germans were in full retreat, with neither prepared defences to the west of the Rhine nor reserves to fill the breeches in their lines.

The tide of liberation was as dramatic as the German *Blitzkrieg* four years before, and most Allied commanders were talking of a final German defeat by Christmas. Surely nothing could save Hitler now?

Hitler insisted that the German Army cling to its positions in Normandy until it was too late for an orderly withdrawal. The result was catastrophic. Instead of the fighting retreat across France, envisaged by his generals, the German army collapsed in rout. US armoured columns fanned out in pursuit, Allied aircraft strafed and bombed every road east.

Massive losses

Between D-Day, 6 June, and the end of August 1944, the German Army lost 221,000 men killed, missing or captured in France. Another 67,000 were wounded.

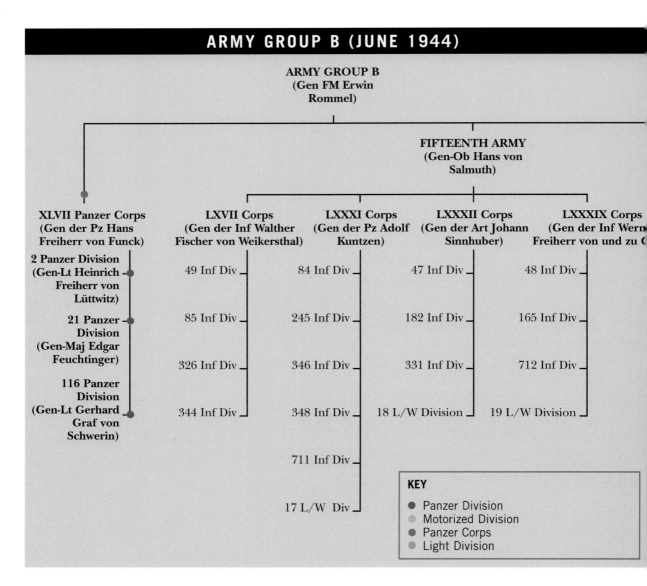

ARMY GROUP B (JUNE 1944)

ARMY GROUP B
(Gen FM Erwin Rommel)

FIFTEENTH ARMY
(Gen-Ob Hans von Salmuth)

XLVII Panzer Corps (Gen der Pz Hans Freiherr von Funck)	LXVII Corps (Gen der Inf Walther Fischer von Weikersthal)	LXXXI Corps (Gen der Pz Adolf Kuntzen)	LXXXII Corps (Gen der Art Johann Sinnhuber)	LXXXIX Corps (Gen der Inf Werner Freiherr von und zu G
2 Panzer Division (Gen-Lt Heinrich Freiherr von Lüttwitz)	49 Inf Div	84 Inf Div	47 Inf Div	48 Inf Div
21 Panzer Division (Gen-Maj Edgar Feuchtinger)	85 Inf Div	245 Inf Div	182 Inf Div	165 Inf Div
116 Panzer Division (Gen-Lt Gerhard Graf von Schwerin)	326 Inf Div	346 Inf Div	331 Inf Div	712 Inf Div
	344 Inf Div	348 Inf Div	18 L/W Division	19 L/W Division
	711 Inf Div			
	17 L/W Div			

KEY
- Panzer Division
- Motorized Division
- Panzer Corps
- Light Division

The *Westheer*, or Army of the West, began the campaign with 50 infantry divisions and 12 panzer divisions. By the time Field Marshal Model gathered up the wreckage, there were only 24 infantry divisions and 11 panzer divisions – divisions in name only, since all had been reduced to a fraction of their authorized strength.

Allied Advances

The Allied armies reached the Seine 11 days before they had expected to, and had freed Paris 55 days ahead of

schedule. The American Seventh Army, which landed on the French Riviera on 15 August, had broken German opposition in the south and linked up with Patton's forces by mid-September. At the same time, the American First Army had closed on the German city of Aachen. They were a full eight months ahead of schedule. Everywhere, British and American troops were embraced as conquering heroes.

The Germans were driven back towards the borders of the Reich. The British Army crossed into Belgium, and

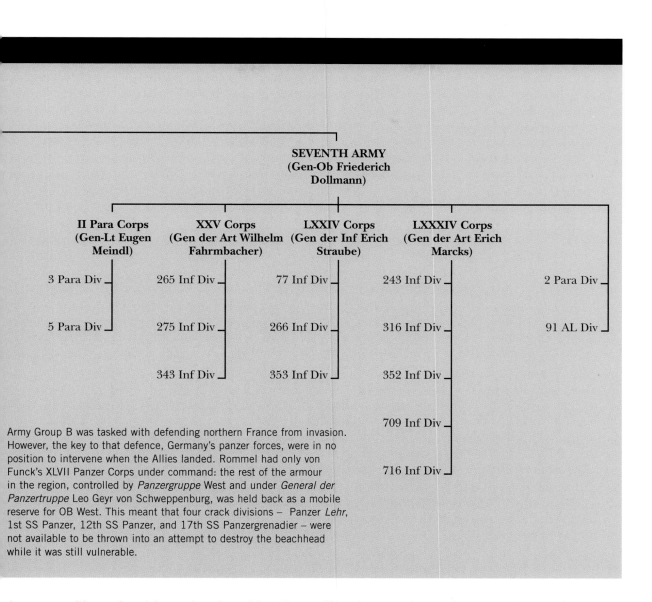

		SEVENTH ARMY (Gen-Ob Friederich Dollmann)		
II Para Corps (Gen-Lt Eugen Meindl)	XXV Corps (Gen der Art Wilhelm Fahrmbacher)	LXXIV Corps (Gen der Inf Erich Straube)	LXXXIV Corps (Gen der Art Erich Marcks)	
3 Para Div	265 Inf Div	77 Inf Div	243 Inf Div	2 Para Div
5 Para Div	275 Inf Div	266 Inf Div	316 Inf Div	91 AL Div
	343 Inf Div	353 Inf Div	352 Inf Div	
			709 Inf Div	
			716 Inf Div	

Army Group B was tasked with defending northern France from invasion. However, the key to that defence, Germany's panzer forces, were in no position to intervene when the Allies landed. Rommel had only von Funck's XLVII Panzer Corps under command: the rest of the armour in the region, controlled by *Panzergruppe* West and under *General der Panzertruppe* Leo Geyr von Schweppenburg, was held back as a mobile reserve for OB West. This meant that four crack divisions – Panzer *Lehr*, 1st SS Panzer, 12th SS Panzer, and 17th SS Panzergrenadier – were not available to be thrown into an attempt to destroy the beachhead while it was still vulnerable.

Antwerp was liberated on 4 September. *Generaloberst* Kurt Student was ordered to establish a defensive line to hold the Low Countries, although his grandly titled First *Fallschirmjager* Army consisted of rear echelon troops, returned wounded and raw recruits.

German resistance
However, the Allies headlong rush was at its zenith. Tenacious resistance by German garrisons in French ports was restricting Allied supplies. The armies of

liberation were short of frontline infantry replacements. Men were exhausted and vehicles were in desperate need of overhaul. The helter-skelter advance slowed, then stopped.

After the debacle of Normandy, Field Marshal Model established the headquarters of Army Group B at Oosterbeek, near Arnhem in the Netherlands. On 17 September he found himself in the middle of the landing zone as the British 1st Airborne Division launched Operation Market Garden. This was a daring attempt by Montgomery to capture the bridges on the lower Rhine, Maas and Waal.

Arnhem battles

However, German reaction was swift: II SS Panzer Corps, the 9th SS Panzer and 10th SS Panzer Divisions were busily refitting after Normandy. Meanwhile, a series of improvised *Kampfgruppen* fought off the airborne assault, stopping Montgomery's attempt to open the gateway to the Ruhr.

Allied advances held

After Arnhem, Army Group B fought off the US First and Ninth Armies in the Hürtgen Forest. Aachen eventually fell on 21 October, but at enormous cost to the US First Army. The Ninth Army's push to the River Roer fared no better, and did not manage to cross the river or wrest control of its dams from the Germans. The entire battle was so costly that it has been called an Allied 'defeat of the first magnitude', with specific credit being assigned to Model and Army Group B.

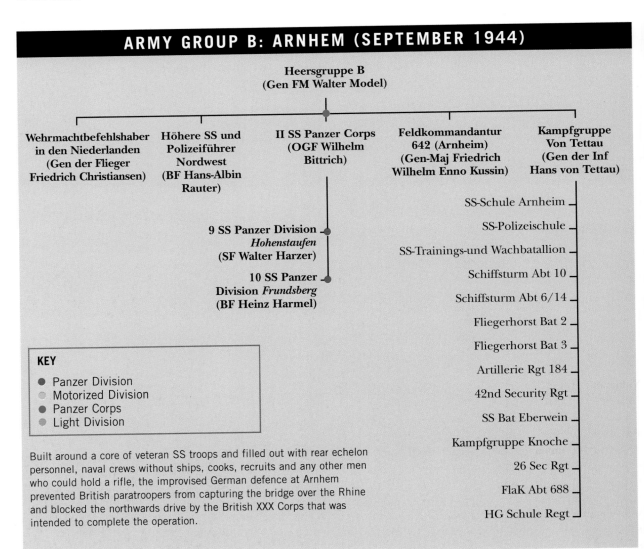

ARMY GROUP B: ARNHEM (SEPTEMBER 1944)

Heersgruppe B
(Gen FM Walter Model)

Wehrmachtbefehlshaber in den Niederlanden
(Gen der Flieger Friedrich Christiansen)

Höhere SS und Polizeiführer Nordwest
(BF Hans-Albin Rauter)

II SS Panzer Corps
(OGF Wilhelm Bittrich)

Feldkommandantur 642 (Arnheim)
(Gen-Maj Friedrich Wilhelm Enno Kussin)

Kampfgruppe Von Tettau
(Gen der Inf Hans von Tettau)

9 SS Panzer Division *Hohenstaufen*
(SF Walter Harzer)

10 SS Panzer Division *Frundsberg*
(BF Heinz Harmel)

SS-Schule Arnheim

SS-Polizeischule

SS-Trainings-und Wachbatallion

Schiffsturm Abt 10

Schiffsturm Abt 6/14

Fliegerhorst Bat 2

Fliegerhorst Bat 3

Artillerie Rgt 184

42nd Security Rgt

SS Bat Eberwein

Kampfgruppe Knoche

26 Sec Rgt

FlaK Abt 688

HG Schule Regt

KEY

- Panzer Division
- Motorized Division
- Panzer Corps
- Light Division

Built around a core of veteran SS troops and filled out with rear echelon personnel, naval crews without ships, cooks, recruits and any other men who could hold a rifle, the improvised German defence at Arnhem prevented British paratroopers from capturing the bridge over the Rhine and blocked the northwards drive by the British XXX Corps that was intended to complete the operation.

The Ardennes Offensive

German troops in Western Europe were under the orders of the Armed Forces High Command or OKW. Operational command was by the *Oberbefehlshaber* West, the commander-in-chief of German forces in Western Europe.

Army Group D was formed on 26 October 1940 in France, its initial cadre coming from the disbanded Army Group C. On 15 April 1941, the status of Army Group D was upgraded, the command of Army Group D being one of the posts of *Oberbefehlshaber* West, the commander-in-chief for the Western Theatre.

In December 1944, Army Group D was under the command of *Generalfeldmarschall* Gerd von Rundstedt. It controlled Army Group G, which had retreated from southern France after the Allied invasion in 1944, fighting through the Vosges Mountains in November 1944, and retreating through Lorraine and north Alsace during December 1944.

The second major formation under Army Group D control was Field Marshal Model's Army Group B, which had retreated through Belgium and France to defensive positions in the Netherlands.

The third Army Group to come under the authority of *Oberbefehlshaber* West and Army Group D was Army Group H. Established in November 1944 by the renaming of Army Group Student in the Netherlands, it was commanded by *Luftwaffe Generaloberst* Kurt Student. The final formation assigned to Army Group D in December 1944 was the Sixth SS Panzer Army, commanded by SS-*Oberstgruppenführer* 'Sepp' Dietrich.

Vulnerable front

Army Group D would be in control of the final major German offensive in the west. By mid-December 1944, the main bulk of the Allied forces, and the attentions of Allied High Command, were concentrated towards both ends of the battlefront. The Anglo–Canadian armies were in the north around Antwerp, and the US First and Ninth Armies were set to close up to the Neder Rhine, where they threatened the vital Rŭhr dams. In the south, General Patton's US Third Army was poised to sweep through the equally important Saar region.

I SS PANZER CORPS – PANZER STRENGTH (DEC 1944)					
Tank type	**Pz IV**	**Pz V**	**StuG**	**FlakPz**	**Pz VI**
1ST SS PANZER DIVISION					
1st SS Pz Rgt	37	34	28	8	45
12TH SS PANZER DIVISION					
12th SS Pz Rgt	37	41	14	0	0
150TH PANZER BGDE					
1/11th Pz Rgt	0	5	0	0	0

Between the two powerful groupings were strung out some 80,000 American troops along 145km (90 miles) of front. The bulk of these consisted of General Middleton's VIII Corps, which had been brought across from Brittany. They were backed by one armoured division, the 9th, which had not yet seen action.

They were stationed here because this part of the front, the Ardennes section, was quiet. It was covered in front by the sparsely settled German Schnee Eifel, and behind by steep wooded hills and foaming trout streams, which had always been regarded as unsuitable country for open warfare.

Three German armies had been created for Hitler's last offensive in the west. By mid-December, they had been

II SS PANZER CORPS – PANZER STRENGTH (DEC 1944)					
Tank type	**Pz III (Bf)**	**Pz IV**	**Pz V**	**StuG**	**FlakPz**
2ND SS PANZER DIVISION					
2nd SS Pz Rgt	0	28	58	28	8
9TH SS PANZER DIVISION					
9th SS Pz Rgt	0	32	33	28	8
10TH SS PANZER DIVISION					
10th SS Pz Rgt	3	41	10	38	0

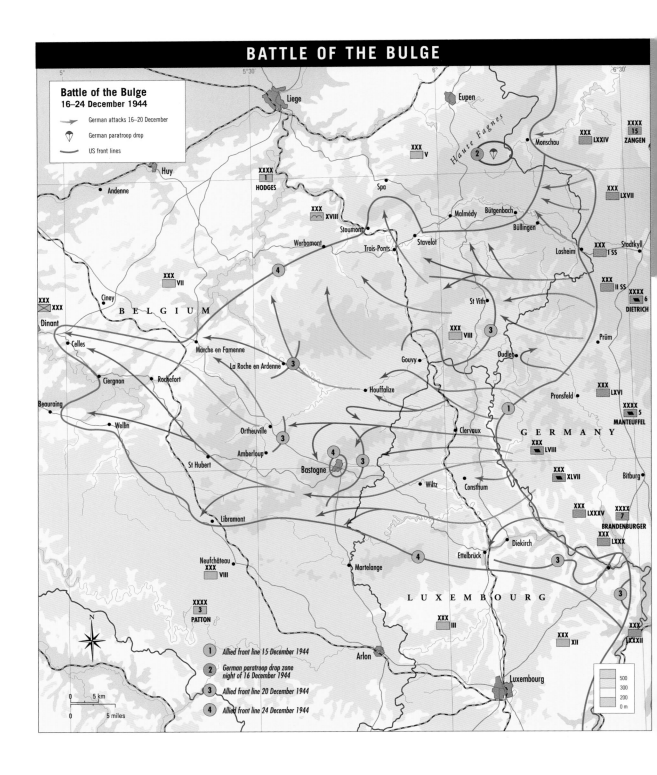

BATTLE OF THE BULGE

Battle of the Bulge
16–24 December 1944

German attacks 16–20 December

German paratroop drop

US front lines

1 Allied front line 15 December 1944

2 German paratroop drop zone
night of 16 December 1944

3 Allied front line 20 December 1944

4 Allied front line 24 December 1944

Liege
Eupen
Monschau
Haute Fagnes
XXX LXXIV
XXXX 15 ZANGEN
Huy
XXX V
Andenne
HODGES XXXX 1
Spa
XXX LXVII
XXX XVIII
Malmédy
Bütgenbach
Büllingen
Stoumont
Werbomont
Trois-Ponts
Stavelot
Losheim
XXX 1 SS
Stadtkyll
XXX VII
St Vith
XXX II SS
Ciney
XXX XXX
Dinant
XXX VIII
Prüm
Celles
Marche en Famenne
La Roche en Ardenne
Gouvy
Oudler
XXX LXVI
Pronsfeld
Ciergnon
Rochefort
Houffalize
Beauraing
Clervaux
XXX 6 DIETRICH
XXXX 5 MANTEUFFEL
Wellin
Ortheuville
GERMANY
XXX LVIII
Amberloup
Bastogne
St Hubert
Wiltz
Consthum
Bitburg
XXX XLVII
Libramont
XXX LXXXV
XXXX 7 BRANDENBURGER
XXX LXXX
Diekirch
Ettelbrück
Neufchâteau
XXX VIII
Martelange
PATTON XXXX 3
LUXEMBOURG
XXX III
XXX XII
XXX LXXXII
Arlon
Luxembourg

N

0   5 km
0   5 miles

500
300
200
0 m

16–24 December 1944

On 16 December 1944, to the astonishment of the Allies, the Germans launched a massive armoured offensive through the Ardennes. Hitler's plan was to use two panzer armies to drive for Antwerp, splitting in half the Allied armies threatening the Reich. Four thinly stretched American divisions were battered by the 16 divisions of the Fiftth Panzer Army and the Sixth SS Panzer Army. German tanks bypassed St Vith in the North, and surrounded Bastogne in the south. However, news that SS men had massacred prisoners of war stiffened American resistance, and German progress slowed. By 20 December, they were still 32km (20 miles) short of the Meuse. Over the Christmas period the skies cleared, and Allied air forces were free to harrass the panzer forces. Within weeks, the Allied forces had fought the Germans to a standstill.

FIFTH PANZER ARMY – PANZER STRENGTH (DEC 1944)				
Tank type	Pz IV	Pz V	StuG	FlakPz
2ND PANZER DIVISION				
3rd Pz Rgt	28	64	24	4
9TH PANZER DIVISION				
33rd Pz Rgt	28	57	14	8
116TH PANZER DIVISION				
116th Pz Rgt	21	41	14	3
PANZER LEHR DIVISION				
130th Pz Rgt	27	30	0	7

marshalled under an exemplary cloak of secrecy and subterfuge opposite that thinly occupied line held by the US VIII Corps.

SS Panzers

In the north were poised the units of the Sixth SS Panzer Army under General 'Sepp' Dietrich. In the middle section of the attack front waited the Fifth Panzer Army under the army general and panzer expert Hasso von Manteuffel. And on the southern flank of the attack, to form the 'hard shoulder' against any possible Allied counterattacks, was the Seventh Army under the dogged General Erich Brandenburger.

Altogether some 200,000 men would take part in Operation *Wacht am Rhein*, equipped with more tanks, more artillery and more ammunition than had been granted to any similarly assembled German force for many months past.

While Operation *Wacht am Rhein* was under way, a second offensive designed to draw Allied forces away from the Ardennes was launched. Operation *Nordwind* was an attack against the thinly stretched, 110km (68-mile) line of the US Seventh Army to the south of the Ardennes. By 15 January, the Seventh Army's VI Corps was almost surrounded in Alsace, forcing the Seventh Army to withdraw to defensive positions on the south bank of the River Moder on 21 January. However, Operation *Nordwind* finally drew to a close on 25 January after the defeat of the Ardennes offensive.

JOSEF 'SEPP' DIETRICH (1892–1966)

A former Sergant in World War I, Dietrich was an early member of the Nazi Party and Hitler's personal driver.

• He commanded *Leibstandarte SS Adolf Hitler* as it grew from a small bodyguard unit to one of the most powerful panzer divisions in the German Army.

• Not an innovative thinker or a particularly gifted panzer tactician, he nevertheless achieved some success with the *Leibstandarte* at Kursk and in Normandy.

• He rose to command the Sixth SS Panzer Army, one of the most powerful armoured formations of the war. He led this unit in the Ardennes and in the attempt to relieve Budapest in February and March 1945.

THE ARDENNES OFFENSIVE

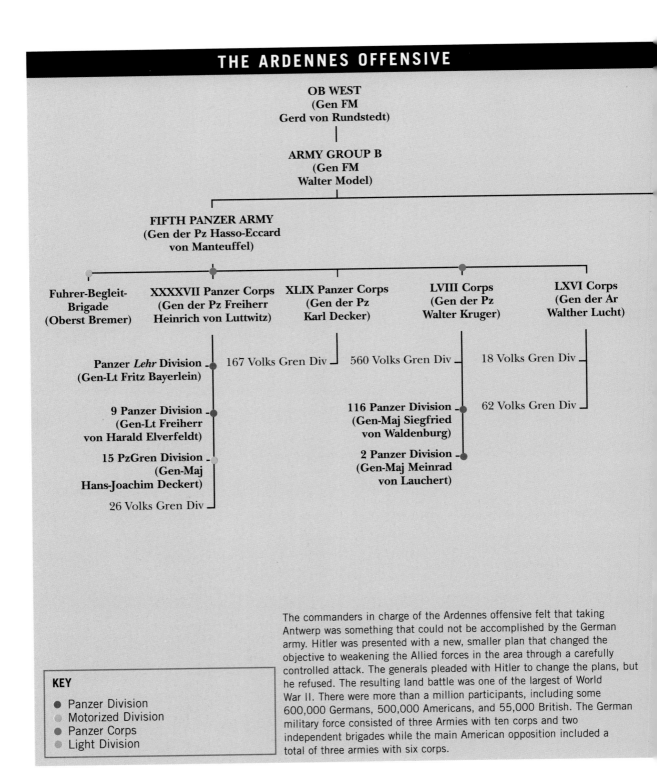

OB WEST
(Gen FM
Gerd von Rundstedt)

ARMY GROUP B
(Gen FM
Walter Model)

FIFTH PANZER ARMY
(Gen der Pz Hasso-Eccard
von Manteuffel)

Fuhrer-Begleit-
Brigade
(Oberst Bremer)

XXXXVII Panzer Corps
(Gen der Pz Freiherr
Heinrich von Luttwitz)

XLIX Panzer Corps
(Gen der Pz
Karl Decker)

LVIII Corps
(Gen der Pz
Walter Kruger)

LXVI Corps
(Gen der Ar
Walther Lucht)

Panzer *Lehr* Division
(Gen-Lt Fritz Bayerlein)

167 Volks Gren Div

560 Volks Gren Div

18 Volks Gren Div

9 Panzer Division
(Gen-Lt Freiherr
von Harald Elverfeldt)

116 Panzer Division
(Gen-Maj Siegfried
von Waldenburg)

62 Volks Gren Div

15 PzGren Division
(Gen-Maj
Hans-Joachim Deckert)

2 Panzer Division
(Gen-Maj Meinrad
von Lauchert)

26 Volks Gren Div

The commanders in charge of the Ardennes offensive felt that taking Antwerp was something that could not be accomplished by the German army. Hitler was presented with a new, smaller plan that changed the objective to weakening the Allied forces in the area through a carefully controlled attack. The generals pleaded with Hitler to change the plans, but he refused. The resulting land battle was one of the largest of World War II. There were more than a million participants, including some 600,000 Germans, 500,000 Americans, and 55,000 British. The German military force consisted of three Armies with ten corps and two independent brigades while the main American opposition included a total of three armies with six corps.

KEY

● Panzer Division
○ Motorized Division
● Panzer Corps
○ Light Division

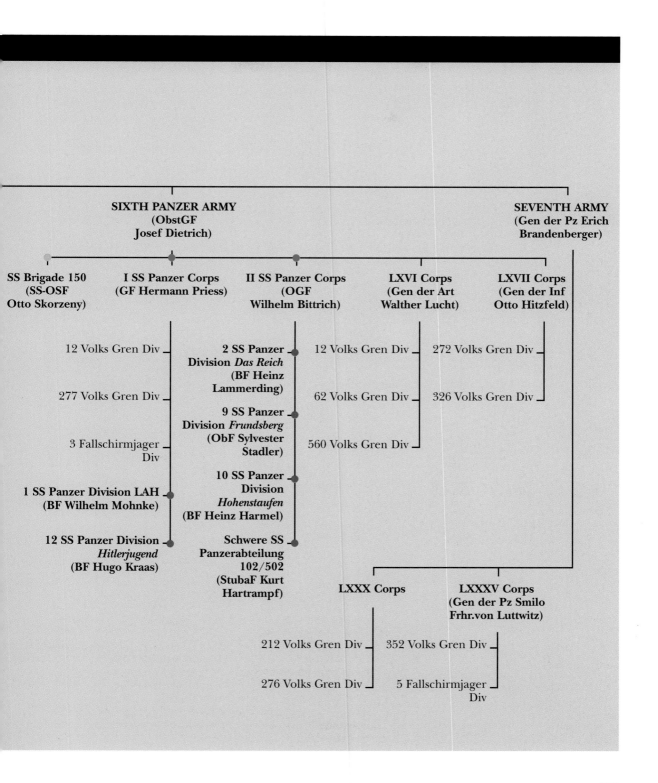

SIXTH PANZER ARMY
(ObstGF
Josef Dietrich)

SEVENTH ARMY
(Gen der Pz Erich
Brandenberger)

SS Brigade 150
(SS-OSF
Otto Skorzeny)

I SS Panzer Corps
(GF Hermann Priess)

II SS Panzer Corps
(OGF
Wilhelm Bittrich)

LXVI Corps
(Gen der Art
Walther Lucht)

LXVII Corps
(Gen der Inf
Otto Hitzfeld)

12 Volks Gren Div

2 SS Panzer
Division *Das Reich*
(BF Heinz
Lammerding)

12 Volks Gren Div

272 Volks Gren Div

277 Volks Gren Div

62 Volks Gren Div

326 Volks Gren Div

9 SS Panzer
Division *Frundsberg*
(ObF Sylvester
Stadler)

3 Fallschirmjager
Div

560 Volks Gren Div

10 SS Panzer
Division
Hohenstaufen
(BF Heinz Harmel)

1 SS Panzer Division LAH
(BF Wilhelm Mohnke)

12 SS Panzer Division
Hitlerjugend
(BF Hugo Kraas)

Schwere SS
Panzerabteilung
102/502
(StubaF Kurt
Hartrampf)

LXXX Corps

LXXXV Corps
(Gen der Pz Smilo
Frhr.von Luttwitz)

212 Volks Gren Div

352 Volks Gren Div

276 Volks Gren Div

5 Fallschirmjager
Div

165

Defence of the Reich: 1945

By the end of 1944, Germany's armed forces were in retreat on all fronts. Still capable of putting up a fight, the *Wehrmacht*'s Panzer forces were equipped with the most powerful tanks in the world, but there was no way they could match Allied numbers.

SS King Tigers in Hungary, 1945. Introduced at the end of 1944, the King Tiger was the best-protected tank of the war, and its long 8.8-cm gun could destroy any Allied tank at ranges of up to 2000m (6562ft).

IN JANUARY 1945, Germany was doomed, as Allied forces to west and east prepared to tear into the heartland of the Reich. Having lost the Battle of the Bulge, the German Army was on the defensive, and Allied armies stood on the borders of Germany itself. They had yet to penetrate the home territory of the Reich, but senior commanders, notably Heinz Guderian, knew that this was the calm before the storm. When the Allies decided to attack, he knew there would be no way that Germany could be saved.

The Allies were still extremely wary of the Nazis. In the Ardennes, the massive German attack had recently succeeded in wiping out one tenth of all American and British armour. The American newsreels were warning their forces in propaganda films that the Nazi beast had not yet been destroyed. To the east, the Soviets were struggling to wrest control of Budapest in one of the most bitter of all struggles of Worl War II. A huge push by the Sixth SS Panzer Army was attempting to break the siege of Hungary's capital. Further north, the Red Army's offensive of the previous year had been halted on the east bank of the Vistula, before Warsaw.

In Germany, Goebbels' propaganda machine was working at full throttle. Morale had received a huge shot in the arm from the Ardennes counterblast, coming as it did at the end of a year of calamities for the Reich.

Newsreels exhorted the population to renewed and continual sacrifices. For the defence of the homeland, the very old and very young were called upon to place themselves in the path of the Allied onslaught. Many of these 'volunteers' were supplied with the one-shot panzerfaust rocket launcher, but little else.

The previous November, a German counterattack had regained the little town of Neummersdorf – to find the place in ruins and the entire population massacred by the Soviets. This bore out all of Goebbels' most blood-curdling prophecies. Most of the poorly trained *Volkssturm* (People's Assault) units did not get the chance to use their weapons – many broke ranks and fled when faced with the horror of a real battle.

Western Front: 1945

Allied plans in the west had been changed by the capture of the bridge at Remagen on 7 March. The bridge could not be immediately exploited, but on 22 March, Patton's Third Army established another bridgehead after a surprise assault at Oppenheim.

Soon afterwards, Montgomery's Twenty-First Army Group crossed the river on a broad front at Wesel north of the Ruhr. The German defences of the Rhine were therefore compromised at two widely separated places, in the Ruhr and at its confluence with the River Main.

Ruhr pocket falls

While the British and Canadian armies pressed on into northern Germany, aiming towards Hamburg, the US Ninth and First Armies surrounded the Ruhr, Germany's industrial heartland. The huge pocket contained the remnants of Army Group B together with elements of Army Group A's Parachute units. It finally fell on 18 April, yielding 325,000 prisoners. The last few German units surrendered on 21 April. Model, 'The Führer's Fireman', committed suicide.

On the evening of 11 April, the US Ninth Army reached the River Elbe, the agreed demarcation line between the Soviet and western occupation zones in Germany. They were only 80km (50 miles) from Berlin.

Orders quickly came down the line that they were not to press for the German capital – it was to be left to the Red Army. The western armies were bound by the inter-Allied Agreement made at Yalta the previous year. American forces in the central sector would stay where they were, while the British and Americans continued to clear northern Germany and the southern US units and French armies overran Bavaria.

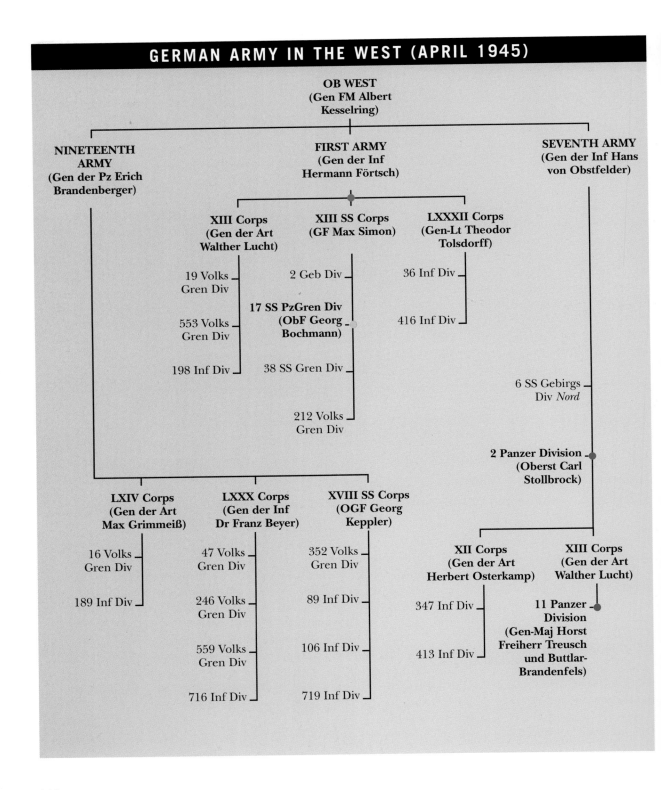

GERMAN ARMY IN THE WEST (APRIL 1945)

OB WEST
(Gen FM Albert Kesselring)

NINETEENTH ARMY
(Gen der Pz Erich Brandenberger)

FIRST ARMY
(Gen der Inf Hermann Förtsch)

SEVENTH ARMY
(Gen der Inf Hans von Obstfelder)

XIII Corps
(Gen der Art Walther Lucht)

XIII SS Corps
(GF Max Simon)

LXXXII Corps
(Gen-Lt Theodor Tolsdorff)

19 Volks Gren Div

2 Geb Div

36 Inf Div

553 Volks Gren Div

17 SS PzGren Div (ObF Georg Bochmann)

416 Inf Div

198 Inf Div

38 SS Gren Div

212 Volks Gren Div

6 SS Gebirgs Div *Nord*

2 Panzer Division (Oberst Carl Stollbrock)

LXIV Corps
(Gen der Art Max Grimmeiß)

LXXX Corps
(Gen der Inf Dr Franz Beyer)

XVIII SS Corps
(OGF Georg Keppler)

XII Corps
(Gen der Art Herbert Osterkamp)

XIII Corps
(Gen der Art Walther Lucht)

16 Volks Gren Div

47 Volks Gren Div

352 Volks Gren Div

11 Panzer Division (Gen-Maj Horst Freiherr Treusch und Buttlar-Brandenfels)

189 Inf Div

246 Volks Gren Div

89 Inf Div

347 Inf Div

559 Volks Gren Div

106 Inf Div

413 Inf Div

716 Inf Div

719 Inf Div

8 February – 21 March 1945

In February 1945, the task for the Allied armies was to cross the Rivers Roer, Our and Saar and to reach the Rhine. By 21 February, Goch, Cleve and Calcar were in British and Canadian hands, and the Americans took Moenchen Gladbach on 1 March and Cologne five days later. On 7 March, the Ludendorff Bridge at Remagen was taken intact by the US First Army. On 23 March, Montgomery's Twenty-First Army Group stormed the Rhine at Wesel, preceded by two divisions of paratroopers. By nightfall, the ground troops had joined up with the paratroopers, and the Rhine bridgeheads were secure. Further south, the Americans launched their own crossings, mostly mounted by fewer men with limited resources. Patton, eager to beat Montgomery across the river, had sent an assault regiment of the US 5th Division, part of his Third Army, to cross the Rhine, in rubber boats, between Nierstein and Oppenheim. Securing the far bank, they were joined by the rest of the Division. By the end of March, Darmstadt and Wiesbaden were in American hands, and US armoured columns were driving for Frankfurt-am-main. Further south, the French had put an Algerian division across the river at Gemersheim. Most German troops knew that the war was lost and were ready to surrender, though a few young volunteers along with diehard SS men continued to fight to the last.

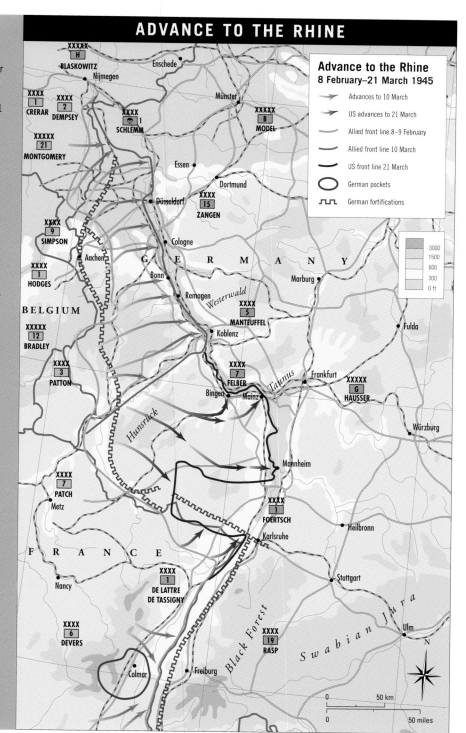

ADVANCE TO THE RHINE

Advance to the Rhine
8 February–21 March 1945

- Advances to 10 March
- US advances to 21 March
- Allied front line 8–9 February
- Allied front line 10 March
- US front line 21 March
- German pockets
- German fortifications

3000
1500
600
300
0 ft

0   50 km

0   50 miles

Eastern Front: 1945

After its incredible successes on the Eastern Front in the summer and autumn of 1944, the Red Army paused to regroup in November and December of that year. However, the German generals knew that the final onslaught was coming.

General Heinz Guderian, who had been appointed chief of staff of the German Army, told Hitler that the Red Army massing against Germany's eastern defences enjoyed overwhelming material superiority: 20:1 in artillery; 11:1 in infantry; and 7:1 in armour. Hitler refused to listen and told Guderian to sack his intelligence chief – to which Guderian retorted that Hitler might as well fire his chief of staff too.

Offensive through Poland

On 12 January, the very day predicted by Guderian, the Soviet offensive was launched. Marshal Konev's 1st Ukrainian Front broke out of the Sandomierz bridgehead to tear a 35km (22-mile) hole in the German defences in southern Poland; at the same time, the 3rd Ukrainian Front attacked East Prussia.

Two days later, Zhukov's 1st Belorussian Front attacked from its bridgeheads over the Vistula and surrounded Warsaw. On 17 January 1945, the Polish capital – razed to the ground on Hitler's orders after the abortive rising the previous autumn – was taken by the First Polish Army. Krakow was liberated the next day. German units assembling for a counterattack at Lodz were caught deploying, and swept back to the Oder.

Baltic coast isolated

East Prussia was cut off. The Third Panzer Army fell back into Königsberg and the Samland peninsula. The beleaguered Germans were joined by the former garrison of Memel, evacuated on 29 January under the guns of the surviving units of the German Navy, including the heavy cruiser *Prinz Eugen*. From the Baltic to southern Poland, improvised *Kampfgruppen* fought desperately, firstly to win time for German forces to make good their escape, and then to break free themselves. They took a huge toll on the advancing Soviet forces. The gunners counted for wave after wave

of Soviet armour. Counterattack followed attack. But the Red Army advance was remorseless, progressing 400km (249 miles) in a fortnight to seize footholds on the west bank of the Oder. From there to Berlin was but an hour's drive on the *autobahn*.

Meanwhile, the siege of Budapest continued. The last German attempt to relieve the city failed on 1 January 1945. Soviet troops fought their way into the eastern half of the city house by house, grinding their way to the Danube at incredible cost. The defenders were split into several pockets that finally surrendered on 18 January. The same horrific process then began on the opposite bank as Buda was conquered with the same combination of flame-throwers, explosive charges and point-blank fire from self-propelled guns. More than 16,000 German and Hungarian troops tried to break out on 16 February, once the end was near. They were wiped out in a series of running battles, and only a handful of individuals escaped to German lines.

January–February 1945

Since Hitler had deployed the cream of the German armed forces in the Ardennes, the *Wehrmacht* had little to counter the new Soviet offensive launched on 12 January 1945. Guderian had proposed to evacuate the divisions of Army Group North stuck in the Courland to the Reich via the Baltic Sea, in order to get the necessary manpower for the defence, but Hitler forbade it. In addition, Hitler commanded that several crack SS divisions be moved from the Ardennes front to Hungary, where they would be used in operation *Frühlingserwachen* (Spring Awakening) to relieve Budapest and secure the Hungarian oilfields. Attacking from the Vistula, the Red Army drove onto German soil for the first time. Silesia fell quickly, and by the end of January, Zhukhov's First Belorussian Front was on the Oder. There, Stalin called a halt, to allow time to prepare for the final attack on Berlin.

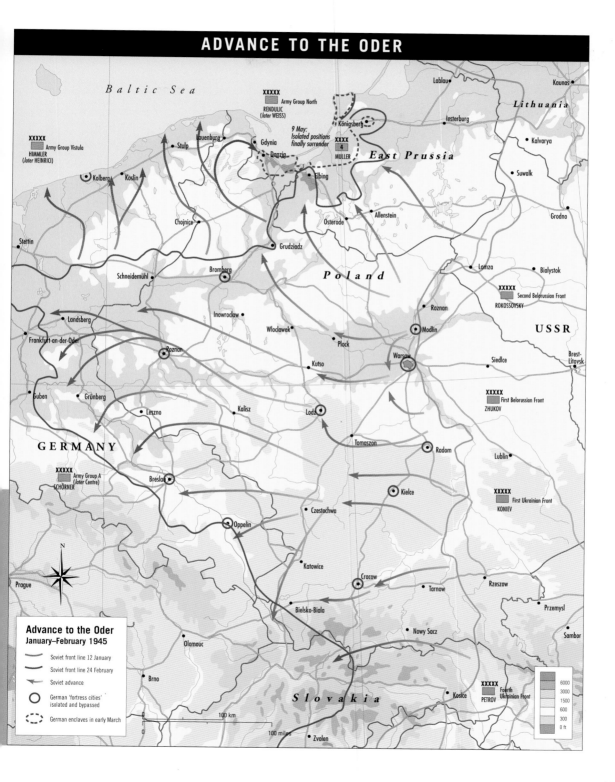

ADVANCE TO THE ODER

Baltic Sea

Lithuania

XXXXX
Army Group North
RENDULIC
(*later* WEISS)

9 May:
Isolated positions
finally surrender

XXXX
4
MULLER

East Prussia

XXXXX
Army Group Vistula
HIMMLER
(*later* HEINRICI)

Lablau

Kaunos

Insterburg

Königsberg

Kalvarya

Suwalk

Grodno

Kolberg

Koslin

Stulp

Lauenburg

Gdynia

Danzig

Elbing

Osterode

Allenstein

Chojnice

Grudziadz

Poland

Lomza

Bialystok

Stettin

Schneidemühl

Bromberg

Inowroclaw

XXXXX
Second Belorussian Front
ROKOSSOVSKY

USSR

Roznan

Landsberg

Frankfurt-an-der-Oder

Roznan

Wloclawek

Plock

Modlin

Kutso

Warsaw

Siedlce

Brest-Litovsk

Guben

Grünberg

Leszno

Kalisz

Lodz

XXXXX
First Belorussian Front
ZHUKOV

GERMANY

Tomaszon

Radom

Lublin

XXXXX
Army Group A
(*later* Centre)
SCHÖRNER

Breslau

Kielce

XXXXX
First Ukrainian Front
KONIEV

Oppelin

Czestochwa

Katowice

Cracow

Tarnow

Rzeszow

Prague

Bielsko-Biala

Nowy Sacz

Sambor

Przemysl

N

Olomouc

Advance to the Oder
January–February 1945

— Soviet front line 12 January

— Soviet front line 24 February

← Soviet advance

◯ German 'fortress cities'
isolated and bypassed

⬭ German enclaves in early March

Brno

Slovakia

Kosice

XXXXX
Fourth
Ukrainian Front
PETROV

100 km

100 miles

Zvolen

	6000
	3000
	1500
	600
	300
	0 ft

ARMY GROUP WEICHSEL (MARCH 1945)

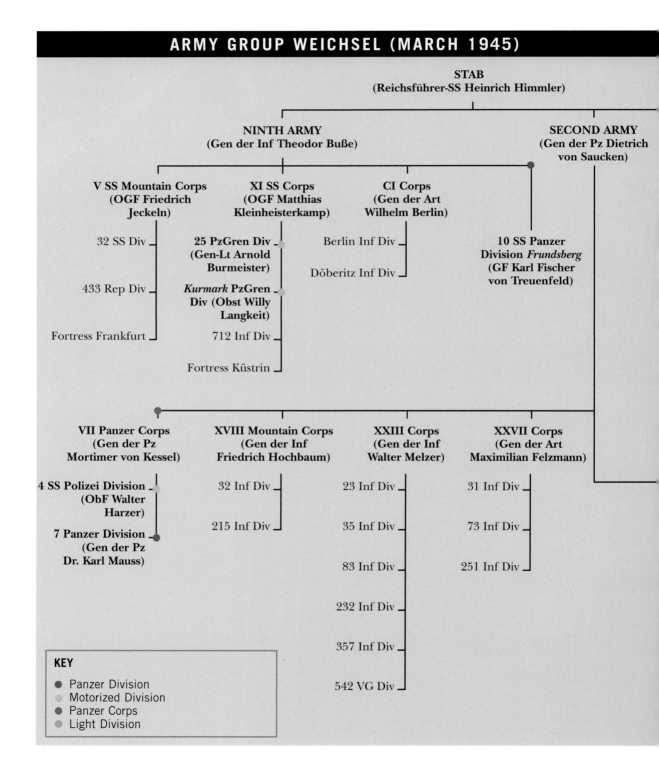

STAB
(Reichsführer-SS Heinrich Himmler)

NINTH ARMY
(Gen der Inf Theodor Buße)

SECOND ARMY
(Gen der Pz Dietrich von Saucken)

V SS Mountain Corps
(OGF Friedrich Jeckeln)

XI SS Corps
(OGF Matthias Kleinheisterkamp)

CI Corps
(Gen der Art Wilhelm Berlin)

32 SS Div

25 PzGren Div
(Gen-Lt Arnold Burmeister)

Berlin Inf Div

10 SS Panzer Division *Frundsberg*
(GF Karl Fischer von Treuenfeld)

433 Rep Div

Kurmark **PzGren Div** (Obst Willy Langkeit)

Döberitz Inf Div

Fortress Frankfurt

712 Inf Div

Fortress Küstrin

VII Panzer Corps
(Gen der Pz Mortimer von Kessel)

XVIII Mountain Corps
(Gen der Inf Friedrich Hochbaum)

XXIII Corps
(Gen der Inf Walter Melzer)

XXVII Corps
(Gen der Art Maximilian Felzmann)

4 SS Polizei Division
(ObF Walter Harzer)

32 Inf Div

23 Inf Div

31 Inf Div

215 Inf Div

35 Inf Div

73 Inf Div

7 Panzer Division
(Gen der Pz Dr. Karl Mauss)

83 Inf Div

251 Inf Div

232 Inf Div

357 Inf Div

542 VG Div

KEY

- Panzer Division
- Motorized Division
- Panzer Corps
- Light Division

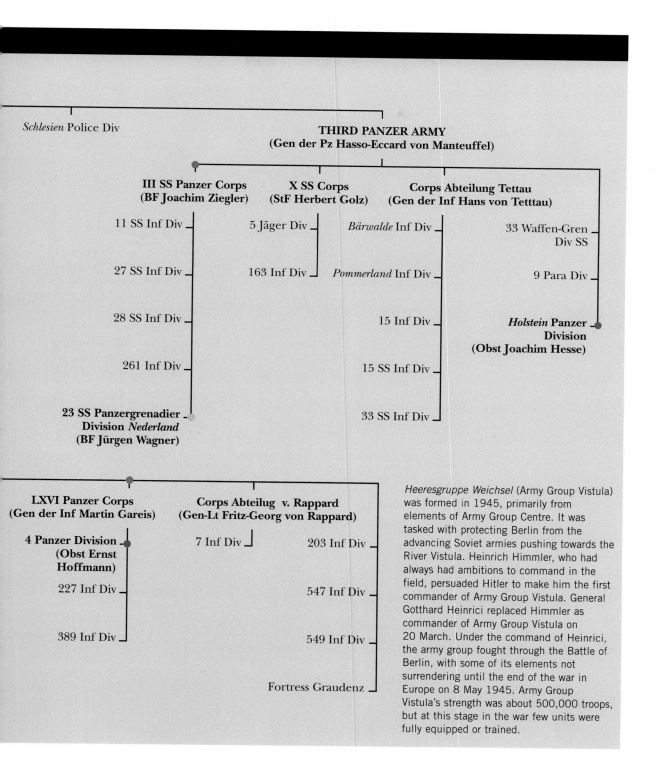

Schlesien Police Div

THIRD PANZER ARMY
(Gen der Pz Hasso-Eccard von Manteuffel)

III SS Panzer Corps
(BF Joachim Ziegler)

X SS Corps
(StF Herbert Golz)

Corps Abteilung Tettau
(Gen der Inf Hans von Tetttau)

11 SS Inf Div

5 Jäger Div

Bärwalde Inf Div

33 Waffen-Gren
Div SS

27 SS Inf Div

163 Inf Div

Pommerland Inf Div

9 Para Div

28 SS Inf Div

15 Inf Div

Holstein **Panzer**
Division
(Obst Joachim Hesse)

261 Inf Div

15 SS Inf Div

23 SS Panzergrenadier
Division *Nederland*
(BF Jürgen Wagner)

33 SS Inf Div

LXVI Panzer Corps
(Gen der Inf Martin Gareis)

Corps Abteilug v. Rappard
(Gen-Lt Fritz-Georg von Rappard)

4 Panzer Division
(Obst Ernst
Hoffmann)

7 Inf Div

203 Inf Div

227 Inf Div

547 Inf Div

389 Inf Div

549 Inf Div

Fortress Graudenz

Heeresgruppe Weichsel (Army Group Vistula) was formed in 1945, primarily from elements of Army Group Centre. It was tasked with protecting Berlin from the advancing Soviet armies pushing towards the River Vistula. Heinrich Himmler, who had always had ambitions to command in the field, persuaded Hitler to make him the first commander of Army Group Vistula. General Gotthard Heinrici replaced Himmler as commander of Army Group Vistula on 20 March. Under the command of Heinrici, the army group fought through the Battle of Berlin, with some of its elements not surrendering until the end of the war in Europe on 8 May 1945. Army Group Vistula's strength was about 500,000 troops, but at this stage in the war few units were fully equipped or trained.

On the Oder and Danube

In spite of the fact that the main strength of the Red Army juggernaut was pointed directly at Berlin, Hitler believed that it was more important to safeguard Germany's last oil resource than to protect the heartland of the Third Reich.

The hot flames of war swept from the ancient Germanic heartland of East Prussia to Berlin itself. The Red Army smashed its way to the Nazi capital in what its historians termed the 'Vistula-Oder operation', an object lesson in *Blitzkrieg* that became a model for future Soviet war plans. Like the original German *Blitzkrieg* into the Soviet Union in 1941, military expertise was combined with incredible savagery in what, from the Soviet point of view, was a war of revenge.

Hitler's grip on reality was slipping, but his belief in his command genius was not. He gave a series of orders that served to shorten the life of the Reich. His favoured method of defence, in the east and the west, was to create a series of *Festungs,* or fortresses. The list of these fortified towns included Stettin, Konigsberg, Tannenberg and Breslau in the East and La Rochelle and Rochefort in the West. They had little strategic value but leeched away German strength by isolating experienced troops who could have been better used in mobile warfare.

Last offensive

Hitler's last military offensive – Spring Awakening – began on 6 March at Lake Balaton, Hungary. Incredibly, Hitler had weakened the defences on the Warsaw–Berlin axis, where the main Soviet thrust would come, in order to reinforce German forces in Hungary. A total of 31 divisions, including 11 panzer and panzergrenadier divisions, took part, although all were substantially below authorized strength.

SS panzers

The strike force included some 800 tanks, most in the Sixth SS Panzer Army, commanded by SS *Oberst-gruppenführer* 'Sepp' Dietrich. Dietrich soon realized that the assault was futile. An early thaw left the Hungarian plain waterlogged, and the operating conditions were impossible for his super-heavy King Tiger tanks.

21ST PANZER DIVISION – PANZER STRENGTH (MARCH 1945)					
Tank type	StuG	Pz IV	Pz IV(70)	Pz V	FlkPz
22nd Pz Rgt	1	31	16	33	4

The last strength of the Reich had been squandered. It defies belief that Hitler could have ordered an attack in Hungary rather than defend his own people who were in such desperate straits further to the North.

Refugees from the east

Five million German civilians fled to escape the Red Army. Two million were evacuated by sea from German-held ports along the Baltic, noted for the worst maritime disaster in history – the sinking of the 25,000-ton liner *Wilhelm Gustloff* by a Soviet submarine. Of the 8000 people aboard, only 650 survived.

15 April–6 May 1945

By mid-April, after a pause to regroup following their successful winter offensive from the Vistula, the massed Soviet armies of Rokossovsky's 2nd Belorussian Front, Zhukov's 1st Belorussian Front and Konev's 1st Ukraininan Front were ready to attack. Stalin ordered both Zhukhov and Konev to prepare for the attack on Berlin, counting on the rivalry between his two greatest Marshals to spur their troops into the city before the Western Allies could snatch the prize. On 16 April 1945, a massive artillery bombardment launched the Soviet attack. In spite of fierce German resistance on the Seelöwe heights to the east of the city, Zhukhov's troops were in the suburbs by 21 April. On 24 April, troops of the 1st Belorussian and the 1st Ukrainian Fronts, which had attacked the southern approaches to the city, finally met on the River Havel. Berlin was surrounded.

ENCIRCLEMENT OF BERLIN

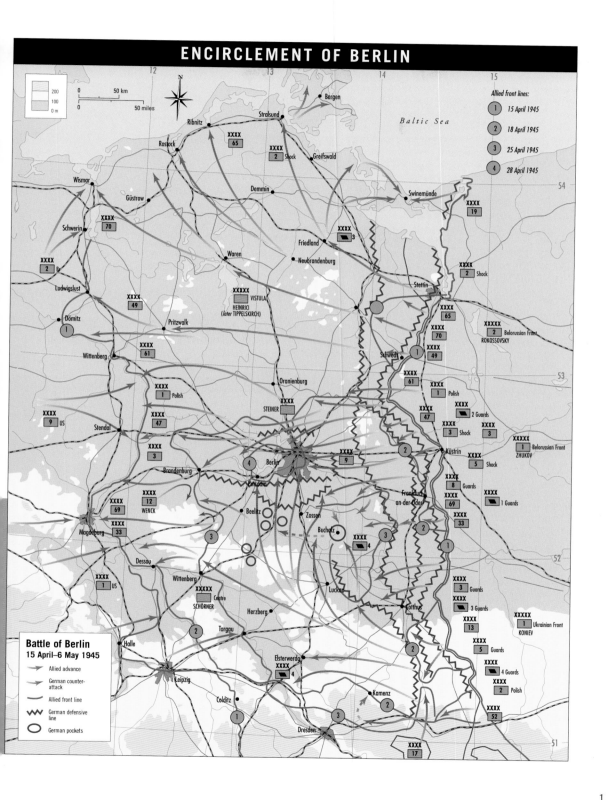

Baltic Sea

Allied front lines:
- (1) 15 April 1945
- (2) 18 April 1945
- (3) 25 April 1945
- (4) 28 April 1945

Battle of Berlin
15 April–6 May 1945

- → Allied advance
- → German counter-attack
- ⌒ Allied front line
- WWW German defensive line
- ◯ German pockets

ARMY GROUP CENTRE (MARCH 1945)

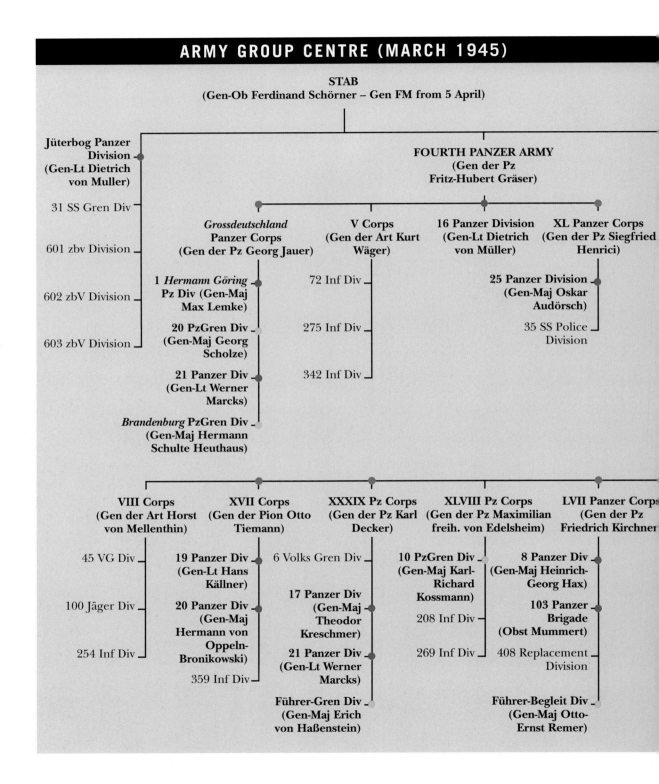

STAB
(Gen-Ob Ferdinand Schörner – Gen FM from 5 April)

Jüterbog Panzer Division
(Gen-Lt Dietrich von Muller)

31 SS Gren Div

601 zbv Division

602 zbV Division

603 zbV Division

FOURTH PANZER ARMY
(Gen der Pz Fritz-Hubert Gräser)

Grossdeutschland **Panzer Corps**
(Gen der Pz Georg Jauer)

1 *Hermann Göring* **Pz Div (Gen-Maj Max Lemke)**

20 PzGren Div (Gen-Maj Georg Scholze)

21 Panzer Div (Gen-Lt Werner Marcks)

Brandenburg **PzGren Div (Gen-Maj Hermann Schulte Heuthaus)**

V Corps
(Gen der Art Kurt Wäger)

72 Inf Div

275 Inf Div

342 Inf Div

16 Panzer Division
(Gen-Lt Dietrich von Müller)

XL Panzer Corps
(Gen der Pz Siegfried Henrici)

25 Panzer Division
(Gen-Maj Oskar Audörsch)

35 SS Police Division

VIII Corps
(Gen der Art Horst von Mellenthin)

45 VG Div

100 Jäger Div

254 Inf Div

XVII Corps
(Gen der Pion Otto Tiemann)

19 Panzer Div (Gen-Lt Hans Källner)

20 Panzer Div (Gen-Maj Hermann von Oppeln-Bronikowski)

359 Inf Div

XXXIX Pz Corps
(Gen der Pz Karl Decker)

6 Volks Gren Div

17 Panzer Div (Gen-Maj Theodor Kreschmer)

21 Panzer Div (Gen-Lt Werner Marcks)

Führer-Gren Div (Gen-Maj Erich von Haßenstein)

XLVIII Pz Corps
(Gen der Pz Maximilian freih. von Edelsheim)

10 PzGren Div (Gen-Maj Karl-Richard Kossmann)

208 Inf Div

269 Inf Div

LVII Panzer Corps
(Gen der Pz Friedrich Kirchner)

8 Panzer Div (Gen-Maj Heinrich-Georg Hax)

103 Panzer Brigade (Obst Mummert)

408 Replacement Division

Führer-Begleit Div (Gen-Maj Otto-Ernst Remer)

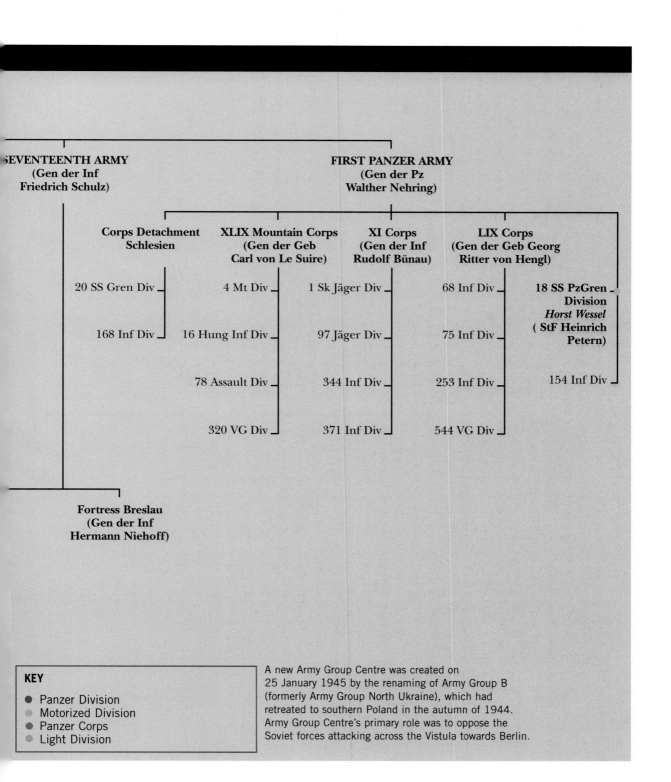

SEVENTEENTH ARMY
(Gen der Inf
Friedrich Schulz)

FIRST PANZER ARMY
(Gen der Pz
Walther Nehring)

Corps Detachment Schlesien	**XLIX Mountain Corps (Gen der Geb Carl von Le Suire)**	**XI Corps (Gen der Inf Rudolf Bünau)**	**LIX Corps (Gen der Geb Georg Ritter von Hengl)**	
20 SS Gren Div	4 Mt Div	1 Sk Jäger Div	68 Inf Div	**18 SS PzGren Division** *Horst Wessel* **(StF Heinrich Petern)**
168 Inf Div	16 Hung Inf Div	97 Jäger Div	75 Inf Div	
	78 Assault Div	344 Inf Div	253 Inf Div	154 Inf Div
	320 VG Div	371 Inf Div	544 VG Div	

Fortress Breslau
(Gen der Inf
Hermann Niehoff)

KEY

● Panzer Division
○ Motorized Division
● Panzer Corps
○ Light Division

A new Army Group Centre was created on
25 January 1945 by the renaming of Army Group B
(formerly Army Group North Ukraine), which had
retreated to southern Poland in the autumn of 1944.
Army Group Centre's primary role was to oppose the
Soviet forces attacking across the Vistula towards Berlin.

ARMY GROUP NORTH (MARCH 1945)

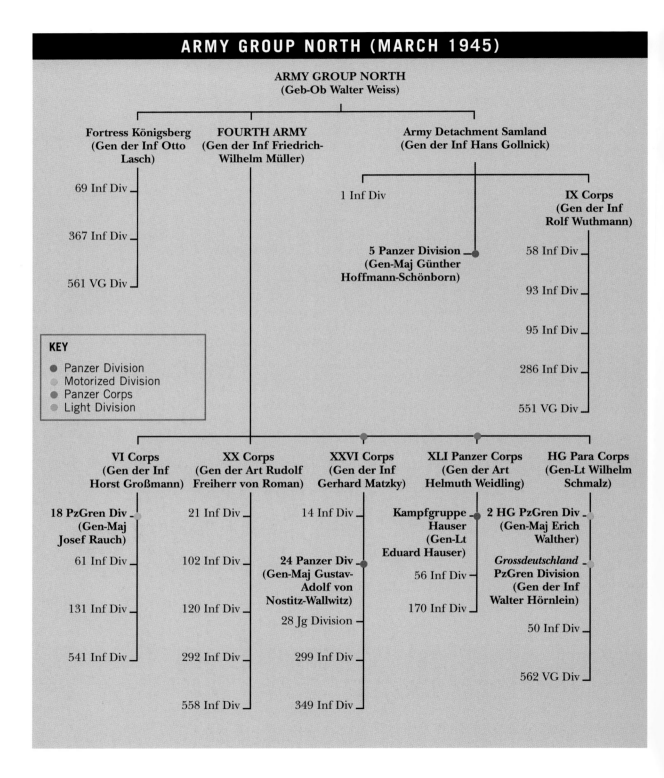

ARMY GROUP NORTH
(Geb-Ob Walter Weiss)

Fortress Königsberg
(Gen der Inf Otto
Lasch)

FOURTH ARMY
(Gen der Inf Friedrich-
Wilhelm Müller)

Army Detachment Samland
(Gen der Inf Hans Gollnick)

69 Inf Div

367 Inf Div

561 VG Div

1 Inf Div

5 Panzer Division
(Gen-Maj Günther
Hoffmann-Schönborn)

IX Corps
(Gen der Inf
Rolf Wuthmann)

58 Inf Div

93 Inf Div

95 Inf Div

286 Inf Div

551 VG Div

KEY

- Panzer Division
- Motorized Division
- Panzer Corps
- Light Division

VI Corps
(Gen der Inf
Horst Großmann)

XX Corps
(Gen der Art Rudolf
Freiherr von Roman)

XXVI Corps
(Gen der Inf
Gerhard Matzky)

XLI Panzer Corps
(Gen der Art
Helmuth Weidling)

HG Para Corps
(Gen-Lt Wilhelm
Schmalz)

18 PzGren Div
(Gen-Maj
Josef Rauch)

21 Inf Div

14 Inf Div

Kampfgruppe
Hauser
(Gen-Lt
Eduard Hauser)

2 HG PzGren Div
(Gen-Maj Erich
Walther)

61 Inf Div

102 Inf Div

24 Panzer Div
(Gen-Maj Gustav-
Adolf von
Nostitz-Wallwitz)

56 Inf Div

Grossdeutschland
PzGren Division
(Gen der Inf
Walter Hörnlein)

131 Inf Div

120 Inf Div

170 Inf Div

28 Jg Division

50 Inf Div

541 Inf Div

292 Inf Div

299 Inf Div

562 VG Div

558 Inf Div

349 Inf Div

Last defenders of Germany

As Allied armies were pushing forwards towards the Rhine and the Vistula early in 1945, German Army groups on the Eastern Front underwent a wholesale reorganization to reflect the realities facing a doomed Reich.

On 25 January 1945, Adolf Hitler ordered the redesignation of Army Group North, Army Group Centre and Army Group A. Hitler's name changes meant that Army Group North became Army Group Courland (*Heeresgruppe Kurland*), Army Group Centre became Army Group North (*Heeresgruppe Nord*) and Army Group A became Army Group Centre (*Heeresgruppe Mitte*).

Army Group Courland

Bypassed by the main Soviet thrusts, Army Group Courland remained relatively intact until the end of the war. Between October 1944 and the Army Group's surrender in May 1945, it fought six major battles against the Red Army.

Army Group North

Army Group North, the former Army Group Centre, which had been rebuilt after its destruction in 1944, had been forced back into East Prussia in January 1945, at which time it was redesignated. On 13 January 1945, almost 1,500,000 Soviet troops, supported by several thousand tanks and aircraft, advanced into East Prussia, Over the next three months, Army Group North was driven into an ever-decreasing pocket around Königsberg in East Prussia. On 9 April 1945, after a fierce four day assault, Königsberg finally fell to the Red Army. Remnants of Army Group North units continued to resist on the Heiligenbeil and Danzig beachheads until the end of the war in Europe.

Army Group Centre

Formerly Army Group A, Army Group Centre bore the brunt of the southern flank of main Soviet thrust towards Berlin. Commanded by *Generalfeldmarschal* Ferdinand Schörner, the bulk of Army Group A was dug into defensive positions along the Oder–Neisse line about 60km (37 miles) east of the German capital, and was quickly brushed aside by Konev's 1st Ukrainian Front.

Army Group *Weichsel*

The Army Group *Weichsel* (the German word for the Vistula River) was formed in 1945 from elements of the old Army Group Centre. It was intended to defend Berlin from Zhukov's 1st Belorussian Front, which was advancing westwards from the Vistula.

In spit of a complete lack of command experience, Heinrich Himmler was appointed the first commander of Army Group Vistula. General Gotthard Heinrici replaced Himmler as commander of Army Group Vistula on 20 March. Under the command of Heinrici, the army group fought through the Battle of Berlin, with some of its elements not surrendering until the end of the war in Europe on 8 May 1945.

Army Group *Ostmark*

At the end of World War II in Europe, Army Group South was redesignated Army Group *Ostmark*. Its units, including the Second Panzer Army, the Sixth SS Panzer Army (which had been rushed east after the failure of the Ardennes Offensive), the Sixth Army and the Eighth Army had been used in the futile attempt to protect the Hungarian oilfields and to raise the siege of Budapest.

The remnants of what had successively been known as Army Group South Ukraine and Army Group South were driven out of Hungary, and most ended the war fighting in and around Austria. However, some Corps-sized units were detached and fought alongside Army Group Centre in Czechoslovakia, where they took part in the battle of Prague – the last major battle of World War II in Europe, which did not end until three days after the general German surrender on 8 May. Army Group *Ostmark* was one of the last major German military formations to surrender to the Allies.

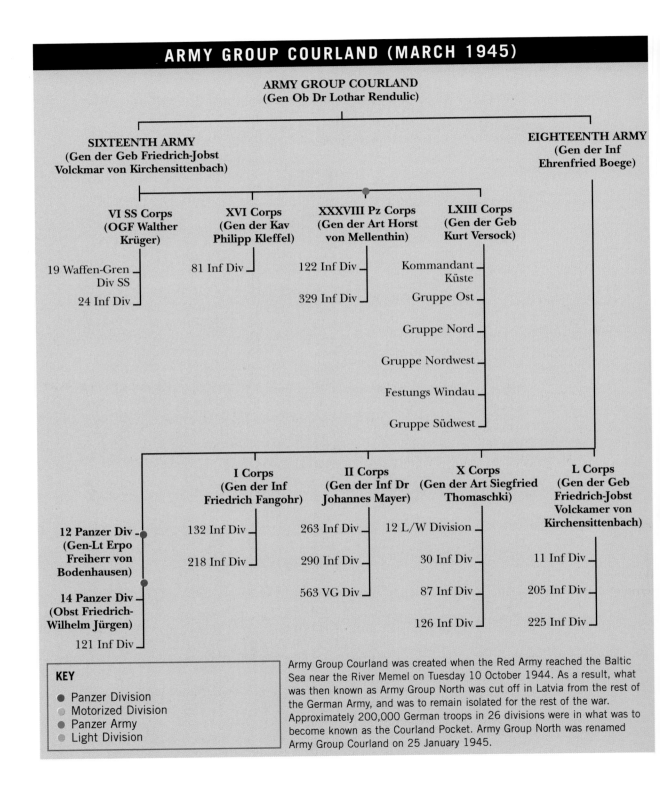

ARMY GROUP COURLAND (MARCH 1945)

ARMY GROUP COURLAND
(Gen Ob Dr Lothar Rendulic)

SIXTEENTH ARMY
(Gen der Geb Friedrich-Jobst
Volckmar von Kirchensittenbach)

EIGHTEENTH ARMY
(Gen der Inf
Ehrenfried Boege)

VI SS Corps
(OGF Walther
Krüger)

XVI Corps
(Gen der Kav
Philipp Kleffel)

XXXVIII Pz Corps
(Gen der Art Horst
von Mellenthin)

LXIII Corps
(Gen der Geb
Kurt Versock)

19 Waffen-Gren
Div SS

24 Inf Div

81 Inf Div

122 Inf Div

329 Inf Div

Kommandant
Küste

Gruppe Ost

Gruppe Nord

Gruppe Nordwest

Festungs Windau

Gruppe Südwest

I Corps
(Gen der Inf
Friedrich Fangohr)

II Corps
(Gen der Inf Dr
Johannes Mayer)

X Corps
(Gen der Art Siegfried
Thomaschki)

L Corps
(Gen der Geb
Friedrich-Jobst
Volckamer von
Kirchensittenbach)

12 Panzer Div
(Gen-Lt Erpo
Freiherr von
Bodenhausen)

132 Inf Div

218 Inf Div

263 Inf Div

290 Inf Div

563 VG Div

12 L/W Division

30 Inf Div

87 Inf Div

126 Inf Div

11 Inf Div

205 Inf Div

225 Inf Div

14 Panzer Div
(Obst Friedrich-
Wilhelm Jürgen)

121 Inf Div

KEY

- Panzer Division
- Motorized Division
- Panzer Army
- Light Division

Army Group Courland was created when the Red Army reached the Baltic Sea near the River Memel on Tuesday 10 October 1944. As a result, what was then known as Army Group North was cut off in Latvia from the rest of the German Army, and was to remain isolated for the rest of the war. Approximately 200,000 German troops in 26 divisions were in what was to become known as the Courland Pocket. Army Group North was renamed Army Group Courland on 25 January 1945.

Fall of Berlin: May 1945

Alarmed at the progress of the Anglo–American forces, Stalin ordered his top commanders to race each other to Berlin – the 'lair of the Fascist Beast'. He deliberately refused to agree unit boundaries between Konev and Zhukov.

The Soviets made intensive preparations for the final attack. They still believed that the Germans had the ability to counterattack in strength and wanted to leave nothing to chance. The two rival commanders had between them 1,640,000 men, with 41,600 guns and mortars, 6300 tanks and the support of three air armies and 8400 aircraft.

Facing them were seven panzer divisions and 65 infantry divisions in some sort of order. There were also 100 independent battalions, formed for the most part from remnants of obliterated divisions.

At dawn on 16 April, a tremendous artillery and air bombardment opened all along the Oder and Neisse rivers. Out of the Soviet bridgeheads stormed the first waves of shock troops. There was no finesse in these massed attacks. The Soviet artillery was arranged wheel to wheel in a row, and thundered away for hours in a massive preliminary barrage.

When the shelling halted, the tanks moved forwards. The T34s lumbered from their hides, the descent infantry squads riding on their hulls.

Storm over Berlin

Konev's troops stormed the River Neisse under the cover of 2000 Soviet aircraft; 60-ton bridges were in position that afternoon and his tanks were ready to exploit the territory all the way to the Spree. Zhukov's attack faltered – the intensity of his artillery barrage notwithstanding. Zhukov allowed impatience to overcome his military judgement, and ordered both his tank armies to attack without waiting for the infantry to break into the defences.

Zhukov could override both his battle plan and his infantry commanders, but even the indomitable marshal could not command the Germans to give in. German anti-tank guns commenced a terrible slaughter of Soviet armour as the vehicles struggled across the swampy plain

FROM THE ODER TO BERLIN (FEB–MAY 1945)		
	Red Army	*Wehrmacht*
Troops	2,500,000	1,000,000
Artillery	41,600	10,400
Tanks	6300	1500
Aircraft	8400	3300

below. When the tanks fought their way on to the German position, they found themselves among minefields and were attacked by infantry teams with panzerfausts.

Seelöwe Heights

Zhukov's men stormed the Seelöwe heights – the last major barrier before Berlin – after 800 aircraft bombed the defences and the gunners unleashed another formidable concentration of fire. However, Konev's tanks had not only reached the River Spree, but his T-34s drove straight into the river where an old map marked a ford. Under fire all the way, they roared across and quickly established a bridgehead on the opposite bank. Berlin lay waiting. Konev's tanks raced north, where Rybalko's Third Guards Tank Army joined Katukovs First Guards Tank Army, part of Zhukov's Front.

By 19 April, Zhukov had advanced 32km (20 miles) on a 64km (40-mile) wide front. As they moved irresistibly forwards, they annihilated the bulk of the German Ninth Army, immobilized in their path by a lack of fuel.

On 26 April, 464,000 Soviet troops, supported by 12,700 guns, 21,000 rocket launchers and 1500 tanks, ringed the inner city. The Soviets massed artillery at a density of 650 guns to the kilometre, virtually wheel to wheel. As the finale began, a pall of smoke from burning buildings and the heat of combat rose 304m (1000ft) above Berlin. The area of the city still in

German hands had been reduced to a strip some 16km (10 miles) long and 5km (3 miles) wide.

Early on 29 April the fighting was less than 0.4km (0.25 miles) away from the Reich Chancellery, which had been demolished by heavy Soviet shells. Meanwhile, 17m (55ft) beneath the surface Hitler exercised what little authority remained to him.

He appointed Grand Admiral Karl Dönitz his successor as Führer. He dismissed Albert Speer for refusal to carry out his orders to turn Germany into a wasteland. He expelled Himmler and Göring from the Nazi party for acts of treason. He appointed Ritter von Greim as chief of the Air Force. He married his long-time mistress Eva Braun and finally dictated his Last Will and Political Testament.

Death of Hitler

Hitler committed suicide at around 3.00 p.m. on 30 April. Above him, the fight for the Reichstag was reaching its climax. The building was brought under the direct fire of 89 Soviet heavy guns of 152mm and 203mm calibre. At 2.00 p.m., men of Zhukov's Third Shock Army had raised the Soviet banner on the second floor of the building. Yet the German garrison of the building was still fighting on.

The battle for the Reichstag raged on all afternoon until, late in the evening, two Red Army men of the 1st Battalion of the 756th Regiment hoisted the victory banner on the Reichstag's dome. Inside the bunker, the deluded Göbbels and Bormann made approaches to the Soviets for a ceasefire, believing that they could parlay for terms other than unconditional surrender.

Final assault

The Soviets refused to negotiate, and at 6.30 p.m. on 1 May every Soviet gun and rocket launcher opened fire on the remaining pocket of resistance. Two hours previously, Göbbels and his wife, who had just poisoned their six children, committed suicide in the Chancellery garden close to Hitler's grave. Their bodies were only partially burned and buried in a shallow grave. Soviet troops had little difficulty in identifying the corpses when they entered the Chancellery garden next day.

At 3.00 p.m. on May 2, General Karl Weidling, the Commandant of the Berlin garrison, instructed it to surrender, and about 136,000 men marched into captivity. They left in the tomb of the Reich the bodies of about 125,000 Berliners who had died in the siege – many by suicide. The cost to the Red Army had also been terrible.

Between 16 April and 8 May, Zhukov, Konev and Rokossovsky's fronts had lost 304,887 men killed, wounded and missing – 10 per cent of its strength and the heaviest casualty list suffered by the Red Army in any battle of the war.

Germany surrenders

Now the war in Europe was almost over. A local armistice had been arranged in Italy and took effect on 2 May. On 3 May, Admiral Hans von Friederburg surrendered the German forces in Denmark, Holland and North Germany to Montgomery. On 7 May, Jodl, despatched by Dönitz from his makeshift seat of government at Flensburg, signed a general surrender of German forces at Eisenhower's headquarters at Reims in France.

Stalin was outraged: he wanted the final surrender to be made in Berlin. Accordingly, the next day, Field Marshal Keitel (his arrogance seemingly untroubled by defeat), Marshal Georgi Zhukov and British Air Marshal Tedder signed a second unconditional surrender. The war in Europe was at an end.

March–April 1945

Launching out of the huge bridgehead stretching up the east bank Rhine from Bonn, Allied troops drove deep into Germany. Elements of the US Ninth Army crossed the Weser on 4 April. By 11 April, they were approaching the Elbe. On 24 April, the US First Army reached its stop line on the Mulde, and the next day sought to link up with Soviet forces at Torgau. Germany had been divided in two. Soon afterwards, on 3 May, troops from the Second British Army of Montgomery's Twenty-First Army Group met the spearheads of Rokossovsky's 2nd Belorussian Front at Wismar on the Baltic. The third act in the dismemberment of the Third Reich came with the Vienna Offensive, which ended on 13 April 1945 with the Soviet capture of the city. The US Seventh Army occupied the Tyrol early in May, linking up with the US Fifth Army, which had advanced from Northern Italy.

GERMANY DEFEATED

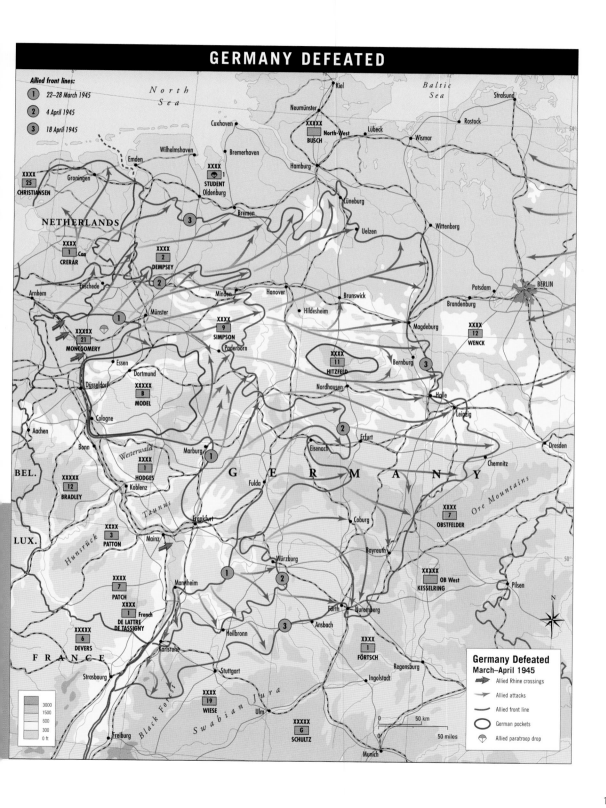

Allied front lines:
1. 22–28 March 1945
2. 4 April 1945
3. 18 April 1945

Germany Defeated
March–April 1945

→ Allied Rhine crossings
→ Allied attacks
— Allied front line
⬯ German pockets
⬙ Allied paratroop drop

0   50 km
0   50 miles

Appendices

Although panzers were a key factor in the success of *Blitzkrieg*, they were never more than a small percentage of German divisional strength. German industry could never meet the Army's demands, let alone match Allied production capacity.

In the early part of the war, the British produced more tanks than the Germans, though these were usually far less capable machines. However, once the industrial might of the United States and the immense natural resources of Soviet Union became factors in the war after 1941, German qualitative superiority was overwhelmed by the sheer numbers of Allied fighting vehicles being delivered to the battlefield.

ANNUAL ALLIED AND AXIS TANK PRODUCTION (UNITS)

Date	USA	Soviet Union	UK	Germany	Italy
1939	–	2950	969	247	40
1940	331	2794	1399	1643	250
1941	4052	6590	4841	3790	595
1942	24,997	24,446	8611	6180	1252
1943	29,497	24,089	7476	12,063	336
1944	17,565	28,963	4600	19,002	–
1945	11,968	14,419	?	3,932	–
TOTAL	**88,410**	**105,251**	**27,896**	**46,857**	**2473**

1941 PANZER DIVISION

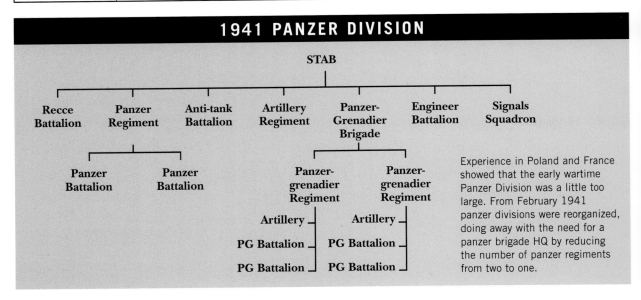

Experience in Poland and France showed that the early wartime Panzer Division was a little too large. From February 1941 panzer divisions were reorganized, doing away with the need for a panzer brigade HQ by reducing the number of panzer regiments from two to one.

1944 PANZER DIVISION

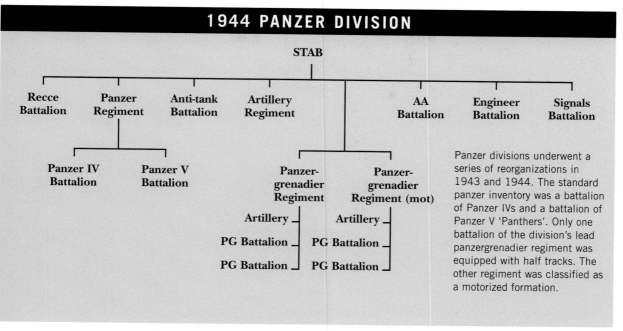

STAB

Recce Battalion — Panzer Regiment — Anti-tank Battalion — Artillery Regiment — AA Battalion — Engineer Battalion — Signals Battalion

Panzer IV Battalion — Panzer V Battalion

Panzer-grenadier Regiment — Panzer-grenadier Regiment (mot)

Artillery — Artillery

PG Battalion — PG Battalion

PG Battalion — PG Battalion

Panzer divisions underwent a series of reorganizations in 1943 and 1944. The standard panzer inventory was a battalion of Panzer IVs and a battalion of Panzer V 'Panthers'. Only one battalion of the division's lead panzergrenadier regiment was equipped with half tracks. The other regiment was classified as a motorized formation.

1943 PANZERGRENADIER DIVISION

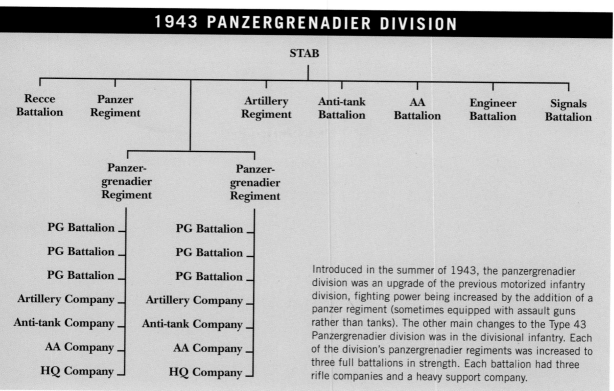

STAB

Recce Battalion — Panzer Regiment — Artillery Regiment — Anti-tank Battalion — AA Battalion — Engineer Battalion — Signals Battalion

Panzer-grenadier Regiment — Panzer-grenadier Regiment

PG Battalion — PG Battalion

PG Battalion — PG Battalion

PG Battalion — PG Battalion

Artillery Company — Artillery Company

Anti-tank Company — Anti-tank Company

AA Company — AA Company

HQ Company — HQ Company

Introduced in the summer of 1943, the panzergrenadier division was an upgrade of the previous motorized infantry division, fighting power being increased by the addition of a panzer regiment (sometimes equipped with assault guns rather than tanks). The other main changes to the Type 43 Panzergrenadier division was in the divisional infantry. Each of the division's panzergrenadier regiments was increased to three full battalions in strength. Each battalion had three rifle companies and a heavy support company.

Tactical Insignia

In 1940 a new, simplified system of divisional markings was introduced. The new system used straight lines that were easy to apply, remember and recognize. A completely new set of temporary symbols were introduced in June 1943 for divisions taking part in the Battle of Kursk.

1ST PANZER DIVISION
The 1st Panzer Division used an inverted 'Y' that was easily recognizable.

2ND PANZER DIVISION
The division's symbol was the same as the 1st Division, with the addition of a short line next to the upright of the inverted 'Y'.

3RD PANZER DIVISION
The division's symbol followed in sequence from the 1st and 2nd Divisions.

4TH PANZER DIVISION
The standard wartime insignia used by the division followed on from those used by the 1st, 2nd and 3rd Panzer Divisions.

5TH PANZER DIVISION
The standard tactical symbol used by the 5th Panzer Division in 1940 followed on from the first four panzer divisions.

6TH PANZER DIVISION
Left: Standard tactical insignia. Right: New symbol introduced for the Battle of Kursk.

7TH PANZER DIVISION
Left: Standard tactical symbol introduced in the second half of 1940. Centre: New tactical symbol introduced in 1941, and used to the end of the war. Right: Tactical symbol adopted for the Battle of Kursk.

8TH PANZER DIVISION
Left: Standard tactical symbol used by the 8th Panzer Division in 1940. Right: Modified variant used by the division from 1941 to 1945.

9TH PANZER DIVISION
Left: Tactical symbol used after the French Campaign in 1940. Right: Modified tactical symbol used from 1941 to 1945

10TH PANZER DIVISION
Left: Standard tactical symbol used in 1940. Right: Modified version used between 1941 and 1943.

11TH PANZER DIVISION
The standard tactical symbol used by the division from its foundation in 1940 to the end of the war.

12TH PANZER DIVISION
This tactical insignia was carried by the division's vehicles from its foundation in 1941 to the end of the war in 1945.

13TH PANZER DIVISION
Like the 12th Panzer Division, the division's vehicles carried the same tactical insignia from 1941 to the end of the war.

14TH PANZER DIVISION
The standard tactical symbol carried by the division from its foundation in August 1941. A similar, slightly elongated version was also used.

15TH PANZER DIVISION
The tactical insignia used in North Africa from 1941 to 1943. It was also seen in black, and in white on a solid red circle.

16TH PANZER DIVISION
Divisional tactical insignia used from 1941–42. A similar symbol was used in Italy in 1943.

17TH PANZER DIVISION
The tactical insignia used from the formation's establishment in Autumn 1940 until the end of the war.

18TH PANZER DIVISION
The standard tactical symbol was related to those of the 16th and 17th Divisions, with additional crossbars on the 'Y'.

19TH PANZER DIVISION
Left: The original tactical symbol was the ancient runic *Wolfsangel* (Wolf's Hook). Right: The new symbol used for the Battle of Kursk.

20TH PANZER DIVISION
From the middle of 1941, the division's vehicles bore a new symbol. Variants had curved and straight lines.

21ST PANZER DIVISION
After returning to Europe from North Africa in 1943, the division fought in Northwest Europe, using this new tactical symbol.

22ND PANZER DIVISION
The division's tactical sign was related to the symbol used by the 21st Panzer Division, simply rotated clockwise through 45 degrees.

23RD PANZER DIVISION
The tactical symbol followed on from the 21st and 22nd Panzer Divisions.

24TH PANZER DIVISION
Left: The division's insignia reflected its cavalry origins. Right: A simplified variant was also seen from 1943 onwards.

25TH PANZER DIVISION
Originally brightly coloured, a simplified version of the symbol was used in Russia.

26TH PANZER DIVISION
The tactical symbol of the division was a representation of a grenadier from the time of Frederick the Great.

116TH PANZER DIVISION
The Division was known as the 'Greyhound Division'.

(130TH) PANZER 'LEHR' DIV
The tactical symbol included the letter 'L' for Lehr (meaning 'demonstration'), inside the rhomboidal military map symbol for armour.

1ST SS PANZER DIVISION LSSAH
In honour of its commander, Sepp Dietrich, LSSAH used a skeleton key ('dietrich' in German) as its divisional symbol.

2ND SS PANZER DIVISION *Das Reich*
Das Reich was one of a number of divisions which used a runic 'Wolf's Hook' symbol.

3RD SS PANZER DIVISION *Totenkopf*
The Death's Head symbolized the division's origins in pre-war *Totenkopf* units.

5TH SS PANZER DIVISION *Wiking*
Wiking division carried a swastika variant of the ancient sun cross runic symbol.

9TH SS PANZER DIVISION *Hohenstaufen*
The insignia included a sword and the letter 'H', standing for the division's honour title.

10TH SS PANZER DIVISION *Frundsberg*
A Germanic letter 'F' for the unit's honour title was superimposed on to an oak leaf.

12TH SS PANZER DIVISION *Hitlerjugend*
The unit honoured its close association with the LSSAH by using a variant of the 'key' insignia.

List of Abbreviations

RANKS

Gen FM	General Field Marshal
Gen-Ob	Colonel-General
Gen der Pz	General of Panzers
Gen der Inf	General of Infantry
Gen der Art	General of Artillery
Gen der Geb	General of Mountain Troops
Gen der Pion	General of Engineers
Gen der Flieg	General of Luftwaffe
Gen-Lt	Lieutenant-General
Gen-Maj	Major-General
Obst	Colonel
SS-ObstGF	SS Oberstgrüppenfuhrer
SS-OGF	SS Obergrüppenfuhrer
StaF	SS Standartenführer (Lt Colonel)
ObF	SS Oberführer (Colonel)

TANK TYPES

Pz I	Panzerkampfwagen I
Pz II	Panzerkampfwagen II
Pz III	Panzerkampfwagen III
Pz III (lg)	Panzerkampfwagen III (long gun/barrelled)
Pz III (kz)	Panzerkampfwagen III (short gun/barrelled)
Pz III (75)	Panzerkampfwagen III (75mm gun)
Pz IV	Panzerkampfwagen IV
Pz V	Panzerkampfwagen V 'Panther'
Pz VI	Panzerkampfwagen VI 'Tiger'
Pz Bef	Command tank
Pz 38(t)	Panzerkampfwagen 38(t)
StuG	Sturmgeschütz assault gun
Pz IV/70	Panzer IV/70 tank destroyer
Flmmpz	Flammpanzer flame-thrower tank
FlakPz	Flakpanzer anti-aircraft tank

UNITS

Inf Div	Infantry Division
Cav Div	Cavalry Division
Gebirgs Div	Mountain Division
Jäger Div	Light Infantry Division
PzGren Div	Panzergrenadier Division
Luft Field Div	Luftwaffe Field Division
Gren Div	Grenadier Division
Volks Gren Div	Volksgrenadier Division
Skijäger Div	Ski Division
Sec Div	Security Division
A/L Div	Air Landing Division
Rep Div	Replacement Division
zbV Div	Special Duties Division
Abteilung	Battalion/detachment
Vf SS	Verfügungs SS (Armed SS)
LAH	*Leibstandarte* Adolf Hitler
HG	Hermann Göring
Rgt	Regiment
Bgde	Brigade
mot	Motorized
Gruppe	Group (ranges from platoon to army size)
Kampfgruppe	Battle group
It	Italian
Rom	Romanian
Hung	Hungarian

Commander Index

Page numbers in *italics* refer to tables and illustrations.

Index

Picture Credits

Art-Tech/Aerospace: 14, 25, 41, 56
Art-Tech/MARS: 24, 40
Cody Images: 6, 12, 72, 134, 135, 148, 163, 166
Library of Congress: 102
Süddeutscher Verlag: 70

All maps supplied by Cartographica © Amber Books.
All illustrations supplied by Art-Tech/Jorge Rosado.

Map Symbol Guide

Army Group	Army Division	Regiment
Army	Airborne	Company
Corps	Armoured Division	Platoon
Artillery	Antitank	Mechanized Infantry
Engineer	Communication	Naval